Dear Reader:

The book you are about to read is the latest bestseller from the St. Martin's True Crime Library, the imprint *The New York Times* calls "the leader in true crime!" The True Crime Library offers you fascinating accounts of the latest, most sensational crimes that have captured the national attention. St. Martin's is the publisher of John Glatt's riveting and horrifying SECRETS IN THE CELLAR, which shines a light on the man who shocked the world when it was revealed that he had kept his daughter locked in his hidden basement for 24 years. In the Edgar-nominated WRITTEN IN BLOOD, Diane Fanning looks at Michael Petersen, a Marine-turned-novelist found guilty of beating his wife to death and pushing her down the stairs of their home—only to reveal another similar death from his past. In the book you now hold, WEALTHY MEN ONLY, Stella Sands reports on a shocking tale of greed and betrayal.

St. Martin's True Crime Library gives you the stories behind the headlines. Our authors take you right to the scene of the crime and into the minds of the most notorious murderers to show you what really makes them tick. St. Martin's True Crime Library paperbacks are better than the most terrifying thriller, because it's all true! The next time you want a crackling good read, make sure it's got the St. Martin's True Crime Library logo on the spine—you'll be up all night!

Charles E. Spicer, Jr.
Executive Editor, St. Martin's True Crime Library

Titles by Stella Sands

Behind the Mask

Murder at Yale

The Good Son

The Dating Game Killer

Wealthy Men Only

From the True Crime Library of St. Martin's Paperbacks

Wealthy Men Only

The True Story of a Lonely Millionaire,

a Gorgeous Younger Woman, and the

Love Triangle That Ended in Murder

STELLA SANDS

St. Martin's Paperbacks

For my sister Andy, a most gentle soul, rest peacefully

WEALTHY MEN ONLY

Copyright © 2012 by Stella Sands.

For information address St. Martin's Press, 175 Fifth Avenue, New York, NY 10010.

EAN: 978-1-250-00615-8

Printed in the United States of America

St. Martin's Paperbacks edition / November 2012

St. Martin's Paperbacks are published by St. Martin's Press, 175 Fifth Avenue, New York, NY 10010.

10 9 8 7 6 5 4 3 2 1

Acknowledgments

So many wonderful people helped me with this book.

For sharing their expertise and experiences, I'd like to thank attorneys Matt Murphy, Angelo MacDonald, John Pappalardo, and Mick Hill; detectives Larry Montgomery, Tom Voth, Dave Byington, and Joe Cartwright; and Matt Murphy's colleagues Dena Basham and Susan Frazier.

For writing insightful articles on the case, I'm indebted to Larry Welborn, Scott Moxley, and Frank Mickadeit.

For the rigorous reading and spot-on comments on this manuscript, I say a hearty "Cheers" to Margaret Mittelbach.

As always, a thank-you to my dear friends Jennifer and Marjorie, for their love and support, and a boundless thank-you to Jess and AF for always being there.

A special thank-you to Kimberly McLaughlin Bayless, who graciously spent many difficult hours speaking with me and sharing stories of her family. Kim's generosity and abiding faith are humbling.

Finally, to Charlie Spicer, April Osborn, Barbara Wild, and Giles Anderson, thank you as always.

Chapter One

Balboa Coves

The Newport Beach area of Southern California isn't for everyone. Curmudgeons and sourpusses will find paltry little to enjoy. But aside from devotees of those two marginal groups, most people agree that Newport Beach is about as close to paradise as it gets—regardless of how you choose to define "paradise."

If it's surf, sand, and sunbathing you're after, the area is pure bliss. With ten miles of perhaps the cleanest beaches in the United States, it boasts the Pacific Ocean's best breaks, especially between Newport Pier and the Santa Ana River. With mountain-size waves, the Wedge, at the extreme eastern end of Balboa Peninsula, offers some of the most breathtakingly unpredictable and insane bodysurfing and bodyboarding to be found anywhere in the world.

If it's perfect weather you crave, the Mediterranean climate warms the soul as it mocks the rest of the country's winter doldrums and cold-weather blues.

Hiking and bird-watching—indeed. Crystal Cove offers a must-walk wooded wilderness, while the estuary on Back Bay beckons birders from all over to observe ospreys, endangered brown pelicans, grebes, and egrets.

With their stunning views, eighteen-hole championship golf courses lure even the most golf-averse putters.

As if all that weren't enough. Newport Beach has

museums, farmers' markets, trendy shops and restaurants, and lively nightlife. It's a postcard-perfect playground by the sea.

And if you happen to be lucky enough to *own* a piece of this paradise, Balboa Coves is the place to be. An affluent community of charming bay-front homes, its sixty or so residences radiate luxury. Although they vary in layout, not one is size challenged and some boast over forty-five hundred square feet. A typical Balboa Coves property might include four bedrooms, 3.5 baths, one hundred–plus feet of azure-water frontage, a luxurious patio overlooking the bay, a private dock, and an oversized three-car garage. These houses are more than homes; each one is someone's dream come true.

Like many upscale Newport Beach communities, Balboa Coves is gated. No one walks or drives into the neighborhood without a gate key or security card. This gives the residents a feeling of extra privacy and safety. But in an area where the crime rate is so low, one might wonder if such a precaution was really necessary.

And it wasn't. Tranquility and uninterrupted peace reigned each and every day in this secluded enclave—well, at least it did until December 15, 1994.

Chapter Two

Thursday, December 15, 1994

At around 7 p.m., Kevin McLaughlin, 24, and his father
Bill, 55, were enjoying the last bites of their dinner in the
kitchen of Number 67 Balboa Coves. It was a gorgeous house.
With a prime end-of-the-block location, it offered privacy,
spectacular south-facing bay views from the sunken hot tub
on the deck, and a dock where Bill tied up his boat. It was
the epitome of dreamy California coastal living.

Bill and Kevin lived in the Balboa Coves house with
Goldie, their perpetually optimistic golden retriever, along
with Bill's fiancée, Nanette Ann Johnston, and her two young
children. Kevin was recovering from an accident, which
was why he was living with his dad. Bill and his ex-wife,
Susan, had been married for twenty-four years before their
contentious divorce in 1991. But now Susan was living in
one of their former vacation homes in Hawaii and Bill was
planning to remarry. Things were settling down.

The topic of conversation between Kevin and his father
during dinner was how well Kevin was doing in his classes
at Coastline Community College. When the two finished eating, at approximately 7:55 p.m., Kevin told his father he was
going upstairs to listen to some music and chill—not the
usual routine for Kevin on a Thursday night. Most Thurs-
days Kevin went to a meeting, but that night he told his father
he simply didn't feel like it.

Nanette would be home later. She had left a yellow Post-it on a lampshade in the formal dining room near the patio. It read: "Bill and Kev. We won our game so we are playing again tonight. See you later, Nanette."

"Restful sleep, Kev," said Bill as Kevin left the kitchen.

Once upstairs in his room, Kevin called his girlfriend, Sandy, to arrange to meet her the following day. Then he put on his headphones, turned up the music, and sprawled across his bed.

Around an hour later, as he was thrumming along to the beat, he heard several thunderous booms. Startled, Kevin took off his headphones. He knew that the sounds weren't part of the tune, but he had no idea what they were or where they came from.

Throwing his legs over the side of the bed, he sat bolt upright. Anxiously he listened for other, similar sounds. But . . . nothing. Not a single noise could be heard from either inside or outside the house. In fact, the silence felt eerie.

With curiosity getting the better of him, Kevin decided to check on his father—although finding him wasn't always easy in their sprawling house. There were three bedrooms on the second floor, with Kevin's being the farthest from the staircase, and three bedrooms downstairs.

Leaving his room, Kevin proceeded down the long hallway, quickly glancing in each bedroom as he passed. The beds were all made perfectly, as usual, with their colorful, plump comforters and pillows. The shades all rested at their customary half-staff position. Except for him, no one was upstairs.

As Kevin made it to the mid-stairway landing, he started doubting himself. Maybe he had only imagined hearing the sounds. *The mind can play some pretty weird tricks*—he knew that for sure. He even considered going back upstairs and crawling into bed. But something made him press on.

Navigating the staircase took some doing. Although he'd been making huge progress since his accident, his brain and body weren't always in sync these days.

Kevin finally made it to the bottom step. From there, he surveyed the grand living room and dining room. Nothing out of the ordinary.

He then headed for the kitchen, his concerns abating. But when he entered the room, he stopped in his tracks. What he saw made no sense. Panic rising, he knew he needed help.

"Newport Beach Emergency," said Dispatcher Anne Donnelly after receiving a 911 call at precisely 9:11 p.m.

"Ohhhh nooo ohhhh nooo!" said a man's profoundly slurred voice.

"Your emergency?"

"Mmmm hhhhh."

"I can't understand what you're saying. Say it again to me, sir. Are you hurt?"

(unintelligible)

"I've got your location. What's the problem there at Sixty-seven Balboa Coves?"

(unintelligible)

"Somebody's dying? Your mother? What's the matter with your mother?"

(unintelligible)

"Your son? Your dad?"

"Ddddd."

"Okay, we have an officer on the way to your house now. Is anybody out there that can talk to me?"

"Nooo."

"Is it your dad? Or a dog?"

"Faaather."

"Okay, we'll have an officer out there any minute. You're at Sixty-seven Balboa. Has he been sick? Do you know what's wrong with him?"

Silence.

"Talk to me. Has he been sick?"

"Nooo."

"Do you know what's the matter with him?"

(unintelligible)

"Is he conscious? Is he breathing?"

"Shahhht."

"Your dog was shot?" asked the operator.

"My daaad."

"Is there anyone there with you? Are you there by yourself with your father?"

"Yessss."

"We're on the way. We're going to help you. Is your dad
breathing?"

"Nooo."

"He is not breathing? Did he fall over? Were you with
your dad when he fell?"

"Aggg."

"Okay okay, just try to be calm. We'll be right there. Is
there an officer at the door? Go to the door. Open the door.
Do you know how to open the door?"

"Yessss."

"How can they get in your door?"

(unintelligible)

"Is your father on the floor?"

"Yeahhhh."

"Do you know what happened to him? Is it his heart?
Heart attack?"

"Gunnnn."

"Did you say a gun? Did he shoot himself?"

"Noooo."

"Where's the gun?"

"Dddnnn."

"Where is he shot? Can you tell where he's shot? In his
head?"

"Noooo."

"I don't understand. Okay, okay. Don't move him. What's
your name?"

"Kkkeeeeenn. Kkkkevvvvvnnn."

"Okay, Kevin. What's your dad's name?"

"Wmmm."

"Do you have a mother? Where's your mother? Does she
live there?"

"Nooo."

"Can you open the front door? Can you go to the front door? I'll stay with you. Go to the front door."

Newport Beach police officer Glen Garrity was working uniformed bicycle patrol in the nearby Lido Beach Plaza area that night when his radio squawked. "Sixty-seven Balboa Coves. Caller saying something about a gun. I'm still on the line with him. Sounds intoxicated or possibly mentally handicapped. Man lying on floor. Possibly shot himself."

Luckily, Garrity wasn't far away. He pedaled hard and arrived soon after the call. As he biked up the driveway, two Newport Beach Police Department (NBPD) officers had just pulled up and exited their patrol car and were approaching the front entrance. The three men met there.

"What've we got?" asked a breathless Garrity.

"Key in the lock," said Officer Mike Pule, observing a shiny key sticking out of the already-wide-open front door.

"And another here on the mat," stated Officer Spencer Arnold as he stared down at his feet.

The officers heard the sound of moans coming from inside the house. A young man was walking toward them, sobbing and obviously highly agitated. Seeing him, the officers immediately sensed that in addition to the man's distress, something else was not quite right. His walk was ponderous and ungainly, and his speech was slurred to the point of incomprehensibility.

Garrity touched him gently on the shoulder. "Come with me," he said. "Let's sit in here." The officer led the young man to the living room, where the two sat down on the couch.

Meanwhile, Officer Arnold remained stationed at the front door while Pule began to search the house for intruders. Seconds later, as more officers arrived, a complete sweep of the home began.

By now, with sirens screaming and cherry lights twirling, nervous neighbors began to congregate along the street.

"Was it a burglary?"

"Must have been. What else?"

"Wonder if anyone was home?"

"Hope not."

"First time I remember anything like this," said Stan Love. "And I've been here over twenty years."

"Never seen anything like this in my forty-five years on the block," responded neighbor Bill Kennedy.

"Hope it's not serious," said Love.

"I was watching a rerun of *I Love Lucy,*" said Kennedy, "and kinda napping on and off when the guy next door called and said he heard gunshots. Five gunshots. I said, 'You must be kidding.' "

"I didn't hear gunshots," said Love.

"You know the folks in the house?" asked Kennedy.

"I've only said 'morning' as he jogged by with his dog. Seems like a nice enough guy."

"Sure is. He's one of the nicest guys you'll ever meet. Lives with his son."

As more neighbors began to gather, rumors started to fly:

An accident in the house—maybe someone fell down the stairs.

A burglary.

Someone was kidnapped.

A domestic dispute of some sort.

A false alarm.

While the neighbors outside pondered what could have taken place, the officers inside continued to examine the premises. When they entered the kitchen, they encountered the cause of the young man's extreme agitation.

There, on the floor in a pool of blood, lay a man on his side. He was wearing a blue bathrobe and slippers. His glasses were off to the side on the floor. He wasn't moving.

One of the officers put his hand to the man's neck and after a moment shook his head. No pulse. There was no question in the officers' minds that the man was dead. They looked closely at the body. "Looks like six of 'em. All in the torso," said police sergeant Kent Stoddard.

"Up close and personal," commented Sergeant Al Fischer.

"See the stippling?" Gunpowder flying off the muzzle of a gun had left tattoo-like marks around two of the wounds—a clear indication the victim was shot at close range.

"Hey, look," said Stoddard, eyeing the floor around the man's body. "Casings." Kneeling down to get a closer look, he could see they were from a 9mm.

"So where's the piece?" asked Fischer.

The officers examined the kitchen, but there was no gun anywhere. Plus, the place was surprisingly intact. No dishes were strewn over the floor. No chairs were overturned. No bits of food were scattered about.

Either the intruder totally surprised the victim, or the victim knew the intruder—but didn't know his or her intentions.

Patrol officers sealed the crime scene and went outside to wait for the detectives.

By 9:30 p.m., after having spoken with the highly upset young man in the living room, Officer Garrity had discovered that his name was Kevin McLaughlin and that the dead man in the kitchen was Kevin's father, Bill McLaughlin. Garrity had also determined that Kevin was not drunk, as he had originally thought. Kevin, he learned, had been in a serious accident a few years previously and experienced brain trauma. He had been hit by a drunk driver while he was skateboarding and was still suffering from motor impairment and slurred speech. But none of this stopped Kevin from remembering or recounting the horror of the preceding hour.

During dinner, Kevin recounted, the conversation with his father had been fine. Everything had been normal. Kevin told Garrity that after dinner he had gone to his bedroom and soon after heard the suspicious sounds. He then headed downstairs to investigate, and finding his father lying on the kitchen floor in his slippers . . . blood everywhere . . . holes in his father's bare chest, he dialed 911.

Kevin said that when the 911 operator advised him to open the front door so the police could get in, he did what he was told. But when he got there, the door was already open.

And that was how the police had found it—the front door

wide open with a key in the lock and another key lying on the mat right outside. Garrity asked Kevin if it was his key that was in the door. Kevin said it was not his key and he had no idea where the key had come from.

Garrity apologized to Kevin for bombarding him with questions at this tragic time, but until more information was gleaned Kevin needed to understand that he was technically considered a suspect—family members, Garrity told him, were always the first to be scrutinized after a homicide. He then asked Kevin if he could bag his hands.

"Do you understand why?" Garrity asked.

"Yeeehhhh," Kevin responded, although Garrity wondered if Kevin really did understand, because the moment after he asked the question the young man's demeanor changed from relatively calm to panicky. "It's routine," explained Garrity, trying to allay the man's fears. "We'll just be checking for gunshot residue."

While Garrity and Kevin were in the living room, members of the Newport Beach Fire Department had arrived and gone directly to the kitchen. After turning the victim onto his back and connecting him to a monitor to register vital signs, the officers declared what everyone else already knew: "Deceased."

At 9:40 p.m., Detective Tom Voth received a call at home from Lieutenant Doug Fletcher at the Newport Beach Police Department. Voth had been assigned to the crimes-against-persons unit (which dealt mostly with domestic violence, robbery, and "a lot of barroom fights") for less than a month when this homicide took place. Before that, he had been a burglary and narcotics detective.

Fletcher advised Voth that a homicide had occurred in Balboa Coves and that Detective Sergeant Steve Van Horn and Detective Bill Hartford were already on their way to investigate. Fletcher told Voth to respond as well.

Meanwhile, at 67 Balboa Coves, at 10:15 p.m., officers were checking everywhere for clues. In the garage, there was a 1991 Mercedes-Benz 300 CE. While searching the sedan,

Officer Rick Bradley located a Davis Industries P-380 pistol under the driver's seat. On close inspection, it appeared that it had not been fired.

Hmmm, wondered the detectives, *what was the victim doing with a pistol in his car?*

At 10:55 p.m., when Detectives Van Horn, Hartford, and Voth arrived on the scene, Officer Arnold briefed them on what he knew. Then Voth and Hartford headed into the living room to speak to Kevin, who was their only witness so far.

After Garrity got them up to speed, Voth asked Kevin to tell him who possessed keys to the residence. After numerous tries, Kevin was able to get across that several family members did, including his sisters and his mother—as well as his dad's live-in girlfriend.

Voth asked Kevin, "Do we have your permission to search the house?"

Kevin hesitated.

"Any weapons here?" they asked.

"Yeeehhhh."

"Can you tell us why?"

"Cccclllllct."

"What kind?"

"Lahhhtz."

After more questioning, Kevin was able to explain that his father owned many guns. Some of them were in the house in Balboa Coves, said Kevin, and others were in another house his father owned, in Las Vegas. Kevin also told the detectives that he and his father had recently fired several of the guns at a shooting range in Las Vegas.

"Anything tonight?"

"Nooo."

When they asked Kevin once more if they could search the house so they could locate all the weapons, Kevin again hesitated—but then he finally agreed.

Kevin took the lead and began showing the officers where the weapons were located. As they looked in the drawers and cabinets, the officers were startled by the number and wide-ranging types of firearms they saw. Among others, there was a Walther P-38 9mm—a WW II vintage semiautomatic pistol, popular with gun collectors and originally manufactured for the Wehrmacht (uniformed armed forces) in Nazi Germany; a Thompson Auto-Ordnance submachine gun; a Poly Technologies 7.62mm assault rifle; two K.B.I. Inc. semiautomatic shotguns; a Springfield Armory M14 rifle; and a Springfield Armory M1.

Mentally ticking off the number—thirty-eight, thirty-nine, forty—the police asked Kevin which of the weapons he and his father had fired at the shooting range in Las Vegas. Kevin said, "M16s, WW Two," but he reiterated that he had not fired any guns that night.

Then Voth got right to the most important question: "Is there anyone you know of who would want to harm your father?"

And without hesitating a second, Kevin replied, "Fishhh-chel."

Outside, a woman pulled up in a car, saying she was the girlfriend of the man who owned the house. "What's going on?" she demanded.

Detective Hartford and Sergeant Van Horn escorted her to the rear of a police car—detective unit #2264—where they noted that she appeared fragile and stunned. Moreover, they could see she was a beauty—petite, in great shape, with blondish-brown hair cascading below her shoulders.

After they asked her full name, she responded, "Nanette Ann Johnston." Hartford then informed her that Bill McLaughlin had apparently been killed inside the house. Johnston looked surprised, even startled, but within seconds she regained her composure.

After apologizing for having to question her at a time like this, Hartford began interviewing her.

"We understand you are the victim's fiancée. Can you tell us how long you have dated Mr. McLaughlin?"

"Approximately four years," she said, lowering her head.

"How long've you lived at the house?"

"Almost four years. Maybe five. Don't remember exactly."

Van Horn paused to give Johnston time to catch her breath and then continued. "Can you tell us what your activities were today, starting around noon?"

Hesitating only a moment, Johnston replied, "At noon I was shopping. I came back here. The housekeeper was here. I had to write her a check."

"Who else was here?"

"She was the only one. I wrote her a check, picked up some stuff for my son, who had a soccer game, and I went up to the game." Pausing for a moment, she continued, "I have two children from a previous marriage to Kevin Johnston—Kristopher, nine, and Lishele, seven.

"The game was supposed to start at six," she continued, "but it started at like six thirty. It was over at about eight. Double overtime. Then I went to South Coast Plaza for Christmas shopping for a few things."

"Do you recall the shops you went to?"

"Nordstrom's, Crate and Barrel. Bullocks."

"Did you use a credit card?"

"Yes. I have the stuff I bought in the car."

"Your kids go with you?"

"I went by myself. My kids stayed with their dad 'cause their school's up there and it was late after the game. They were supposed to come with me, but the game went later than we thought."

"Tell me a little bit about Kevin," said Van Horn.

After taking a deep breath, Johnston said, "Kevin was hit by a car on Newport Boulevard two or three years ago in October, the day before Halloween, and suffered a brain injury. Mostly it affects his motor skills. He's a little slow. Forgets things sometimes."

"But he understands?"

"If you're talking to him, he understands. He has some short-term memory problems."

"Describe his relationship with his father," said Hartford.

"Like any father–son relationship. They yell at each other sometimes. Get along most of the time."

Hartford then paused before questioning Johnston again. "What does Mr. McLaughlin do for a living?"

"Pretty much retired. I handle all the business. We've been working on a couple different deals. He doesn't go to a full-time job. Collects royalties."

"For?"

"An invention he sold. A kidney machine."

"Kevin mentioned his dad does a bit of business in Las Vegas."

"He has a house there. He doesn't do any business."

"What does he do?"

"All the times I've gone with him, we go to shows."

"Casinos?"

"No, he's not a gambler."

"What kind of shows?"

"Gun shows."

"What's his date of birth?"

"October 12, I'm guessing here, 1939. Not sure exactly."

"Somebody mentioned a name, Fischel."

"Yes, Hal Fischel," stated Johnston. "That's a guy he's been in a lawsuit with for three years. He was one of the original guys in the invention. They bought him out. That was the agreement. But when the company was sold, he came back and sued them to try to get more money."

"Did Mr. McLaughlin ever threaten him?" asked Van Horn.

"Not that I ever heard."

"Who has keys to the house?"

"The maid, Mary Berg, myself, maybe [a] couple of neighbors. I think Mr. Kennedy, an old gentleman who lives right there. Kevin. Bill's daughters, Jenny and Kim. Kim's in Japan, though. Jenny lives in Laguna Niguel."

"Other keys around?"

"In the dock box," said Johnston. "I think just one key. Inside a can or something. I think it's just a key by itself."

"On a key chain?"

"I don't know. Never used it. I never had to use it. Bill used it once. We usually come in and out through the garage door."

"He has a house in Vegas?" asked Van Horn.

"Two houses. One right next door to the other. It's vacant."

"Any idea how many guns in the house?"

"Most are in Vegas. He has a list on the computer. I personally don't like guns. I have kids in the house. I asked him if he would move them to Vegas."

"How many houses do you have in Newport?"

"I have one house on Seashore Drive. Nobody lives there full-time."

Continuing, in rapid-fire succession, Hartford kept the questions coming. "The McLaughlin family—who are the members?"

"One son, two daughters. And an ex-wife. Sue. She lives in Hawaii."

"What's their relationship?"

"Friendly."

"Any officers come here to your house for a domestic dispute?"

"No, never."

"Have police ever been here before, for anything?"

"The house on Seashore got broken into the year before last, Thanksgiving. When I went there, the lights were on. I called police. Didn't want to go in. Turned out, somebody was staying there. Messed up the place. Just vandalism. Other than Kevin's accident and cops coming to find out about that, the police haven't ever been here."

"Anybody else stay here, part- or full-time?"

"No, just us. Kevin has [a] room of his own." Then pointing upstairs, Johnston said, "Right up there with the lights on."

"Your kids have rooms of their own? One room, two rooms?"

"Two rooms."

"Can we take a look at your shopping receipts real quick? One thing we need to do to eliminate you is to do some tests on your hands for gunshot residue. Do you understand? We have to do that—always a possibility."

"I have no objection."

The interview went on for several more minutes, during which time Johnston said that Bill had several insurance policies. "I believe most of the policies are in the safe."

After ascertaining the combination, the officers asked Johnston if she had keys to the house.

"Yes, they are on my key chain. I go in through the garage, but they're on the key chain."

Finally, the officers asked, "Do you have any idea at all why this happened?"

"I wish I had something to tell you. I wish I knew. I can't tell you anything."

"Do you have a place to stay?"

"I'll stay at the other house. Forty-four-oh-three Seashore Drive."

"We're gonna have an officer come and do that test on your hands right now. All right, Miss Johnston. Thank you. This officer will take care of you."

By now, Johnston was barely able to hold her head up. The interview ended at 12:20 a.m. and clearly Johnston was exhausted. After Johnston's hands were tested for gunshot residue, Hartford accompanied her to her vehicle. Inside she located the receipts for her purchases earlier that evening and gave them to the detective. One was from Crate & Barrel, made at 9:29 p.m., and another was for clothes purchased at Bullocks, at 9:45 p.m.

While Hartford and Van Horn were interviewing Johnston, other Newport Beach detectives were interviewing several Balboa Coves residents about their observations at the time surrounding what they now knew was a homicide.

Rose Clark stated that she observed a white and black sports car parked just outside the gate.

Sander Domaszewicz stated that his mother saw an unknown Suburban with at least one person in it inside the residential area at the time.

Mildred Powers stated that she heard five shots within approximately four seconds of one another.

Al Vaziri, who lived at 66 Balboa Coves, stated that while he was in the kitchen he heard "more than three shots," which sounded like firecrackers. "I was scared," he admitted.

"Where were the shots coming from?" asked the detective.

"The residence directly east of me—the McLaughlins' home," Vaziri responded. He then stated that he looked out toward the bay and it was dark and he didn't see anything unusual. He went back to the room where his mother was, locked the door, and then telephoned neighbor Bill Kennedy at Number 65 and asked him if he had heard shots. "Bill said he hadn't heard anything unusual."

Other neighbors interviewed that day said that they neither saw nor heard anything out of the ordinary.

At 12:50 a.m., Officer Arnold escorted Johnston and Kevin to the residence at 4403 Seashore. It was a stunning little beachfront home with approximately 2,377 square feet right on the white sands. Normally, the waves lapping against the shore would have been like music to Kevin—he loved the ocean with every fiber of his being. But that night, the sound of the Pacific had never seemed so lonely.

Soon after midnight, video technician Jan Anderson and photo technician George Reise began taping and photographing the crime scene. Crime scene investigator Joe Heppler dusted for fingerprints all over the front door, the kitchen counter, the windows, the telephone, and many other places in the huge home.

Back at the police department Van Horn, Hartford, and Voth discussed whether or not to call the victim's daughter Jenny McLaughlin at such a late hour and Van Horn said, "Let her get some sleep. We'll call her in the morning." Then Van Horn informed Voth that he had been assigned to be the case manager—homicides were not common in Newport Beach, so it would be a team effort, involving numerous detectives. Their assignments would be made further up the chain of command, but Voth would be in charge of coordinating the investigation, as well as presenting any evidence to the district attorney.

After catching only an hour or two of shut-eye, at 9 a.m. Voth telephoned Jenny, but there was no answer.

In the end, it was Kevin who reached his sister Jenny by phone and told her the horrible news. She was at work—and at first couldn't fathom it. Wondering if she had understood Kevin correctly, she asked him several times to repeat what he was saying. When it sank in, she immediately got in her car and, in a daze, began driving to the Seashore home.

Shortly after 9 a.m. California time, the phone rang on the table in the tiny apartment where Kim McLaughlin lived in Tokyo—it was 2 a.m. there. She had been teaching at an international school in Japan for four months, loving every moment of it. That evening she had just returned home from a fun evening out with her colleagues.

"Hello," she said.

"Hi, Kim. It's Mom," and then Sue McLaughlin paused to catch her breath. "There's something very terrible that I need to tell you. Your father has been killed."

"What!" screamed Kim.

"No one knows what happened. You need to come home immediately."

Kim couldn't believe what her mother was telling her. She listened to a few more details, then told her mother she would book the next flight. After saying good-bye, she threw the phone at the wall, crying hysterically. *What is Mom talking about?* she wondered. *Dad called me four days ago to chat and tell me how much he missed me. He said that he couldn't wait to see me at Christmas. Everything was fine. How can this be?*

In a panic, Kim called her friends to help her organize her things and then began frantically packing up. She took a plane home the next morning. "It was the hardest plane ride of my life," she said later.

All of the McLaughlin children were in shock. They could barely believe what had happened. And they couldn't make any sense of it. *Why would anyone want to kill their father?*

Chapter Three

William McLaughlin

William McLaughlin had not been born rich, but there was no question that by 1994 he was a very wealthy man. He owned multiple homes, two boats, and a small plane—a six-seater, single-engine Piper Malibu that he piloted himself. The official estimate of his wealth at the time of his death was about 30 million.

Born on October 12, 1939, McLaughlin grew up in a working-class family on the South Side of Chicago with his two brothers, Patrick and John, and his mother and father. At times, Bill's family was so poor that they would go to relatives' homes for meals. He joined the Marines at 18 and after a three-year stint enrolled in Loyola University (now Loyola Marymount University, the largest Catholic university on the West Coast) and obtained a degree in biology in 1965.

"Bill was the first person in our family to attend college," said his brother, Patrick proudly. "He was always self-made. He wanted to be the kind of guy that would make a difference."

In 1964, McLaughlin entered the medical industry as a salesman—and eventually he did make an impact. "He was one of the best salesmen I ever met," said Dave Burke of Costa Mesa, who worked for McLaughlin in the late 1960s, when McLaughlin was national sales manager for Extracor-

poreal, a dialysis products company later acquired by Johnson & Johnson. "He knew his products inside out," said
Burke, "and could discuss them with a doctor on the same
level."

On February 12, 1966, McLaughlin married Susan, a
beautiful, capable, intelligent, and sensitive woman he had
met a few years previously. Soon after, they welcomed three
beautiful children into their family: Kimberly, in 1966; Jennifer, in 1968, and Kevin, in 1970.

Over the next decade, the proud parents watched as their
precious children grew into intelligent and loving adults. The
family took vacations together, went to church together, and
gathered together around the table for long, satisfying meals,
filled with conversation. On weekends, their Balboa Coves
home, bought in 1975, served as a communal meeting place
for the kids' friends as well as the parents' friends. "It was
an open, welcoming house where everyone was appreciated
and accepted," said Kim.

In 1977, after working as a salesman and marketing executive for several medical-device companies, McLaughlin
began thinking about the medical-product development area
and how he might impact the industry. "His greatest success
would come as an entrepreneur," stated an article in the *Los
Angeles Times*.

That year, working at Medical Device Laboratories, a
firm he founded, he developed a new dialysis catheter. Later
that year, he sold the device to C. R. Bard, a New Jersey
manufacturer of medical devices.

And that was the beginning of McLaughlin's successful
career as an inventor.

Soon after, he learned that the Red Cross was looking
for a faster and safer method for collecting plasma from
blood donors, so in 1978 McLaughlin worked with scientist
Halbert Fischel of Hughes Aircraft to develop such a
method. The two formed HemaScience Laboratories, Inc.,
in 1981.

One member of the team, Don Schoendorfer, recalled,
"Fischel came up with this brilliant idea for a filter that

separated plasma from blood." By 1982, Autopheresis-C or Plasmacell-C, as they called it, was born. It enabled "blood to be extracted from a donor, the plasma removed, and the remaining blood returned to the donor in one continuous, automated process." Before this invention, blood was brought to a laboratory, where the plasma was separated from it by centrifuge. That method brought about serious risks not only because it was a longer process but also because if a donor's blood was mislabeled and switched by mistake with another's before it was returned the person could die.

"We started in my garage in Santa Ana," said Bill Miller, one of the partners. "After the prototype blood separator was developed, Hillman Company, a capital venture firm in Pittsburgh, pumped in the money to help the company seek approval from the Food and Drug Administration to market the product in the United States."

After only a few years, however, trouble developed between Fischel and McLaughlin. They began disagreeing over their original partnership agreement, with each suing the other. The two men finally reached a settlement, part of which involved Fischel leaving the company.

After the team gained marketing approval from the FDA for the device in June of 1986, Baxter Healthcare acquired HemaScience Laboratories, Inc., along with the licensing rights to the blood device. According to reports, they paid "tens of millions of dollars." Under the agreement with Baxter, McLaughlin was paid a royalty on every Plasmacell-C sold, which brought him over $2.5 million a year.

"We were very excited and broke out the champagne and had a little celebration in the garage," recalled Miller. McLaughlin's accountant, Brian Ringler, had a slightly different version. He said that McLaughlin told him that the team *spoke of* breaking open champagne but that McLaughlin "became so busy with business that he never stopped to revel in his victory."

Before Baxter acquired the device, only around one hundred thousand blood separators had been sold. Within two years, however, the annual sales figure soared to 2 million. Today, sales are over 9 million and the device is being used by blood banks worldwide. Indeed, McLaughlin had succeeded in his dream to make a difference.

By 1990, McLaughlin was wealthy enough to own homes in Hawaii and Las Vegas, along with an avocado ranch in Fallbrook, in San Diego County.

Although McLaughlin's business life was progressing nicely, married life was not as successful. Susan was not happy. She began feeling unfulfilled, even marginalized.

Kim McLaughlin summed up her parents' situation: "Both my mother and father put everything they had into raising us. Like many couples, during that time, they didn't work full-time on their relationship. So once we all went off to college and once my father sold his business and moved back home again, they were trying to relearn who they were as individuals and as a couple. My mother realized she wanted to be more independent. . . . Because my mom and dad didn't communicate so well with each other, my mom felt she couldn't get her independence any other way than by leaving."

In April 1990, after twenty-four years of marriage, Susan, then 54, filed for divorce. Susan reported that her husband "fought against [my] wish to get divorced, saying he wanted to maintain the family." More than that, McLaughlin was a devout Catholic and believed strongly that marriage was for life, whatever the ups and downs. The divorce knocked him for a loop.

A messy legal battle followed, with heated arguments concerning assets. In court papers filed by Susan, she claimed that her husband would call "early in the mornings and try to bully me into taking a one-million-dollar settlement." She said that Bill had threatened "not to share his hard-earned money" and to take "unpleasant tactics if she didn't settle."

During the proceedings, the arguments became so

contentious that Susan sought assistance to "prevent her husband from transferring any of their holdings and from harassing her."

In his court papers, Bill asked that the court "not hinder my ability to manage the family estate. My wife has never been interested in the business of the community (property) or how the money was made."

On May 5, 1990, as part of the divorce proceedings, Bill McLaughlin listed his gross yearly income as $1.2 million, with $47,933 a month net as disposable income. His attorney valued McLaughlin's holdings at $8.1 million, but documents revealed that potential liabilities from loans and lawsuits were approximately $9.4 million.

That same year, things took an additional turn for the worse for McLaughlin. Hal Fischel sued both him and Baxter Industries. It was Fischel's belief that he had been cheated out of royalties from the device he and Bill had put out into the world. Fischel was seeking $840 million in damages. McLaughlin counterclaimed that Fischel had tried to sell the plasma technology to a competitor.

The lawsuit lasted for four long "contentious and extended" years, stated McLaughlin's lawyer Paul Gale, during which time, as it was in arbitration in San Francisco, "it consumed a great deal of William's life" and caused McLaughlin deep pain.

The divorce between Susan and her husband was settled more quickly—although it was equally as upsetting—and finalized on December 31, 1991. In it, Susan received around $4.5 million in assets, which included a home in Hanalei, Hawaii, which the couple owned, a 1986 Isuzu Trooper, and a $300,000 payment.

Bill received their twenty-one-acre avocado ranch in San Diego; the home at 67 Balboa Coves; two Las Vegas properties; a $1 million money market account; his Piper Malibu aircraft, two boats, two Mercedes-Benzes; and a 1986 Chevrolet station wagon. He also received the right to all earnings in the future that would come from royalties from HemaScience. Records showed that at the time he was receiving around $100,000 per month.

While the royalties continued to roll in, the lawsuit wore on. Millions of dollars were at stake—perhaps his entire livelihood. However, in 1994 it appeared that the lawsuit was about to be settled—in McLaughlin's favor. An arbitration panel had preliminarily ruled that Fischel should forfeit $9 million in royalties to McLaughlin. It looked like the clouds were finally parting. In spite of the severity of Kevin's accident, he was getting better. And now Fischel might be off Bill's back! He was about to be able to enjoy the fruits of his success again.

According to practically every person who knew him, Bill McLaughlin was a fine, upstanding, religious, and generous man. Friends described him as "wealthy yet down-to-earth," a man who "brought homemade sandwiches to business lunches."

"He was a sharp guy and very successful," said Brian Ringler, McLaughlin's friend and accountant for ten years. "You couldn't ask for a better person."

Neighbor Stan Love said that McLaughlin and his son came to his Christmas party on December 10—only five days before the murder. Love said McLaughlin appeared to be in good spirits and that he went out of his way to take care of Kevin. "He often walked with his arm around his son," said Love.

While living in Balboa Coves, McLaughlin served on the Balboa Coves Community Association in the 1980s and, according to Love, was "always interested in helping with what he could."

Not only was Bill McLaughlin well liked, but he was also generous. He donated money to Anaheim's Servite High School, to Maryknoll, and also to his college alma mater, where he endowed two scholarships for needy students.

About the only slightly negative comment heard about McLaughlin came from an associate who worked with McLaughlin two decades previously. He admitted that

McLaughlin could be "overbearing and sometimes cold-shouldered employees who didn't meet his standards. He could be a nice, charming guy or a mean son of a gun." But still, McLaughlin's associate added, "nothing he ever did would warrant such a horrific ending."

Chapter Four

Friday, December 16

On the morning after Bill McLaughlin's murder, his daughter Jenny arrived at 4403 Seashore Drive, a little more than a mile from Balboa Coves. As soon as he saw Jenny, Kevin came out of the house and the siblings hugged. "I can't believe it, Kev. Is it really true?" asked a devastated Jenny.

Kevin was too distraught to answer.

Johnston remained in the house, and at one point she peeked out the front door at Jenny and Kevin. However, she did not come out.

Shortly after, Jenny drove to the police station. Once there, she stopped at the front desk. "I'm Jenny McLaughlin. It's my dad who—" She couldn't finish her sentence before breaking down in tears.

Detective Voth and Sergeant Van Horn brought her to the Detective Divisions captain's office. After expressing their condolences, they asked her for any information she might have that could help lead them to a suspect.

Trying to pull herself together, she responded softly, "I can only think of one person. Hal Fischel."

Jenny was the third person who mentioned Fischel as a possible suspect. He was definitely someone to interview.

Although Voth did not relish doing it, he then asked Jenny about her whereabouts at the time of her father's murder. It was mandatory to rule out members of a victim's immediate family as soon as possible.

"I was riding my horse at the Nellie Gail Stables in Laguna Niguel until approximately seven thirty," she said, sobbing. "Then two friends and I went back to my home in Laguna Niguel. They stayed until ten fifteen or maybe eleven."

After getting the friends' names, Voth said, "Could you tell us a little about your father's relationship with Nanette Johnston?"

"It seemed fine. There didn't seem to be any problems," she replied.

"Did your father have any dating relationships other than with Johnston at the present time?"

"No. Not that I'm aware of."

After thanking Jenny for her time, Voth said she was free to leave. He told her he would be in touch and that she should call him with any information she thought could be relevant. Upset and bewildered, Jenny returned to her car, where she cried uncontrollably. The reality of the situation was beginning to sink in.

Most days, the channel behind 67 Balboa Coves was a picture-postcard scene of tranquility and beauty. Boats dotted the waterway, either moored at private docks or sailing on their way to Newport Harbor—one of the largest recreational boat harbors on the West Coast. But on this day, something far less benign than usual was taking place.

Believing that the gun used in the murder *could* have been tossed into the waterway, Detective Bob Stephens was tasked to find the nearest scuba dive team to Balboa Coves. To that end, he spoke to Lieutenant Eric Bauer at the lifeguard station at Newport Beach and requested the assistance of their department's dive team. Bauer signed on and said that his team would be at the victim's residence at 1 p.m.

Stephens learned that the Navy stationed in San Diego had its own underwater dive team, which was experienced in using metal detectors. He sought approval from Washington D.C., to allow divers from there to come to Balboa Coves and also search the waters. After the okay was given, Stephens was told the team would arrive the next day.

Now with two dive teams poised to troll the waters around 67 Balboa Coves, detectives were hopeful that the murder weapon would be found in a matter of hours—and that that would be the first step in leading them to the killer.

After the calls were made, Stephens went to the crime scene and conducted a search of the victim's boat—a white fiberglass eighteen-foot 1988 W.D. Schock electric-powered hull—moored at the McLaughlins' dock. Stephens looked over every inch of the boat, but several hours later he was disappointed to have to report that he had found no useful evidence—no gun, no tossed-off clothing, no blood splotches—nothing that he felt could help them solve the case.

While Stephens was at the McLaughlin home, the family's gardener, Jay Shim, arrived. Stephens questioned him about his keys and then checked to see if the gardener's key for the gate also fit into the front door of the home. It did not.

Apparently, the victim had the workman's key made this way for security reasons.

While the boat search was taking place at Balboa Coves, a more solemn task was taking place at the Orange County coroner's office. There, beneath bright lights, a postmortem examination of William F. McLaughlin's body had begun. Senior criminologist Elizabeth Thompson, two forensic technicians, and Detective Hartford were in attendance, attentively observing as Dr. Richard Fukomoto performed the autopsy.

On the autopsy report, the cold, hard facts appeared. The doctor wrote that the deceased arrived in a sealed body bag on a gurney in the main autopsy room. "He was nude. His hands were bagged. EKG pads were on his chest." (Paramedics had placed them there at the crime scene in an effort to revive the victim.)

The doctor noted that there were six entry wounds in the front of McLaughlin's body—four to the abdominal area, one to the left chest, and one to the upper right chest. The doctor further noted that "a through and through gunshot wound was in his left index finger."

Clearly, Bill McLaughlin had been facing his attacker at the time of the shooting and he had raised his left hand immediately before or during the shooting. Did he raise his hand in greeting—or was it to defend himself?

Dr. Fukomoto recovered "three expanded hollow-point slugs" from the body. The "expanded projectiles had the appearance of 9mm Hydra-Shok pistol slugs." (Hollow-point bullets are specifically designed to create wide wound channels and are advertised as having maximum "stopping power." Translation: They are meant to kill.)

The report detailed that stippling patterns were observed to the left of the right chest wound and around the lower right abdominal wound. "Tattooing," as a result of barrel debris surrounding one of the entry wounds to the abdomen, indicated that the "distance between the barrel of the weapon and the deceased was less than two feet."

There was also a gash in the deceased's head, apparently from falling down after being shot.

It seemed that the killer had walked into the kitchen, strode right up to Bill McLaughlin, and pumped six lethal bullets into his body. Sergeant Fischer, one of the first officers on the scene, had been right. This was *up close and personal.*

Dr. Fukomoto determined that the deceased bled to death as a result of "the aorta being struck by one of the expanded bullet slugs."

At 12:45 that afternoon, detectives, using the combination supplied by Nanette Johnston, opened the safe in the hallway closet on the second floor of the victim's home. There they found what appeared to be several insurance policies, other legal papers, and a promissory note signed by Johnston for a $35,000 loan from William McLaughlin. Insurance policies often led detectives in the direction of the perp. Monetary gain often served as a powerful motive.

Searching the house in greater detail than they did many

hours earlier, they located fourteen more firearms in the
closet in the northeast upstairs bedroom. Among them were
a .45 submachine gun, a Colt Sporter rifle, and six PWA
Commando AR-15s.

Quite a collection! Detectives wondered if any of the
firearms would prove key to solving the crime.

Detectives were now planning their immediate course of action. They *definitely* wanted to interview Hal Fischel. As of
now, he was the most promising person of interest. They
also wanted to hear more from McLaughlin's fiancée about
the kind of relationship they had, as well as Johnston's
thoughts on any other people who might have had a vendetta
against McLaughlin. And they certainly wanted to review
the insurance policies and take a careful look at the gun collection.

So far, it didn't appear anything had been taken from the
house. The killer had been in and out very quickly. A robbery gone wrong certainly didn't appear to be the case.

Later that afternoon, after having been summoned by
detectives for a follow-up interview, Johnston arrived at the
NBPD.

During the hour-long interview, Johnston never broke
down in tears. Among other things, Johnston told Sergeant
Van Horn and Detective Voth that she had been taking care
of Kevin since his accident; that in her opinion, a lot of
Kevin's friends were "dope-smoking, fair-weather friends";
that she had met Bill's ex-wife only once in the hospital when
Kevin was recuperating; that she, Johnston, was in charge of
all of Bill's accounts; and that Bill had not been investing
much lately because of a lawsuit with a previous partner, Hal
Fischel, in which "a lot of Bill's money was tied up."

When asked for more information about the lawsuit,
Johnston stated that it was "bogus" and that Fischel had sued
McLaughlin several times over the years, believing that he
was owed money for an invention he had purportedly come
up with when the two were partners. Johnston mentioned
that McLaughlin had bought out Fischel for $2 million years

ago and that just last month the court awarded McLaughlin $9 million, which, Johnston stated, was being held in a special account until all the paperwork was completed.

Asked what she knew about McLaughlin's whereabouts on the days before the murder, Johnston stated that Bill had left for Las Vegas at ten o'clock on Wednesday morning, the fourteenth, and that he had flown his own plane there. "He doesn't file a flight plan," she noted. "He usually returns home around six p.m. on Thursday evenings."

Voth suggested that she change the locks at the Balboa Coves residence, but Johnston told him she had no intention of staying at the house ever again. She remarked that a lot of keys had been given to various workmen and had not been returned. She was taking no chances. After all, she had two small children to protect.

The detectives thanked her for coming in. But in truth she hadn't given them much new to go on.

So far, we've got a fiancée, a disabled and possible druggie son, a disgruntled ex-partner, and an angry ex-wife. The detectives wondered if one of them might have information that would help solve the crime. They also wondered if one of them might have done it.

Chapter Five

Kevin

Kevin McLaughlin was not doing so well in the wake of his father's death. It had been terrifying, horrifying. He had watched his father's blood pour onto the kitchen floor. And then when Kevin called 911 he couldn't get the operator to understand. *If only I could have protected him ... If only things were the way they used to be.*

Kevin had more than one reason to want to turn back the clock. Before becoming disabled—unable to get words out, struggling to walk in a straight line—he had been an athlete. His life as a child and teenager had epitomized the California dream. Handsome, with blond hair and poignant blue eyes, he had been outgoing and adventuresome. Growing up a stone's throw from the beach, he had started surfing at age seven—and eventually become a bona fide big-wave rider. Baja. Puerto Escondido. Hanalei Bay. A bumper sticker on his car read: "The ocean is my playground." He also scuba-dived, skateboarded, fished, skied, and snowboarded. His sister Kim described him as "the life of the party—silly, funny, and quirky." He had a great family, lots of friends, and girls had often come knocking on his door.

But on October 30, 1991, when Kevin was just twenty-one, tragedy struck. As he was skateboarding—an activity he excelled in—a drunk driver, careening along at over sixty miles per hour, hit Kevin, knocking him over the front windshield.

When medics arrived, Kevin was unconscious. He was first raced to one hospital, but because he was in such dire condition he was immediately airlifted to another hospital.

The prognosis was not good.

Kevin remained in a coma for three and a half long months as his family sat by his side night and day, praying, talking to him, singing to him, and holding his hand. His father visited the hospital every day he could, talking to his son, trying to draw him back to consciousness. But the doctors were not optimistic.

Then one sunny day, miraculously, Kevin woke up. He seemed to recognize his family. He smiled. He mumbled. He moved his limbs. The doctors were incredulous—and also wary. They knew the road back to his old life would be long and challenging.

Kevin remained in hospitals for another year and a half as he relearned to walk, talk, swim, ride a bike, read, write, and take care of himself. Every step was difficult, but Kevin soldiered on. At times, he was angry and frustrated, but he never gave up, even though there were many times he wanted to. He worked through his frustrations and lack of coordination and balance until he was able—slowly, slowly, slowly—to walk, then run a bit, then even stand up on a surfboard.

"It was a miracle he survived," said his sister Kim later. "Doctors told us he might never wake up from his coma, but we knew he would." With his strong will and love of life, the family felt certain he would one day say hello to them again.

Once he got out of the hospital, Kevin continued to take daily physical therapy and speech sessions, and he improved so much that he was beginning to attend college, taking special classes for people with brain injuries, had a girlfriend, and was able to enjoy some of the things he did before the accident. Although life was not as he wished it to be—not by a long shot—Kevin had bucked the odds. His family was ecstatic.

While getting back on his feet, Kevin was living with his

father, his father's girlfriend, and sometimes Johnston's kids from another marriage. It usually worked out pretty well, with everyone respecting the others' space.

Still, there were bumps. Sometimes Kevin felt he needed something extra to get through the day—a little weed here, a few beers there. He had had a penchant for partying before his accident and didn't think it was a big deal, but his family members soon became concerned. Around a year before the murder, his father learned that Kevin was smoking pot and abusing alcohol. Bill McLaughlin told his son, in no uncertain terms, that his behavior along these lines was unacceptable. Kevin, on the other hand, really didn't see the problem.

What he did see, however, was that his father was extremely upset and angry. In early 1994, McLaughlin had written out a contract between himself and his son, in which he wrote that if Kevin did not give up using drugs and alcohol he would be placed in a board-and-care facility and his family would stop supporting him.

Yes, it was tough love. But it seemed that the agreement was having some effect, because Kevin started attending an AA meeting soon thereafter. In fact, most Thursday nights that's where he would be. Clearly, Kevin was ready to take another step toward full recovery.

However, on Thursday, December 15, 1994, Kevin simply didn't feel like going out. He wanted to stay at home and listen to music. He was feeling pretty happy. It was nice having dinner with his dad after his trip to Vegas. Kevin was pleased that his father hadn't even bugged him about missing his meeting that night.

Dad must have something important on his mind or he would've started in on me, thought Kevin after they hugged good night.

Chapter Six

Saturday, December 17

The first time members of the general public heard anything about a murder in Balboa Coves was when they picked up the newspaper on the morning of December 17.

"Man Is Shot to Death in His Balboa Coves Home" read the headline of an article in the *LA Times*.

"Newport Millionaire Slain in Gated Home," stated a headline in the *Orange County Register*. "The entrepreneur's son finds him shot six times at their house in the Balboa Coves community." The article went on to report that the police would not say whether or not they had any suspects.

Neighbors interviewed for the article recalled that Bill McLaughlin always locked his door. His neighbor Bill Kennedy, 79, said that although McLaughlin had a dog, it probably wouldn't have offered much protection. "It was awful friendly," he commented.

One neighbor recalled, "Last time I talked to him, he had asked me what I wanted for Christmas. He was a very nice person, and very strong."

The murder stunned the community, who was used to reading headlines about surfing contests and pricey home sales.

Following up on the one person of interest who had been mentioned by several different people, Detectives Hartford

and David Szkaradek interviewed Halbert Fischel, Mc-
Laughlin's former business partner, at his home in Santa
Barbara.

Fischel was a top contender because he and McLaughlin
had been engaged in a bitter lawsuit for four years, starting
in 1990, and Fischel had recently found out that the arbitration panel's preliminary decision had favored McLaughlin—to the tune of $9 million.

*Was it possible that Fischel, or someone Fischel hired,
could have killed William McLaughlin?*

While being interviewed at his home, Fischel fully
cooperated with the police, calmly answering every question.
Asked about his whereabouts on the night of the murder,
Fischel stated that he was at home—and his wife confirmed
it. Later, when following up on this alibi, eyewitnesses told
detectives that they had seen Fischel in Santa Barbara—some
150 miles north of Balboa Coves—right before the time of
the murder.

During the interview, Fischel told detectives that McLaughlin had frozen him out of the company after he, Fischel, had
invented a plasma separator in March 1982. Fischel stated
that he had sued McLaughlin and received an out-of-court
settlement, but he would not reveal the amount. Fischel
stated that he sued McLaughlin again and Baxter Healthcare in June 1990 for royalties concerning the development
of the plasma separator and that the case was still in litigation.

When asked his opinion of McLaughlin, Fischel said he
had no comment. He did, however, follow that statement
with the fact that he would not dispute the opinion of someone who did *not* like McLaughlin.

*Clearly, there was no love lost between Hal Fischel and
Bill McLaughlin,* thought the detectives. *But would he go so
far as to hire a killer to take revenge on his nemesis? From
a financial perspective, Fischel didn't stand to benefit from
McLaughlin's death. And his ironclad alibi served to move
him several notches down on the list of potential suspects.*

* * *

By late afternoon, the underwater search of the canal—from the Newport Boulevard Bridge to approximately forty yards west of the McLaughlins' property line—was in full swing. Interested onlookers craned their necks from their decks and nearby roads, curious to see if the divers would come up with anything. The entire neighborhood was on edge—sorry, of course, for the victim's family and friends but also concerned about their own safety. After all, a murderer was on the loose and, they wondered, what was to stop the person from coming back to *their* house and killing *them*?

By the end of the weekend, their concerns turned into grumblings, which turned into outright criticism. Perhaps the Newport Beach police weren't doing enough to solve the crime—or, even worse, they simply weren't up to the task.

Chapter Seven

Monday, December 19

Nearly four full days had passed since the murder took place, and the police still weren't naming any suspects. In fact, they weren't offering up *any* information about the progress—or lack thereof—concerning the case. "The investigation is on-going," were the only words coming from the NBPD. "We will reveal any pertinent information at the appropriate time." This statement did little to allay the fears of the Balboa Coves residents, many of whom feared for their lives.

However, regardless of how it appeared to the public, the NBPD was not sitting idle. If Fischel wasn't panning out as a suspect, it was time to check on the fiancée's alibi. In an attempt to find out more about the soccer game where Nanette Johnston said she had been right before the murder, detectives called Johnston's former husband and asked him to come to the station. Maybe Kevin Ross Johnston, known as Ross, could add some details that could point them in the right direction.

When Ross arrived, Detective Hartford began by asking him about his relationship with his ex-wife. "It's a good one," he said. "Amicable, especially regarding the children. We both put the kids first."

Switching to the night of the murder, Detective Hartford asked, "Were you with your ex at the game?"

"No. Nanette came with her friend."

"Who is that?"

"Eric."

Ross went on to say that Eric had been Johnston's friend for the past year and a half and that he had attended several of the children's soccer games with her.

"Can you tell us something about him?"

"Well, he's kinda muscular. In his twenties. She's with him a lot, but I never met him personally."

"Do you recall the time the game ended?"

"Let's see. Around eight twenty, I think. Yup. Eight twenty. I remember that exactly because Nanette came over to me and asked if I could take the children for the night. Her friend was late for an appointment. She said the appointment was at eight. So I looked at my watch and saw that indeed, he was late already."

After the interview with Ross ended, Hartford had one important question on his mind: *Who was this Eric whom Nanette Johnston was with at the soccer game?* Detectives decided to surveil Johnston's home to find out.

Later that day, at around 3 p.m., Detective Hartford interviewed Kim McLaughlin. Kim was clearly distraught but managed to give some details about her father. She described him as very social, a person who loved to attend parties. She commented that her father was "such a wonderful person, an amazingly loving father, and my best friend."

"Can you tell me what your feelings are towards Ms. Johnston?"

"I can't say that I like her very much. In August, when my dad and I were having a chat, I told him Johnston was mooching off him. He told me, 'I understand women. I know they're attracted to me for my money.'"

Kim stated that her father had recently been complaining about Johnston and about the fact that *he* was practically raising *her* children. Kim specifically recalled her father stating, "Nanette's going to the gym and taking care of the kids is getting old."

As the interview was winding down, the detective asked

Kim if she had any idea who might have a motive to kill her father.

"Hal Fischel," she replied without hesitation. And then she added, "And Nanette."

That made four fingers pointing toward Fischel and something new: one finger pointing toward Nanette.

The plot was definitely thickening.

Chapter Eight

Tuesday, December 20

It was now five days before Christmas and the investigation at the NBPD was heating up. Detectives decided that in addition to continuing to interview persons of interest, perhaps the key to solving this murder would be the *keys* themselves.

McLaughlin's killer had used not one but two keys to gain access to the home. Both were left at the scene. One was chrome colored, left in the house's front-door lock. The other was brass colored, left on the mat just outside the front door. Both keys appeared to be new.

The chrome-colored key, detectives soon discovered, opened not only the McLaughlins' front door but also the east side-gate to the house. The brass-colored key opened a pedestrian gate into the Balboa Coves community, located around fifty feet from the McLaughlin home, near a basketball hoop.

Where had the keys come from? Were they copies? Maybe they could trace the keys to a specific hardware store or person and then they might be able to find the killer. One key had the word "ACE" stamped on it; the other had it embossed on it, suggesting they were copies made at an Ace Hardware store.

That evening as part of the surveillance on Nanette Johnston, Newport police detective Dave Byington followed Johnston to 4403 Seashore Drive. Byington then exited his car and surreptitiously walked behind the house. Standing on the sand only feet from the ocean, he was able to look into the living room window of the home. He saw what looked to him like a happy holiday scene—Johnston and her two children decorating a Christmas tree and placing brightly wrapped presents underneath. Byington was surprised.

A killer is on the loose. The killer has just murdered this person's fiancé. Isn't she afraid for her life? For her children's lives?

Apparently not. Apparently, life goes on.

Chapter Nine

Wednesday, December 21

Six days after the murder, a memorial service was held for Bill McLaughlin at Our Lady of Mount Carmel, a Catholic church in Newport Beach, the same church that the family had attended when the McLaughlin children were growing up.

Over a hundred people filed solemnly into the church, located directly on the water. The service was a somber affair. Most of the attendees still hadn't been able to process the fact that their friend, business associate, neighbor, relative—loved one—was dead. "No one ever, ever in a million years would have expected that," said one neighbor. A business associate said he was "dumbstruck," describing McLaughlin as charming, with a warm smile. "He was a man who always asked about all our families."

The service was emblematic of McLaughlin's deep connection to his faith. "Father Bill Barry, a man who had always been in our lives and who lived next door, said mass with Father Dean and Father Sai, my dad's best friends," said Kim. "Plus, his best friend at Loyola Marymount, Father Donald Merrifield, also offered mass. I remember thinking what a great honor it was for my dad for all these priests to be there. That was very special for our family."

Commenting on the people who spoke at the funeral, Kim said, "I can only remember my brother, who gave a beautiful tribute to my dad. He talked about what a great friendship they had and what a great dad he was." Continuing, Kim stated, "Truth is, I was in complete shock. I remember very little of it. I remember trying to greet people and it was all a blur."

During the ceremony, the entire McLaughlin family was gripped with sadness, sobbing uncontrollably. Kevin, in particular, was inconsolable. He was also very, very angry at what happened.

Nanette's children were also inconsolable. They were screaming and crying loudly. Kim later said, "They must have been missing my dad so much."

Nanette, on the other hand, did not break down at all. She appeared stoic and never shed a tear. "She just seemed a little detached," said Kim later.

After the ceremony at a memorial reception, Judy Palmer and David McLaughlin, a niece and nephew of Bill's, sat down at a table with Johnston's son, Kristopher.

"Mom's boyfriend plays football," Kristopher animatedly told David.

"Your mom's boyfriend?" asked an incredulous David.

"Yeah."

"That's strange. I thought Uncle Bill and Nanette were going to get married. Who's the boyfriend?"

But by then Kristopher had already walked away.

Apparently, it was no big deal to Kristopher that his mother seemed to have a boyfriend on the side. But it *was* a big deal for David. David usually spoke on the phone with his uncle at least once a month, and his uncle Bill had never told him anything about Johnston having another boyfriend. In David's mind, Johnston and McLaughlin were dating each other exclusively—and there had even been talk of marriage.

Although Kristopher had no idea his comment would spark a fire, it did. When David and Judy told their father, Patrick, what Kristopher had said, Patrick, too, was stunned.

That evening, Patrick contacted the police. "Maybe this information can help you," he said as he told them about what he had heard.

Although the NBPD was already aware of this possible "other" man in Johnston's life, they were becoming increasingly more concerned about why Johnston had kept this information from her fiancé and his family.

If this Eric was simply a friend, why wouldn't she tell McLaughlin about him? What was she hiding?

After the funeral, detectives continued to tail Johnston. They followed her first to Champion Motorcycles, which was about two miles away in Costa Mesa. After she walked into the showroom, a detective shadowed her inside, ostensibly to buy a motorcycle for himself. Watching her actions closely, he saw Johnston talking at a table with a salesperson and filling out paperwork. After she wrapped up the transaction, the detective spoke to the salesperson. It turned out that Johnston had just signed a credit card receipt labeled: "Exchange only: item: sale $7,052.70." After quickly interviewing the salesperson, the detective learned that Johnston had bought three dirt bikes.

On the day of her beloved fiancé's funeral, Johnston was out buying three dirt bikes. Wasn't she supposed *to be in mourning?*

Detectives then followed Johnston to a Wells Fargo bank. An investigator followed her in and watched as Johnston withdrew some money—as it turned it, a $3,000 advance on a McLaughlin credit card.

Very odd that right after a funeral Johnston was going on with life as usual. However, everyone processes grief in his or her own way—and it was dangerous to jump to conclusions.

Chapter Ten

Nanette Johnston

Nanette Johnston was born Nanette Ann Maneckshaw on July 3, 1966, in Chicago, to Adi Maneck Maneckshaw, 27, and Carol Marcia Maneckshaw, 25. Soon after, Nanette's family moved to Phoenix, Arizona, where she grew up and attended high school. Her family included a brother, Jim, and a sister, Michelle.

In 1983, when she was 17, Nanette met 22-year-old Kevin Ross Johnston, known as Ross, at a twenty-four-hour Nautilus Health Spa in Mesa, Arizona. According to Ross, Nanette was gorgeous, sexy, outgoing, and really intelligent. The following year, they married, moved into an apartment, and soon had their first child, Kristopher. In 1987, they had their second child, Lishele. At the time, neither had much money, but they did have a lot of love.

Soon, however, trouble appeared in the marriage. Ross discovered that Nanette had not only been seeing other men, but she was also placing ads in singles newspapers in an attempt to meet wealthy men. One time, he even found a business card of Nanette's on an expensive foreign car. On the card, Nanette had written: "You caught my eye while driving down Scottsdale Road. If you are unmarried, I'd love to meet you. I'll be at 'What's Your Beef?' tonight looking for you. Nanette."

That did it. Ross had had enough. The two separated and

Ross moved to Lake Forest, California, with their two children. Soon after, however, Nanette contacted him and told him she wanted to reconcile. Apparently, she was ready to change her cheating ways. Ross figured that he'd give it another chance.

Nanette moved to Lake Forest, and for the first few months things were going well. However, all that changed when Ross discovered that Nanette was once again placing ads in singles magazines and had taken out a PO box in Mission Viejo in order to receive the responses. Now, totally fed up with her behavior, Ross asked her to leave. In May 1990, Nanette moved from Ross's home to an apartment in Costa Mesa.

Single life seemed to agree with her. While on her own, Nanette liked to frequent bars and clubs. One night in November 1990, she went alone to The Red Onion in Newport Beach, where she eyed a handsome bouncer. The two started up a conversation, and by the time the evening ended it was clear that something serious was beginning. Tom Reynolds was smitten by Johnston. She was nothing short of a bombshell, she was smart, and she clearly liked him. The relationship developed quickly, and approximately three weeks after they met Johnston moved into his place. One thing was perfectly clear: Johnston had a knack for charming the pants off men—literally.

The couple lived together between November 1990 and January 1991 and all during that time, Reynolds was totally taken by her. "She would sit there and tell you she was going to be queen and you would believe it. You'd get ready for the coronation," said Reynolds.

Once, after Reynolds had won a lot of money gambling in Las Vegas, he wired it all to Nanette and asked her to deposit it in his bank. When he returned home, he discovered that she had deposited $2,500 less than the amount he sent her. He was disturbed, but he decided to give her the benefit of the doubt.

However, not long after that, as he was cleaning out some things in early January 1991, he found canceled checks, which had been written to a singles magazine. Not only that. Reynolds also discovered that Nanette was dating three or four other men. In fact, a previous boyfriend of Nanette's contacted him and said she owed him money. "He warned me about her."

Reynolds had had just about enough. He ended the relationship at the end of January 1991 but that wasn't the end of it. Later, he was forced to declare bankruptcy as a result, he said, of her making so many large charges on his credit card. Reynolds also stated that when she moved out she attempted to take some of the furniture that belonged to him.

Once again, Nanette was single, and once again, it didn't take her long to find herself a new man.

Only three months later, in May 1991, after having placed yet another ad in a singles magazine, Nanette received a response from Bill McLaughlin. To Nanette, he seemed like the man of her dreams. Although they were nearly thirty years apart in age, the two enjoyed many of the same activities and got along just fine. In fact, they got along so well that in August she moved into his Balboa Coves home with her two children. Nanette seemed to fill a deep void in Bill's life. He'd been lonely since his divorce, and Nanette was outgoing, congenial, and an engaging companion. Plus, she took over some of the day-to-day accounting duties that his wife used to deal with, freeing him to stay abreast of the many business dealings he was involved in. Besides, he loved her kids.

The two seemed to be getting along so well that McLaughlin bought a second home, on Seashore Drive, close by, so Nanette could have her own place to stay in if she wished. As it turned out, however, she spent most of her time at the Balboa Coves home, where her two kids had their own separate bedrooms. Life was certainly sweet for Nanette.

One day in June 1991, Nanette picked up her children at Ross's home, driving an Infiniti. Immediately Ross knew she had met a wealthy man. Then in July Nanette paid Ross a past-due debt of $28,000 she owed his parents. Now Ross was certain that she had met a rich man.

His feelings were corroborated when he was reading over court papers concerning the custody of their children. In the papers, Nanette wrote that she lived at 67 Balboa Coves, and it was then that Ross knew she had, indeed, met a *very* wealthy man. When Ross asked her where she had gotten the money to pay back the debt, she said that the man she was living with, the man who was serving as her mentor, Bill McLaughlin, had given it to her in return for her assisting him in negotiating a business deal.

Although she appeared to be living the life with Bill McLaughlin, Nanette still found time to hunt for other men. She was a fitness fanatic—obsessive about keeping in shape—and going to the gym and doing various sports were great ways to engage the attention of new prospects. Not one to remain monogamous for long, in early 1992 Nanette met Richard Baker while she was Rollerblading by Newport Beach. He was immediately smitten by this outgoing, beautiful, and intelligent woman. In March 1992, he asked her if she would like to attend the wedding of one of his friends. She agreed and the two flew off to Arizona for a romantic weekend of their own.

According to Baker, Nanette told him that she and McLaughlin had a platonic business relationship, in which he was acting as her mentor. She also told Baker that she had made her own money through a hairbrush she invented, which removed water from the hair. She also claimed to be part owner of the Seashore Drive house and that she was interested in buying out McLaughlin's portion. To Baker, she was quite the catch.

Baker said that he asked Nanette to introduce him to McLaughlin on at least five different occasions, but she never would. He thought that was odd but it certainly didn't raise any red flags. He stated that he had been inside the Balboa Coves home at least ten times during his relationship with Nanette. He would arrive at the Pacific Coast Highway gate and buzz the residence, and Johnston would open the gate for him. Baker said that he always entered through the garage door by ringing the bell or knocking on the door and

Johnston opened it by remote from the inside. Baker said he had sexual relations with Johnston at least ten times in a first-floor bedroom of that residence.

Baker stated that their relationship ended after Kristopher called him Dad. That was definitely *not* what Baker had signed up for.

So once again, Nanette was on the prowl, even though she was still living with McLaughlin. One day, while her children were taking a fitness class at the Sporting Club at Lakeshore Towers in Irvine, she was intrigued by their hunk of a teacher, one Eric Naposki. It was mid-1992. It seemed that Nanette was about to spin her magic yet again.

And that's exactly how it seemed to Naposki—magical. After spending some time together over the next several months, the two became lovers and could barely keep their hands off each other. They could often be seen kissing and hugging in public.

Back at the McLaughlin house, things seemed to be going along swimmingly as well. Obviously, McLaughlin didn't know anything about the antics of his live-in girlfriend as the two traveled to Las Vegas and took other vacations together. They often went out to dinner with McLaughlin's friends. They were getting along so well that McLaughlin took out a $1-million life insurance policy and listed Johnston as the sole beneficiary. Plus, he made her a co-trustee of his multimillion-dollar estate. Not only that. McLaughlin bought Johnston an enormous diamond engagement ring. It seemed that the pair intended to get married.

In spite of McLaughlin's daughters' misgivings about Johnston—a young woman after his money, they said—McLaughlin assured them they had nothing to worry about. He knew what he was doing, he assured them, and he had definitely found himself a fine life companion.

Chapter Eleven

Thursday, December 22

The day after the funeral, a headline in the *LA Times* read: "Newport Entrepreneur's Death Baffles Community: Police are investigating victim's dealings. Neighbors believe the shooting was not a random act."

However, the thought that Bill McLaughlin possibly knew his shooter did not assuage the anxiety of the residents of Balboa Coves. In fact, fear had reached a near-hysterical pitch, with neighbors buying new locks for their doors, investigating "renting" guard dogs, and finding out how much it cost to hire a guard for the community 24/7.

After all, a killer was still on the loose, and if Bill McLaughlin's death was *not* premeditated, who knew who would be next?

The days before Christmas are customarily a festive time of putting final touches on Christmas trees, doing last-minute shopping, baking cookies, and sneaking nips of eggnog. However, December 22 was anything but cheery at the McLaughlin home in Balboa Coves.

That morning, Detectives Hartford and Voth stopped by to interview the victim's brother, Patrick, who was staying there with other members of the McLaughlin family. Extremely upset, Patrick was nevertheless able to provide the officers with some pertinent information. When asked if his brother ever spoke to him about Johnston, Patrick stated, "I had one discussion with Bill in which we discussed Nanette."

"What did he say about her?" asked Voth.

"He said he had no intention of marrying Nanette."

"In so many words?"

"In those exact words."

What exactly had been going on between McLaughlin and Johnston? the detectives wondered. *Had McLaughlin discovered Johnston was unfaithful? Untangling these relationships wasn't going to be easy.*

Later that day, the detectives spoke to Nanette at the Seashore Drive home. They asked to see her key ring to determine what keys were on it. Voth noted in his report: "I checked to see if a key that matched the description of the security gate key for the complex was on the ring. I could not find a key that matched that description. She had one 4403 Seashore key and a key for the Cadillac (which Bill McLaughlin had bought for her to drive), no exterior gate key, and I think a house key. There was no key to the pedestrian access gate."

This gave detectives pause. *Could it be that Johnston gave her key to someone? Could it be that that person had a new key made—one that was left at 67 Balboa Coves on the night of the murder? Could it be that Nanette actually knew the killer?*

Several detectives continued to surveil Johnston's comings and goings. "At approximately 1620 hours," stated the police report, "Nanette and her two children arrived at her secondary residence [4403 Seashore Drive, Newport Beach]." After Johnston exited the car and went inside the house, "there was no activity at all," the police report stated, "until later in the afternoon, at 1645 p.m. Then, a 1991 black Nissan Pathfinder pulled up and a man got out. The children ran out of the house and hugged and kissed him. Then the children and the man went inside Seashore Drive."

The detectives on surveillance duty passed on the plate

number to Voth, who set in motion a records check to see who owned the vehicle. Meanwhile, the officers watched as the man left the house "at 1655," got into his car, and drove away. The officers tailed him.

A short while later, when the contact information came back on the license plate detectives learned that the car was registered to a "John F. Naposki" of Heritage Court, Yorktown Heights, New York, and that there was an outstanding warrant for "an Eric Naposki" arrest for a traffic violation: "Failure to Appear on vehicle code violations in the amount of $343.00."

The detectives were elated. The warrant provided the perfect opportunity to bring Eric in for questioning.

What exactly, the detectives wondered, *had Eric Naposki been doing on the night of the murder?*

The detectives followed Naposki for several hours and ultimately tailed him to the Thunderbird Nightclub in Newport Beach.

The Thunderbird had been open for only a few weeks—it was a flashy new hot spot, with multiple party rooms, plenty of alcohol, and an interior décor that featured columns draped in faux tiger fur. It catered to some of Newport's rowdier club rats—and it was located just 131 yards, some 393 feet, from Bill McLaughlin's front door.

After Naposki parked and went inside at around 9 p.m., detectives sat and waited outside in their car. *This was turning into a stakeout.*

Chapter Twelve

Friday, December 23

At around 2 a.m., as Naposki was saying his good nights to several people standing outside the nightclub, detectives contacted officers from the NBPD, who had been alerted ahead of time to be nearby. They planned to stop him for the outstanding traffic violation and, more importantly, try to find out details of his whereabouts on the night of the murder. Around fifteen minutes later, as Naposki was driving home, the uniformed police pulled him over.

"You know why we stopped you?" asked one officer.

"No," responded Naposki calmly.

"We've got an outstanding warrant for your arrest. A three-hundred-forty-three-dollar Newport Beach warrant for failing to appear on a traffic citation on June 19, 1993."

"Okay," said Naposki.

"We'd like you to come with us."

Although surprised, Naposki put up no resistance. He was cuffed and put into the backseat of their car. His Pathfinder was taken away for impoundment.

On the way to the station the officers didn't engage Naposki in any discussion—and they took him to a cell at the NBPD.

At 3:55 a.m., Naposki was escorted from his cell and brought to Interview Room Number 4, a small, windowless room with a desk and four chairs. Naposki's chair looked directly at the door.

Within minutes, Detectives Van Horn and Voth walked in, and Naposki immediately wondered why *two* detectives were needed to conduct an interview about a traffic violation. He had the sinking feeling that he knew the answer.

He was read his Miranda rights; then one detective asked him, "Where do you live?"

"One-four-nine-oh-one Newport Avenue. Apartment one fifty-six. Tustin."

Then, within seconds, Naposki amended what he said. "But I moved out two days ago. I'm staying at the Ramada Inn at Seventeenth and Superior."

"Why'd you move?"

"They were raising the rent, so I left."

"Can we search your hotel room?" Naposki said that would be fine.

"What do you do for a living?"

"I used to play pro football. Now I have a security business, Coastal Elite. I work as a security guard and operate a uniformed security company. I'm also head of security for the Thunderbird Restaurant, in Newport Beach."

Apparently, Naposki hadn't been at the club for the oyster shooters and premium vodka.

"Do you own any firearms? asked Voth.

"No, I don't do any armed work," Naposki responded without hesitation.

Voth asked again, "You sure you don't own any firearms?"

"Oh, yeah," Naposki responded, seeming to have just recalled a gun he owned. "I have a .380-caliber semiautomatic handgun. Got it in Texas."

"Where's it now?"

"I gave it to my dad for his protection. He got mugged in New York hauling asbestos."

The detectives then turned to the subject of Nanette Johnston. "Can you tell us a little about your relationship with Ms. Johnston?"

"Nanette's a pretty good friend of mine."

Van Horn asked, "Can you define 'good friend'?"

"Yeah, we've been friends for two and a half years."

The detectives next asked Naposki about Bill McLaughlin. "Never met Mr. McLaughlin," Naposki stated. "I've never been to his residence."

Asked what he knew of Johnston's relationship with McLaughlin, Naposki responded, "I knew of his partnership with Nanette as far as business goes and stuff like that. From what I gathered it was kind of a mentor, almost like a father-slash-daughter-type thing."

"So you didn't see it as a romantic relationship or a boyfriend-slash-girlfriend?"

"No. I didn't," Naposki answered. "You know, I didn't involve myself in that. . . . I didn't think, you know, [it was my business] because we weren't romantically involved."

"So you're just a friend who's helping her out?"

"Pretty much."

Detectives continued to press Naposki about his relationship with Johnston. When asked again to give more details, Naposki hesitatingly offered a different version. "Hmm," he said after thinking it over for a few seconds. "I would say we're pretty close."

"Would you describe it as a dating relationship? A boyfriend, girlfriend relationship?"

"Yeah," he admitted. "I wouldn't say solo total—like I have girlfriends, you know, and people that I date, also. I would say a dating relationship that has potential, you know, to get better, to be more, but we've both been married before."

"Okay. I'm still somewhat in the dark as far as you say it's a dating relationship that has potential to be more," said Van Horn. "Is it serious?"

"Well, you know, I don't want to embarrass her in any way," responded Naposki.

"Okay. We're not talking to her, okay?" declared Voth.

"I know. I know, but, you know, I mean I don't want to embarrass myself by saying I like her, you know, something like that."

"Okay."

"[Nanette was] someone I might have hugged tonight at the club and made a date with or something like that. I'd say, you know, a girlfriend."

Under further questioning, Naposki revealed something that took the detectives by surprise, especially considering that he had just defined his and Nanette's relationship as loose and casual. "I planned to purchase an engagement ring and propose to her on New Year's Eve," he told them. However, he added, "because of the victim's sudden death, I decided to hold off asking her to marry me."

First, Naposki tells us they're just friends. Then, he says Nanette's a girlfriend whom he might hug. Now, she's a potential fiancée. What gives?

"Have you given any gifts or rings to Nanette?"

"I didn't get a ring. I just felt a little weird."

"Did you propose to her?"

"No, never."

Switching topics once again, the detectives asked Naposki where he was on the night of the homicide.

"With Nanette at her children's soccer game in the city of Diamond Bar. After the game," he continued, "she dropped me off in Tustin between let's say nine and nine fifteen. I changed my clothes and drove to my job at the Thunderbird Nightclub."

"What time did you arrive?"

"I'd say between nine thirty and nine forty-five."

"So how far is the Thunderbird from Mr. McLaughlin's home?" asked Voth.

"I'd say a few minutes walking."

After nearly an hour of questioning, the detectives felt they had gotten enough information and decided to end the interview. However, just as they finished thanking Naposki and were about to exit the room, Naposki volunteered another piece of rather extraordinary information "You know, I bought a gun this year," he told them. "I gave it [to] one of my guys four to five months ago, to a guard to take it on a job around June of 1994, and he fuckin' lost it. He said it was stolen at his house."

The officers were intrigued. "What kind of gun?"

"Beretta 92 F, 9mm handgun. Cost me seven hundred dollars. Got it from a gun dealer in Los Angeles. Kevin Mc-Daniel."

Keeping stone-faced, although definitely interested in this news, they asked, "So who's the guy that lost it?"

"Name's Joe David Jiminez. Had the gun three weeks, never fired it."

"What kind of friend was he?"

"Shitty." Then, after a pause, Naposki added, "He could have sold the fuckin' thing for all I know."

"Were you paid back?"

"You kiddin'? He tried to sell me a bulletproof vest."

"Can you tell us something about this Joe David?"

"Yeah. He's about thirty years old. Lives in Huntington Beach. The guy said that an acquaintance of his by the name of Brian Dirky may have taken it."

"You report the gun missing?"

"No. I was hoping it would show up."

"Have you had any handgun training?"

"Well, I did some ROTC."

At that point, the detectives got word that officers searching Naposki's car had noticed two areas with discoloration. One appeared to be dried bloodstains on a green towel. The other was several brown and red stains on the carpet. Voth decided to press Naposki on it. "We're wondering if you could clear some things up for us," he said.

"Sure," said Naposki.

"Mind telling us why there's blood on a towel in there."

Without a second's hesitation, Naposki replied, "I cut myself shaving." He then pointed to the area on his chin that he claimed to have cut. Neither Van Horn nor Voth saw a cut or scab.

"Okay," Voth continued. "How about the stains on the carpet?"

They were from "a spilled café mocha."

"Okay," said Voth. "If that's the case, would you consent to having a sample of your blood taken, just so we can rule some things out?"

"Sure. No problem."

Although Naposki seemed unfazed by the stains, detectives felt that perhaps they would reveal something incriminating.

If the blood in the car was McLaughlin's, then the case would take a whole new turn. Not only would Naposki have to explain why he said he had never met McLaughlin, but even more important, he would have to explain why a total stranger's blood was in his car.

Naposki then asked the detectives if he could have the notebook that was inside his Pathfinder. It was his daily planner as well as a personal diary. They said he would get the notebook back in due time—along with the rest of his belongings.

The interview now over, the detectives thanked Naposki for his cooperation and said they would be in touch. Naposki was then taken back to his cell.

A few hours later, a friend of Naposki's posted bail of $343, the cost of the failure-to-appear citation, and Naposki was once again a free man.

Detectives then started mulling over what they had just learned.

Naposki began by saying he didn't own any firearms. Then he admitted he owned a .380. Later, he stated he also owned a 9mm. Why would a person fail to reveal what guns he owned, unless, of course, he had something to hide?

Naposki also began by saying he and Nanette were just friends, but by the end of the interview he admitted that he had planned to propose to her. Why would a person lie about the person he was in love with, unless, of course, he had something to hide?

That afternoon, detectives received a forensics report from the sheriff's ballistic lab office. It was the analysis of the three bullets that had been found lodged in Bill McLaughlin's upper body during his autopsy, as well as the shell casings found at the crime scene.

Under the "Examination" section, the report stated that the bullets retrieved from the body were "damaged 147 grain 9-mm Luger caliber Federal brand Hydra-Shok." All had the headstamp "9mm Luger FC."

In the "Results" section, the report stated: "The six bullets [casings] were fired from the same firearm."

In an attempt to narrow down the kind of gun that could have been the murder weapon, the report listed twenty-eight different firearms "as possibly having been used to fire the bullets"—including a Beretta 92 F—along with the following statement: "Additional firearms may exist which may not be in the above reference data base."

The detectives had already surmised—from the casings found at the crime scene—that a 9mm had most likely been involved in the murder. *But Naposki hadn't known that. Why would he spin a tale about his long-lost 9mm Beretta?*

Regarding the Federal Premium Hydra-Shok ammunition, the detectives knew all about what that meant. "The unique center-post design of the Hydra-Shok Hollow Point delivers controlled expansion while the notched jacket provides efficient energy transfer for maximum penetration," states midwayusa.com, an Internet site devoted to gun-related items. Another site, policelink.monster.com, points out that this kind of ammunition is the choice of law enforcement agencies nationwide because it "provides efficient energy transfer to penetrate barriers while retaining stopping power. The deep penetration of this jacketed bullet satisfies even the FBI's stringent testing requirements."

Obviously, whoever killed McLaughlin wasn't taking any chances. The person had been locked and loaded to put McLaughlin down permanently.

After learning about the 9mm bullets and casings, detectives began rethinking the information Naposki had given them early that morning.

As the interview ended, Naposki told us he also owned a 9mm. Why hadn't he told us that upfront? And was the gun

really "lost" as he had claimed? The detectives vowed to
find out.

That evening, detectives interviewed Mary Berg, the
McLaughlins' housekeeper. Unlike almost every other person they had spoken to, Berg had some rather harsh things
to say about her boss. She stated that the victim was a very
demanding person to work for. "I have never been given a
raise, and only once in the last few years have I received a
Christmas bonus," she stated.

Lately, Berg said, McLaughlin had become very careful,
wanting his doors closed and locked when she left the residence. She said she believed Johnston and McLaughlin were
engaged, because she saw a ring on her finger. Berg said she
didn't believe McLaughlin had been with any other women
while he was with Nanette.

Berg stated that McLaughlin had bought Nanette a car
several years before, but she "rolled" it. "It was a long time
before he bought her a new car."

Chapter Thirteen

December 24–31

As Christmas approached and traditional carols played incessantly in stores and over the radio, the gaiety of the season seemed to heighten the McLaughlin children's despair and disorientation. They were heartbroken. Their father was dead. The truth of it was still impossible to comprehend, but one thing they knew for sure. They needed to get away from Balboa Coves and put some distance between the house where their father had been killed—where blood had pooled all over the kitchen floor—and where they slept at night.

In an attempt to heal themselves, the McLaughlins decided to travel to Hawaii to spend a few days there as a family. Although they could not stay at their mother's house—it had been damaged in a hurricane a few months prior—they rented a house on the beach.

"We all needed to be together and to get away. We were very scared," said Kim. "Someone had entered our house and killed my dad. . . . We had *absolutely* no idea who did it. . . . The only person he was even butting heads with was Fischel—he was the only person we knew who even disliked my dad or even disagreed with him in any way, shape, or form. So we were really baffled. Was this a random event?" Perhaps the tranquil water and calm surroundings would bring them the peace they so desperately needed.

Before they left, they thought it would be a good idea to

call Nanette and let her know of their plans and also to tell her that if there was anything she needed, she should not hesitate to give them a call. "We're going to Hawaii," Kim told Nanette "to have some downtime and try to ingest all this and clear our heads. Maybe we'll figure out how we're going to get through this." Then, after a pause, Kim continued. "And, while we're gone, if you need to take your things out of the house, please feel free to go in."

The McLaughlins thought that Nanette, too, would most likely be trying to process all that had taken place and attempting to get her life back on track. Perhaps, they thought, this could best be accomplished if she gathered her belongings from the Balboa Coves home and brought them to the Seashore Drive home. Also, the McLaughlins were trying to get a handle on their father's possessions and felt that the job would be easier if Nanette removed hers—they certainly had no interest in going through her things. And if they were honest with themselves, they would admit they wanted Nanette out of their lives. They had long sensed she was a phony, and her continuing presence in the house was making it hard for them to grieve.

Christmas in Hawaii for the McLaughlins was anything but celebratory. Although the family tried hard to find ways to enjoy themselves, they came up short. What was the purpose of buying presents? What was the reason to sing songs and bake special treats? Why bother putting up a Christmas tree? After all, they were missing the man who had given them so much. They were missing the man who had given them life.

They also talked about the shooting and tried to make sense of it. *Could his gun collection have had something to do with it?* Their father had been avidly collecting guns for two years. As a former Marine, he found them fascinating. "He was collecting them and cataloging them," said Kim. "We'd roll our eyes and say, okay, if that's what you're into. It was weird—big old antique rifles. But Dad had these fascinating stories to go along with each and every one, so we learned a lot about their history. So with all that gun stuff around, we thought that maybe some crazy gunman decided to come in and kill my dad." Their father's murder was so unimaginable, so unreal, it seemed like anything was possible.

Most days, the McLaughlins took long silent walks along the beach hoping that somehow a moment of clarity would come to them, explaining why their loved one had been killed. At other times, the family sat together and prayed. They also cried a lot and anxiously wondered how they would ever have the strength to come to terms with the events of December 15.

While the McLaughlins were in Hawaii, the detectives in the NBPD were following up on any lead that came their way—and the leads kept coming and coming.

After they copied and reviewed the notebook found in Eric Naposki's car, they saw that several pages had writing on them. Among the jottings was a "top-ten list of rules." The rule page was dated February 13, 1994.

Rule 1: Build a relationship of trust and love with Krista & Kayla [his two children from his previous marriage]. Support them both financially and emotionally. They must miss you like you miss them. Do not forget them, just the past!

2. You must be honest about things in your life: relationships, career goals, family, and friends.

3. You must stay disciplined and focused on your short-term goals, so the long-term goals have a chance.

4. Once you get your ass out of this financial disaster, do not overextend yourself anymore. Money is not important if you don't need it to have fun. Enjoy the free things life has to offer. Go back to basics.

5. Your body and athletic ability was a true gift from God! Use it to its utmost ability. Make it strong and perfect so you can enjoy all it has to offer. Your body is your [unreadable] that allows your soul to prosper.

6. Develop strong spiritual ties to life and all its meanings. Remember: No Excuses, None, Never!

7. Do not be sidetracked by bullshit. Keep your dreams alive.

8. Keep a positive mental attitude. You only live once. Make it count. Your [*sic*] 27 now. Don't waste time anymore.

9. Do not be afraid to succeed or to fail. There is no difference. It is how hard and honest you work!

10. Be one tuff [*sic*] son of a bitch. Respect everyone. Fear no one!

Other pages had notes on them, such as "Figure out Rent situation/New Place; Collect $500; Insurance New York; Truck Payment Soon—mail overnight; Phone store; leather store." On one page was a list of money that he was owed or he owed: "Tom: $100; Todd: $444; and Jimmy B: $180"; along with "Call Arthur for meeting; look into Irvine Studio w kids." Still another page included a daily schedule for running, working out with Nanette; showering; lunch; office; working out again; dinner; and so on.

A couple of pages later were some random letters and numbers that looked to Voth like a license plate: "2WWL034." Later, Voth commented, "That one really piqued my interest. I decided to check out my hunch and run the numbers through the California system."

Half an hour later, the results came back. The numbers and letters were, indeed, a California license plate. And to whom was the license plate registered? William McLaughlin. In fact, the license was registered to McLaughlin's 1991 Mercedes-Benz.

The detectives were shocked.

Why would Naposki have McLaughlin's license plate number written down in his notebook when, according to Naposki, he had never met McLaughlin, nor had he ever been to his home? And could this have been why Naposki asked for his notebook when his Pathfinder was impounded? What was Naposki hiding?

During Christmas week, detectives also looked into the Chubb Life Insurance Company policies that were in the safe at 67 Balboa Coves. After reading them carefully, Voth discovered another important piece of information. Nanette Johnston was named as a beneficiary on one of the policies. In the event of Bill McLaughlin's death, she was to receive $1 million.

That's a lot of money, Voth thought. *And a lot of motive.*

Continuing to do background checks on Johnston and Naposki, Detective Craig Frizzell learned that they were both members of the Sporting Club at Lakeshore Towers, a swanky new gym located in a high-rise office complex in Irvine. He contacted Carrie Piecuch, the club's director of member services, and asked if she would speak to him about the pair. She readily agreed.

"About a year ago," Piecuch told the detective, "Naposki was employed at the club as a personal fitness instructor. He worked here for approximately three months, until we were forced to terminate his job." Piecuch went on to explain that the management was upset because Naposki continued to park his motorcycle on the sidewalk adjacent to the front office after he had been repeatedly warned not to do so. One day, continued Piecuch, after Naposki had once again parked his motorcycle outside the gym, the club had a tow truck come and tow it away. "When Naposki learned of this," Piecuch stated, "he became extremely upset and threatened to do bodily harm to those responsible." That, coupled with "his overall bad attitude," Piecuch stated, as well as his "having a big ego and being a hothead," led the club to terminate his services.

Since then, Piecuch related, Johnston and Naposki had routinely worked out at the club and Naposki had "been on his best behavior."

Continuing their investigative work, Voth located Joe David Jiminez at Jiminez's parents' home in Texas. Jiminez was the man Naposki mentioned during his interview as the person he had given his 9mm to. Detectives began their interview by stating that they had previously interviewed Naposki. "He mentioned he lent you a 9mm."

Quiet for a moment, a confused Jiminez said, "No. It wasn't a 9. It was a Jennings .380-caliber handgun."

"Are you sure?" asked Voth.

"Positive."

"Not a 9mm?"

"Absolutely not."

"Where's it now?" asked the detective.

"I sold it to a friend, Art Menaldi, after Naposki didn't pay me for a job. I needed the money."

"Can you give us his contact information?"

"Sure."

After detectives completed their interview with Jiminez, they called Menaldi. Art was at work, said his brother, but he would be willing to help them out.

"Do you know if your brother got a gun from Joe David Jiminez?"

"I know he did. In fact, I have it now. I can run it down to the station if you want."

Detectives were eager to see what Minaldi would bring in—and if it was indeed a .380. "Bring it," the detectives said.

Within an hour, Menaldi's brother Dominic brought a "blue steel, semi-automatic Jennings Firearms Bryco 38, .380 caliber" to the police station.

"This is the gun Jiminez gave my brother," Dominic said emphatically.

Supporting the fact that Naposki had given him a .380, after Jiminez returned from Texas to Los Angeles a few days later he came to the police station and turned over six rounds of ammunition to Voth—"Federal Hydra Shok copper jacketed, hollow-point bullets, made for a .380 semi automatic pistol"—which, he said, came from the firearm Naposki had given him.

Once again, detectives were forced to question Naposki's statements during his interview.

Who was telling the truth about the gun—Jiminez or Naposki? Did Naposki give Jiminez a .380, as Jiminez stated, or a 9mm, as Naposki stated? And, if it was a .380, why did Naposki lie?

What exactly was Eric Naposki's deal?

Chapter Fourteen

Eric Naposki

Eric was born on December 20, 1966. He grew up in the projects on Heath Avenue in Kingsbridge Terrace in the Bronx. It was a tough, dangerous neighborhood, and Eric literally ran home every day after school to avoid encounters with druggies and gangbangers.

His mother, Ronnie Lee Salesky, was 19 when Eric was born, and Eric never knew his father. There was no male influence in his life until he was nine. That was when John Naposki—all six feet, three inches, and 280 pounds of him—walked into their lives. John married Eric's mother in 1977 and immediately adopted Eric. According to Eric, "John found the son he had always dreamed of. And I found the father I always wanted. He was a fantastic dad."

Eric grew up to be a big kid and a talented football player. In fact, he lived and breathed football, starting out in the Pop Warner football league and then "I had to go to three high schools in order to keep playing football."

First Eric played at Tuckahoe High School in 1982. Football coach Jim Capalbo recalled Naposki as one of the biggest sophomores on the varsity team. "He was popular, good-looking, and earned good grades. He had the desire to be a good athlete.

"He was quickly plugged into the starting lineup," said Capalbo. "He was the kind of kid you'd want on your team.

If I gave you a list of which kids would go bad, he'd be at the bottom. He wouldn't even be on there." Capalbo recalled seeing Eric's father attending most of his games and pushing his son to succeed.

When Tuckahoe's football program folded in 1983, Naposki moved to Yonkers so he could continue to play football, at Lincoln High School. However, soon after Lincoln dropped football, too, when a team member had a heart attack. Trying to keep their son's football dreams alive, a year after that, the family moved once again, to Eastchester. And here, Eric shone on the field.

During his senior year at Eastchester High, Eric made fourteen touchdowns, gained over 876 yards on offense, and had over one hundred tackles. Eric led the state in rushing.

As a result of his successes, Eric was eyed by a number of universities to play for their football teams. He was offered partial scholarships by New Hampshire, New Haven, and Buffalo, but he accepted a full scholarship from the University of Connecticut, a Division 1-AA school, in the now-defunct Yankee Conference.

Eric was thrilled—and proud. He had worked hard and achieved his goals of going to college *and* playing football.

It was a heady time for the Bronx native and he loved being in the "country" at UConn. Plus, he got to play football.

While Eric was in college, his girlfriend since the fifth grade, Kathy O'Connell, would often come to visit him. He loved her deeply, and one weekend in his sophomore year, when Eric was 18, O'Connell got pregnant. He had always planned to marry her—and now with a baby on the way it seemed to be the right time. The two tied the knot and vowed to live together in good times and in bad.

However, being married and staying in college wasn't easy. Eric tried hard to make it work, but he wasn't able to support his family. One of the rules of his football scholarship was that he wasn't allowed to work so there was no way he could afford an apartment and put food on the table. Moreover, the coach wasn't playing him as much as he wanted. *If he was going to make it to the NFL, he needed to be seen!*

So in his junior year, he gave up the scholarship and left school and the team. Then, he had a crazy idea. He would try out for the NFL on his own. How? He decided to sneak into a mass tryout for the New England Patriots—literally getting onto the field through a hole in the fence at Sullivan Stadium—and grabbed a number. He ran the forty-yard dash in 4.5 seconds—blazingly fast for a linebacker. The Patriots ended up signing him. Finally, his dream of playing in the NFL had come true! "Over two hundred people tried out in New England—and I was picked," said Naposki proudly. "I was the youngest player in the NFL!"

But there was still no guarantee. He might still be cut at the Patriots' training camp or even in the preseason. "My dad came to the last preseason game and he said afterwards, 'That's the best game you ever played. If they cut you, it doesn't matter. You are so good.'" That meant a lot to Eric— but he certainly didn't want to be cut.

In fact, Eric survived the final cut and was put on the Patriots' roster as an outside linebacker. However, six weeks into the season he was badly tackled in a game he started and landed in the hospital with broken ribs and a lacerated liver. The injuries were so serious that the doctors warned that he could die. All through the days and nights in the hospital, his wife stayed with him. "With her help," said Naposki, "I made it through."

Getting into the pros had been his lifelong dream, but ultimately his NFL career didn't really gel. Although Eric was a big guy—six feet, two inches, and 230 pounds—and very fast, he was small for a linebacker, and this worked against him in spite of his skills. All told, he played in five games with the Patriots in two seasons, before he was traded to the Indianapolis Colts, in 1989, where he played in only one game. Over the next few years, he was given tryouts with the Dallas Cowboys, the New York Jets, the Washington Redskins, and the Seattle Seahawks, but in each case he was eventually dropped.

However, in 1991 an opportunity opened up. The World

League of American Football had been formed in 1990, with teams in both the United States and Europe. In 1991, Eric went to Spain to play for the WLAF Barcelona Dragons—and he stood out. He was a star player, supported by cheering crowds and children mobbing him when he went out to eat. He had a fan club called La Penya Naposki. After one game, Eric was quoted as saying, "I was just running onto the field, and people started to scream. I didn't know what they were doing. I even looked around to see who was following me, to see who they were cheering for, but there was nobody. Suddenly, I realized it was me." Eric was perplexed. "I mean, I'm a linebacker. We're not used to that kind of fanfare."

On the field, he was a freight train. Fellow linebacker and sports commentator Matt Millen said of Naposki's success at sacking opposing players, "This guy is scary and will hit you." He was so outstanding that he was awarded MVP.

However, his good fortune didn't encompass his personal life, nor did it last long. In 1991, Eric and his high school sweetheart, Kathy, got divorced, and Kathy stayed in Connecticut with their two children. Plus, physical issues plagued him big-time. He had a groin injury, then an ankle injury. On top of that, the WLAF suspended operations after his second season and his NFL tryouts had gone nowhere.

It was now 1992 and Eric felt like a beat-up rag doll and wanted to regroup. He decided to go to Orange County and start serious rehab. He hoped one day to return to football, but for now he simply wanted to get his body into shape. To do that, he joined a gym and worked tirelessly day in and day out to heal and strengthen his muscles. "That's where I met Nanette," Eric said later. "There was no sexual attraction. She was kind of like stuck-up, appeared richy rich, as if she's too good for this.

"When I met her and we started to work out, she was dating a few guys," said Eric. "Right away, that tells me she is single." To Naposki, Nanette came across as intelligent, attractive, fun loving, and very wealthy. She told him that she liked to dance, ski, and scuba dive. "Plus," added Naposki, "she was very interested in my life and that made me feel really good."

To support himself, Naposki started a security business, and soon began to get accounts with various nightclubs. One of them, the Roxbury, required that Naposki's men wear suits to work—something Naposki didn't have the money for. When he told Nanette about his problem, she immediately gave him $5,000 no strings attached. "She was a very good friend to me," Naposki said.

As the days and weeks passed, Johnston and Naposki began to hang out together more often. "We went naturally from friendship to relationship, to having lunch, to having lunch and sex. Nanette had what you would call an extreme appetite for lovemaking, and I could barely keep up."

At the end of 1993, Nanette invited him to go to her sister's New Year's Eve party in Maryland. "Of course, I accepted. We had a great time, and the next day, we went to New York. . . . I was falling in love with Nanette then. She was best thing since sliced bread. We aligned well—country music; working out; running. I adored her children. Me and Kristopher were very close. Our relationship reminded me of myself and my dad.

"In February 1994, I started living with buddies. Nanette and I were hanging out," said Naposki. But things only got truly serious between them after Naposki returned from an aborted tryout for the Canadian Football League in June. "I was playing good, but my groin and my arch were bad, so I eventually went home and settled into an apartment in Tustin." Not long after, the pair went on a short vacation to Jamaica. Nanette paid for the whole Caribbean getaway. *And why wouldn't she?* She said she was a millionaire—and based on the way she dressed, the $60,000 Cadillac she drove, and the ease with which she spent money in general, it appeared to be true.

Upon their return, the couple couldn't find any place to be alone, since Eric was living with roommates and Nanette was living with her older "mentor" in a "purely business relationship." So Nanette urged Eric to get his own place, which he did.

According to Eric, "We were getting closer and closer and the relationship was getting deeper and deeper. Nanette slowly started telling me some things about the 'mentor' with whom she was living. In September . . . she had a fat lip and bruises on her arms. She told me 'Bill' was drunk [and that he] came down to her room with a weapon; forced himself on her; tried to penetrate her, but wasn't successful so he penetrated her with [the] weapon." Despite this revelation, Nanette and her children continued to live in Bill McLaughlin's house in Balboa Coves. According to Eric, Nanette was willing to stay on in the house because for her the positives still outweighed the negatives.

During Thanksgiving of 1994, Naposki and Johnston traveled east to visit Naposki's parents, arriving on November 21 and leaving on the 25th. Nanette's children came with them. To Eric's parents, Ronnie and John, the pair looked so happy. Ronnie thought that Nanette was very smart and very nice. She believed that Eric had finally found the one.

Soon after they returned to California, in early December, Eric got a job as head of security at the Thunderbird Nightclub, located—as it turned out—only a couple of minutes' walk from Bill McLaughlin's home.

And on December 15, Bill McLaughlin was dead.

Chapter Fifteen

January 1995

In early January, the McLaughlins returned from their two-week respite in Hawaii and drove directly to 67 Balboa Coves. They knew they had to face this new reality and were poised to do their best. After settling in, Kim, Jenny, and Kevin went upstairs to their father's office, where they expected to find everything right where it was when they left. After all, the papers and equipment in this room belonged to their father, and if Nanette had taken the time to clear out her belongings, surely she wouldn't have found many of her own items to remove from the office.

However, as they entered the room, they saw that it was practically empty. Gone was their father's huge, old computer. Gone was his bulky fax machine. Gone were the many documents that were always strewn all over his desk and tables. Gone, too, was their father's favorite and highly treasured baseball—signed by Babe Ruth.

As they continued surveying the room, they noticed that some things were *not* gone. Not gone were many photographs of Nanette and Bill together, smiling, with their arms around each other. That seemed odd to Kim and Jenny—leaving behind such poignant remembrances of Nanette's beloved fiancé—but they tried not to think negative thoughts about Johnston. After all, their father had been living with her for four years, and although they may have had their own concerns about the "affair," they had always wanted to support their father and to believe he had picked a good woman as his partner.

During the following days and weeks, Kim and Jenny began the difficult task of trying to sort out their father's finances. They had a lot to deal with, especially because his investments were so wide-ranging. Knowing that Johnston had been aware of much of what their father had been dealing with financially, they decided to start by asking her what she knew.

"Jenny and I hadn't been in the loop for a while," said Kim later. "It had been between my dad and Nanette, so we were trying to get a handle on things. We knew tax time was coming up and we were trying to get things in order because we had bills to pay. We'd leave messages on Nanette's machine saying we're looking for this or that document for Brian, our accountant, but she wouldn't return our calls. She constantly tried to avoid us."

When detectives learned this, they decided to find out more about McLaughlin's finances by sidestepping Johnston and getting in touch with McLaughlin's accountant, Brian Ringler. Ringler was not only in charge of preparing McLaughlin's taxes but also helped him out with all of his financial dealings. Although it was primarily a business relationship, Ringler and his wife would sometimes go out for a social evening with McLaughlin and Johnston, having dinner and lounging over coffee and dessert.

Ringler told Detective Hartford that McLaughlin received regular royalties from his invention. Those monies, Ringler stated, went into an investment account managed by U.S. Funds under the name of "W. F. M. Holdings, Ltd. Partnership," which Ringler referred to as McLaughlin's "big" account.

The accountant pointed out that McLaughlin had another account, at Primerit Bank, which was set up to take care of small matters, such as credit card bills and the like. In this account, set up in the McLaughlin Trust, Johnston was a trustee. As such, Ringler stated, Johnston had signing authority. He did not believe that Johnston had signing authority on the U.S. Funds account.

When asked how much money McLaughlin might have in the "big" account, Ringler commented that it could have over a million dollars, depending on when the royalty checks arrived. In the smaller account, Ringler stated, the amount could range from very little to around $50,000.

Ringler told Hartford that just a few days previously he had received a call from Johnston, in which she told him that funds were low in both accounts. Ringler said he thought that was strange, because he felt there should have been a substantial amount of money in the U.S. Funds account. He knew McLaughlin received his royalties in December and "that usually lasts for three months."

Ringler continued, "I was aware of his property taxes and the various bills that he owed, so I asked Johnston if she would mind getting me the last three monthly statements from the W. F. M. Holdings account. I was certain that there would be a lot of money there."

In mid-January, Detective Voth received an unusual request from Bill McLaughlin's ex-wife, Sue. She was very upset—as upset as she had been when she first learned of Bill's murder. During the past three weeks, she told Voth, she had noticed that Kevin was becoming more and more distant and she sensed that his use of drugs and alcohol was increasing. After speaking with several of Kevin's friends, Sue felt that some of these so-called friends seemed to be enabling him in his drug dependency. She asked Voth if there was anything he could do to help.

Voth said later that he "counseled her, offering her information I had learned as a narcotics detective. I also asked a fellow detective, who was trained to counsel juveniles with drug and substance problems, to call her."

What was causing Kevin to unravel? Was it pure and simple grief and the horror of experiencing his father's murder? Or was it possible Kevin knew more than he was telling?

Around that same time, Kim received a copy of her father's will and immediately handed it over to Voth. Voth was eager to check out the disbursements to see who, if anyone, *could* have had a financial motive to want McLaughlin dead.

The will, he saw, had been filed in Las Vegas on March 2, 1992, and was signed by McLaughlin's attorney David Dundas, as a witness. According to the document, Kimberly Sue McLaughlin and William McLaughlin's brother, Patrick, were named co-executors. Kimberly was to receive her father's 1991 Mercedes-Benz and two-thirds of the estate, after the bequeathment to Johnston, which the will stated included $150,000, a 1991 Infiniti, and a year's free rent in the home on Seashore Drive. After the year, "the house was to revert to McLaughlin's daughters, Kimberly and Jennifer."

Further, according to the will, McLaughlin's younger daughter, Jennifer Kate, was to receive the final third of McLaughlin's estate.

McLaughlin's son, Kevin Patrick, was to receive nothing. (Detectives were told later that Kevin had not been in the will to preserve his SSI eligibility. SSI, or Supplemental Security Income, is a Federal income supplement program designed to help the disabled and aged, who have little or no income, by providing cash to meet their basic needs.)

The will concluded: "Anyone who contests the will is disinherited."

Although the will did not place a value on McLaughlin's estate, court records from his 1990 divorce estimated his worth at $8 million. Police put the total as high as $55 million.

With this information in hand, the detectives dispassionately sifted through potential suspects and motives, considering nothing but the cold calculus of financial gain.

Based solely on the will's disbursements, Kevin would have no monetary reason to want his father dead. Of course, Kevin might have been angry about being disinherited, and anger could be a powerful motive.

Nanette, on the other hand, could *benefit financially from McLaughlin's death. She would get $1 million from life insurance, $150,000 from the will, and some perks like free rent and a new car. On the other hand, if she had married Bill McLaughlin, she might have benefited even more from his being alive.*

Kimberly and Jennifer would *benefit monetarily, so they might have a financial reason to commit murder. However, to even think that they had something to do with their father's demise seemed absurd.*

And what of the will? What were the circumstances surrounding it? Taken at face value, it looked like Kevin had been cut out. But was that really what was going on? Kevin had had his near-fatal accident in October 1991, suffering severe brain trauma and landing in the hospital for months. His father had just confronted the fact that life can be snuffed out in an instant. The will, which was dated March 1992, had been crafted right in the middle of that terrible time. Was Kevin being disinherited? Or was Bill McLaughlin making sure that if he suddenly wasn't around his severely disabled son would be taken care of? Perhaps Kevin's third of the estate was being entrusted to someone Bill McLaughlin knew would take care of Kevin if Kevin couldn't take care of himself.

And what about the bequest to Nanette? McLaughlin had known her for about a year when the will was drawn. In the event of his untimely death, Bill gave her enough to live on for a year or two or even three if she could be more frugal— enough time to get back on her feet. But apparently there was a limit to McLaughlin's generosity when it came to Nanette.

Increasingly frustrated that an entire month had passed since the murder and still no suspects had been identified, Voth wrote in his notes: "On 1/3/95 I asked Jenny to contact her siblings and Nanette to consider a reward. She said that she would call me back."

On January 3, Kim called Detective Voth and reported

that the McLaughlin family and Nanette were planning to put up a $40,000 reward for information leading to the arrest and conviction of a suspect in the case. On the thirteenth of the month, the flyer was finalized. According to detectives, the delay in not having the flyer released sooner was due to Nanette's failure to commit the funds for her portion of the reward.

In mid-January, Voth received information that there had been a lot of activity on the victim's Visa and MasterCard. These charges had taken place *after* the victim's death. To make certain that nothing untoward was taking place, Voth called Kim and Jenny to ask if they had been using the cards.

"No," they responded. "We never used our dad's credit cards."

"Do you have any idea who is using the cards?"

"Most likely, it's Nanette," they responded.

Voth suggested that Jenny stop all credit cards in her father's name and notify Nanette. Jenny told Voth it was her belief that Nanette was racking up huge charges, which she was not entitled to do.

Continuing to find out as much as they could about Naposki, on January 15, Detectives Byington and Voth met with Robert Frias, a co-worker of Eric's who had lived with Eric during the past few years, until Eric became serious with Nanette, in approximately March or April of 1994. When asked about Johnston, Frias said that Naposki told him that Johnston made her money through pharmaceutical sales and from inventing a medical device. Frias also said that he, Johnston, and Naposki had gone shooting together at a gun range.

Having learned that Frias had a storage locker, detectives ordered a search warrant for the unit. After they conducted a thorough search, they had to admit they found nothing to incriminate Naposki. Frias was clearly frazzled, though, unable to fathom why his storage locker would be of any interest to the police.

After the police searched his unit, Frias immediately

called Naposki to tell him what had occurred. Frias told Naposki that the detectives had searched his locker for over three hours, looking for a gun, a black gun, a clip-type gun.

Frias also called Naposki's roommate, Leonard J. Jomsky. Jomsky said he had spoken to Naposki, who told him that the police were trying to "pin a murder" on him.

Continuing their investigations, on January 16, detectives asked Kevin to come to the NBPD for an in-depth interview.

Asked once again to give as many details as possible about the day of the murder, Kevin stated that he had been watching TV when his father returned home from Las Vegas. When he came in the door, Kevin asked his father how the trip was and he replied, "Fine."

But now Kevin added a detail the detectives hadn't heard before. He said that immediately prior to hearing gunshots he heard their dog barking "three to four times from inside the residence." Kevin stated that he thought that this was unusual because the dog rarely barked inside the house. He said he then heard several shots.

When asked how long he thought it had taken him to get from his bedroom to the kitchen, Kevin said he thought it was approximately three minutes from when he heard the shots until he called the police.

The officers then switched topics to his father's relationship with Johnston. Kevin stated that Nanette had her own room at the Balboa Coves residence, "but I frequently saw her leave her room and go into my dad's room at night."

Kevin also added these new details about Nanette: She never had any friends come to the house to visit; Nanette had lived with them for six to eight months (this was nearly accurate, since Kevin didn't return to the Balboa Coves home until late 1993; Nanette and Bill had lived together for over three years); he and his father had a running joke that when Nanette "turned thirty, he [McLaughlin] would dump her"; he had paid for Nanette's breast implants; and the morning after the murder Nanette took Kevin to breakfast. He said that was unusual because she had never done that before, nor had she ever made him breakfast. He surmised she took him to breakfast to be "friendly" to him after the homicide.

Although it was often hard to understand him because his brain injury continued to slur his speech, Kevin also told the police that Nanette had been acting suspiciously. Instead of sharing his grief, she was shedding crocodile tears. Maybe he couldn't explain it properly—but he *knew* she had something to do with his father's murder.

On January 18, Detective Voth went to Tustin Ace Hardware, located at 115 West Main Street in Tustin, to speak with the manager about the keys found at the crime scene.

First, they showed manager David J. Vandaveer various photographs and asked if he recognized any of the people in them. Vandaveer identified one as the person who worked security for them on October 7 through the ninth at Tustin Tiller Days—an event for Tustin residents to celebrate Orange County's agricultural heritage, as well as an opportunity to raise funds to benefit a wide variety of local needs. Vandaveer stated that the photo was of "Eric." He said that he didn't know the man aside from his working security, but Vandaveer mentioned that Eric had come into the store two or three times after that to have keys made.

Vandaveer said that his employee Michael Rivers might know more about Eric. When questioned, Rivers admitted that yes, he had had some dealings with Eric Naposki. In fact, Rivers claimed that Naposki came into the store one day and asked him for a "special order." Naposki wanted to know if Rivers could make him a silencer for a gun.

"What kind of gun was it?" Voth asked.

"9mm."

"Did he say why he wanted a silencer?"

"He said it was for a movie. I charged him around two dollars and fifty cents. It only took about ten minutes."

A silencer? For a 9mm? First, Naposki didn't mention he owns any *guns. Then, he admitted he owns a 9mm, but he said he gave it to Jiminez. Finally, Naposki had a silencer made for the 9mm.*

However, the date that the fake silencer was made for Naposki's 92 F was long after the date Naposki said that the gun had supposedly been stolen. Things were not looking good for the ex–pro football player.

Eager to speak to Nanette Johnston again—especially about all the new information they had received from and about Eric Naposki—detectives drove to her residence on Seashore Drive on January 19.

Once there, Lieutenant Mike Jackson, Sergeant John Desmond, and Detective Hartford began their interview.

"Can you tell us something about the man you went to the soccer game with?"

"His name's Eric Naposki."

"Do you have a relationship with him?"

After hesitating for a few moments, she said that she did.

"And how would you describe the relationship?"

"Let's see. We started out as friends. He played football and did a lot of traveling. Then a dating relationship began about a year and a half ago, after the football season ended, around mid-June." Johnston went on to say that she had spent "not a whole night with Naposki" at his apartment in Tustin on a few occasions.

Asked what that meant, Johnston stated that she left at around six or seven in the morning.

Surprised about this information, the detectives asked her about a seeming contradiction. "In our earlier interview, you stated you were engaged to the victim, Mr. McLaughlin. Is that true?"

"We were supposed to be married already, but because of the lawsuit Bill was involved in, we put it off. Bill put everything in my name to protect his assets just in case he lost the lawsuit."

Still confused, the detectives asked, "Did Naposki know you were engaged?"

"No." Then after a moment, she added, "I never wore the ring [McLaughlin gave me] when I was with him."

"Why didn't you tell Naposki?"

"'Cause I never thought about it. Because he wouldn't like that." Then Johnston added, "Naposki believed Bill and I just did business together."

So this woman is basically telling us that she is engaged to one man, dating another man, but not telling the second man that she is engaged? Hmmm.

Asked what she believed Naposki knew about Bill, she admitted that she may have led Naposki to believe that she and Bill had a strictly business relationship. Asked what else she told Naposki about herself and her finances, Johnston stated that she told him she had a six-figure income, she owned the residence at 4403 Seashore Drive, she owned the Cadillac, and she was an independent businesswoman.

Asked if Bill McLaughlin knew of her relationship with Naposki, she said that she and Bill had a "kind of unspoken agreement" that she would have affairs and that was okay as long as she was discreet. She said Bill told her she could have these "friends" as long as it didn't embarrass him. She described McLaughlin as not jealous and said they had a "really good relationship."

When questioned why she hadn't mentioned Naposki to them when they first asked about her activities preceding the murder, she stated that she didn't feel it was relevant. "Since no one specifically asked me, I didn't think I needed to bring [Naposki] up."

The detectives asked if she had ever traveled anywhere with Naposki. Johnston stated that they had gone to her sister's wedding in Maryland, which coincided with a visit to his parents. In June 1994, Johnston said, the two traveled to Jamaica for a vacation. She admitted that on that occasion she had told Bill she was going to Chicago to visit her grandmother. She and Naposki took the short visit to Chicago to visit her grandmother, she said, and then they went to Jamaica. Two weeks after the murder, Johnston added, "we went to San Francisco just to get away."

Next, detectives showed Johnston some pages from Naposki's notebook. On one, McLaughlin's license plate number was scrawled on the top.

"Why do you think Naposki wrote down Mr. McLaughlin's license plate number in his book?"

"Most likely," Johnston replied, "he had written it down after the murder so that he could do a little background work on the victim—to see if maybe he was involved in drugs or something else that could potentially cause me and my family some danger."

After the interview ended, the detectives had a whole lot of new information. *For certain, Nanette was cheating on her fiancé! She didn't mention the boyfriend to us until after we brought him up. Maybe she was ashamed at having a man on the side? Or maybe there's another reason. Plus, she doesn't seem particularly upset. Is there something more here than meets the eye?*

At around 2 p.m., Detective Hartford interviewed another member of the McLaughlin family. This time, it was the victim's ex-wife. Since the family had returned from Hawaii earlier in the month, they had all been staying together at the Balboa Coves home.

"When were you married?" the detective asked Sue McLaughlin.

"On February 12, 1966, but we filed for divorce in April of 1990. The divorce was finalized on December 31, 1991."

When asked why she and her husband split up, she said their relationship was imbalanced. She described herself as "a weak persona" while Bill was "very strong and domineering." She felt the relationship was crushing her and the stress had led her to develop a drinking problem. After the relationship ended, she had started attending AA meetings.

The divorce, she added, had been particularly unpleasant when it came to financial matters. Elaborating, Sue stated that she believed Bill was being ungenerous, given the wealth he had accumulated during the course of their marriage. However, from Bill's point of view, she said, "he thought I was gouging him." Eventually, Sue stated, "we worked out a settlement."

The detective inquired about Bill's habits. "Was he a drinker?" Sue recalled that Bill drank alcoholic beverages on a daily basis, mostly beer in the afternoon and late evenings. But he drank hard liquor only on rare occasions. Her ex-husband, she noted, was very disciplined. She stated also that during the marriage she took care of the finances for the home, such as paying the bills. Nanette, she said, had quickly slipped into that role—managing the household expenses— soon after moving in.

Feeling that Naposki was now a strong person of interest, Detectives Hartford, Frizzell, and Voth conducted a second, taped interview with him that afternoon in his bedroom. Earlier that month, Naposki had moved into an apartment with friend Leonard Jomsky. Naposki welcomed the detectives to the apartment and seemed willing to tell them all he knew.

"We wonder if you could straighten something out for us," they began. "In our last interview, you mentioned that you gave your 9mm to Jiminez. When we spoke to the gentleman, he told us that you gave him a .380."

After he thought this over for a moment, Naposki's composure changed and he became defensive. "I lied."

"Okay," said Frizzell, "so where is your 9mm?"

"I have no idea."

"You have no idea?"

"That's my statement. I don't want to talk about that anymore," Naposki said curtly.

"Do you remember the last time you saw it?"

"I don't know."

"I don't want to go around in circles about it anymore," said Frizzell.

"I don't want to talk about that," declared Naposki emphatically.

Seeing that Naposki's mood had drastically changed and hoping that he wouldn't lawyer up, detectives decided to change the subject.

"So, what did you think about the relationship between Johnston and McLaughlin? What did you think was going on between them?"

"This is my statement," said Naposki, who was becoming increasingly less cordial. "There is no way in the world that I knew anything was going on between those two until after the murder, when I started thinking [you all] were looking at me for a reason. Not just because I'm a big tough boyfriend, because that doesn't give me motive to do anything wrong. So I asked Nanette the question, 'Is this a love triangle situation that I didn't know about?' And Nanette said, 'It is just like I said it is [a business relationship with McLaughlin].' We went to Jamaica together. Am I a jealous guy to do something like that? Hell no!"

"Why wouldn't she tell you about Bill?"

"Maybe because she's scared to lose me. She might be playing me. She thinks if I find out I might break up with her." After a short pause, Naposki continued. "I wouldn't be with a girl that's with another guy. Bring her to my house. Introduce her to my parents. Make plans to spend time with her if that was the situation."

Naposki continued, more animated and more angry. "Of course, I work right across the fuckin' street. It makes it really easy for me to go [to McLaughlin's home]. Do you guys think I'm a fuckin' idiot? Would I do something like that and then walk across the street to work?"

"You told us previously you didn't know Mr. McLaughlin. Is that the case?" the detectives asked.

"I was never at Balboa Coves. I was never at Bill's house. Never, ever. Never, ever in Bill's house. I never met the man."

Later in the interview, detectives returned to the subject of the guns. They reminded Naposki how they discovered the discrepancy in his story concerning the 9mm after speaking with Jiminez. Naposki interrupted the detectives. "I understand. I understand the discrepancy."

"It's a big discrepancy," said Frizzell, "and these are the kinds of things that we need to clear up so we can let you go. Help us take you off our suspect list."

"I have no idea where it is or when it was taken, okay? Or what happened to it, period." Naposki stated that he had used the gun for an earlier security job he had, protecting a man's family during the wedding of his daughter in Mexico, but since then, he stated, he had not seen it.

"Did you confuse the guns?" the detectives pressed, trying to hide their incredulity. They then showed Naposki photos of the two different guns. "Here's our .380 and here's the 9mm Beretta 92 F. How could you confuse giving Joe David a 9mm and not a .380?"

"I didn't confuse it, obviously. I just told you—"

"You misled us?"

"Well, I misled you, yeah, 'cause I felt scared, you know."

Voth said, "Well, Eric, you got to know that's gonna focus some activity in your direction as soon as we disproved that and figured out it was a lie."

"That's fine. That's the deal. I misled you, yeah. I misled you, big deal."

"Yeah," said Voth quietly, "that's a really big deal."

Taking time to let those words sink in, Frizzell finally tackled the question that was uppermost on his mind. "Hey, pal," he said. "You don't have an alibi."

"I thought I did. I got paged that night by the alcohol manager."

Although this seemed like a revision of Naposki's original story, they urged him to continue. "Okay, then take us through your activities on that evening again."

Clearly exasperated, Naposki nevertheless once again recounted his movements on the evening of the murder. "We left the game at eight thirty-five. We moseyed to the car. She dropped me at my apartment around nine o'clock. I got situated, grabbed my papers for work, drove by Leonard Jomsky's house to see if they were home, got a page from my bar manager, returned the page from a pay phone at Denny's."

"This is kinda different from the first interview we had with you," said Voth, consulting his notes. "Then you told us that after you got to your apartment, you changed and went straight to work. Now you're saying you drove three miles up the Fifty-Five Freeway to Leonard Jomsky's house, got a page, drove over to Denny's, and returned the page, right?" Jomsky lived north of Naposki's apartment, while the Thunderbird Club was to the south.

Naposki responded, "Why don't we look at my phone bill and maybe you guys can leave me alone."

Detective Voth agreed that that would be a good idea. "Show us your phone bill. Then we can be done with this."

Without waiting for that to happen, and switching topics again, Frizzell said he was curious about the "random" numbers found in Naposki's notebook. "How did the license plate number of the victim's vehicle happen to find its way onto your notepad?"

Naposki stated, "I called somebody and they called me back. I don't want to get into it. I acquired it after [the victim's] death." Naposki went on to say, "I don't want to reveal my sources. It was about me doing some checking, why the guy was knocked off, if my girl was in trouble."

"How did you obtain the license plate number?"

"Uh, I don't want to go into my sources."

"Well, so somebody gave it to you?"

"I don't want to talk about that."

At the end of the interview, Naposki voiced his displeasure about the searching of his car and the taking of his notebook: "Instead of just bringing me the book and saying, 'What's this?' we play the old mind-fuck game between each other. That night, okay, I mind-fucked you with the gun, and you mind-fucked me with what happened to me that night. I don't even know if it's legal, all of what you did, as far as taking my notebook and photocopying it and all that kind of stuff, you know. I bet it wasn't legal. I believe it was illegal search and seizure. There was no reason, no probable cause, to steal my notebook."

Detectives chose not to go into details with Naposki about what was legal or illegal in a search and seizure. They knew the law. They knew they had every right to do what they did. And they also didn't ask him about the silencer that he had made. They were holding that question in reserve.

Finally, as the interview was winding down, Naposki laid on another bombshell. He told detectives that he had purchased a *second* Jennings Firearms .380 at about the same time as he bought the first one and at the same gun shop in Dallas, Texas.

For a person who initially told us he didn't own any firearms, we now learn he has at least three. If we just let this guy keep talking, maybe he'll dig his own grave.

After the interview, Naposki must have sensed that things had taken a decidedly negative turn. A few hours later, he called the NBPD and told the detectives he had hired an attorney. "My attorney advised me not to talk with you anymore unless he was present." When detectives asked him if he would still be willing to give blood, Naposki stated that he would speak to his attorney and get back to them.

Johnston must have felt the very same way. On January 26, the law offices of Barry O. Bernstein contacted Voth advising him that they were now representing Nanette Johnston. "Please do not speak with our client without our prior approval or presence."

It seemed that Naposki and Johnston were both now feeling some heat—as well they should.

Chapter Sixteen

February 1995

After hearing Naposki's new alibi, detectives knew it was important to pinpoint the exact time of the shooting. After all, regardless whether or not Naposki looked suspicious, if he *absolutely* could not have gone from the soccer field to Balboa Coves in time to commit murder he would have to be eliminated as a suspect. The 911 call had been placed at 9:11, but how long was it between the firing of the gun and Kevin's placing the call? Following up on Kevin's interview, detectives called Kim and Jenny McLaughlin and asked if they would time Kevin walking from his bedroom to the kitchen. The detectives were beginning to think that perhaps Kevin's account, that it had taken him about three minutes to make the trip, might not be spot-on. If timing became a key issue in this case, detectives wanted to make sure they had an accurate accounting.

On February 8, Kim called Voth and said she timed Kevin walking from his room to the kitchen. It took him fifty-two seconds, she stated.

On February 11, Newport Beach police sergeant Andy Gonis was quoted in the *OC Register* as saying, "[Johnston and Naposki] are suspects at this point. They are not necessarily the only suspects." The article went on to report that neither person has been arrested because "detectives lack physical evidence to tie the pair to the crime—including the

9mm gun used to shoot McLaughlin." The motive, according to the article, was $1 million in insurance money.

This was the first time that there was any mention in the press about a 9mm having been used in the murder.

On February 18, Kim once again called Voth with some new, alarming information about her father's bank account. "I've just discovered that since November 1994 six hundred forty thousand dollars has been taken from my dad's royalty account." She said that no one in her family had withdrawn that amount of money. Kim told Voth that she planned to call the bank to investigate the matter further. Kim also said that residents in Balboa Coves had been calling her saying that a private investigator named James Box had been asking them questions.

Although Johnston and Naposki were considered suspects, neither could be arrested because there was no direct evidence linking them to the murder.

Yet.

But detectives were eyeing Johnston after they discovered some new and potentially incriminating information.

First, there were details about finances.

Although McLaughlin's accountant, Brian Ringler, had asked Johnston for McLaughlin's November, December, and January bank statements, he received only the November and January ones. Looking over what he had in hand, Ringler noticed that according to the November 1994 statement, the ending balance on the "big" account was around $650,000. The ending balance on the January 1995 statement was around $40,000. That meant that during December $610,000 was taken out of that account. Curious about why so much money had been withdrawn, Ringler requested the December statement from the bank itself, instead of bothering Johnston again.

Then he called the detectives.

At the time he ordered the records, Ringler told them, he was just trying to do cash flow projections to find out what kind of money the McLaughlin family would need to keep the estate going and to pay the various bills. Ringler stated that he never thought for even a second that something untoward might be going on with McLaughlin's funds.

"After receiving the statement," Ringler told detectives, "I saw that there were a couple of very large checks made out—but I didn't know to whom. The statements didn't give that kind of information, so I requested copies of the big checks."

When detectives asked him what he learned after he saw the actual copies of the checks, Ringler said, "Well, right off, I saw that one was made out to Nanette Johnston Trust in the amount of two hundred and fifty thousand dollars. It was dated December 14, 1994—the day before the murder."

"Anything else?"

"I also noticed that there were a lot of discrepancies between the checks themselves and a QuickBooks computer register Johnston kept of the checks. On the computer report, for example, it might say 'Void' for a certain check, yet when I looked at a copy of the check itself, it was made out to 'Nanette Johnston.' One printout read 'one thousand dollars,' but the actual check was for three thousand dollars. Another printout read 'one thousand dollars,' but the check cleared the bank at five thousand dollars."

Ringler went on to say that the $250,000 check made out to Nanette Johnston Trust was signed in an "unfamiliar" script. Also, many of the checks, he said, had cleared after the murder. "I know banks are slow," Ringler stated, "but I wouldn't expect them to be that slow."

Continuing, Ringler said, "The first check discrepancy I saw was in February of 1994. In the check register, the payee was noted as 'Primerit,' but on the actual check, the payee was 'Nanette Johnston.' Looking further, I surmised that the closer it got to McLaughlin's death, the more frequently the irregularities increased, as well as the amounts. When I totaled up all the discrepancies, I found there to be three hundred and forty-one thousand, two hundred and seventy-two dollars and eighty-one cents."

After thanking the accountant for the information, detectives decided to put a handwriting expert on the case. They wanted someone professional to compare the signatures on all of McLaughlin's checks to McLaughlin's own handwriting to make sure that they were *all* penned by William McLaughlin—or not.

The answer wasn't long in coming.

On February 23, the handwriting expert Charles Beswick completed his examination of the "known and questioned signatures of Nanette Johnston and William McLaughlin; and also the known and questioned hand printing of Nanette Johnston and William McLaughlin."

The expert reported that, in his opinion, fourteen checks that were signed "W. F. McLaughlin" were actually penned by Johnston. The date, payee, and dollar amounts were penned by Johnston on many; and on some, only the signature seemed to have been forged.

Apparently, Nanette had been forging checks for nearly a year, helping herself to barrelfuls of McLaughlin's cash.

Following the money is usually key when it comes to homicide cases involving forgery. Could it be that Nanette used the money to hire someone, say a hit man, to do away with McLaughlin? Anything seemed possible.

That month, as detectives continued to follow up on every tip that came their way, Voth received an anonymous call from a person who wanted to tell him about the character of Nanette Johnston. The caller stated that in April 1990 Johnston was fired from the company where she was working—a company that handled advertising for Donnelly Directory phone books—due to her "forging customers' signatures" on advertising contracts.

And that *still* wasn't all.

Eager to ascertain more information about Nanette Johnston, detectives called in one of her ex-boyfriends, Tom Reynolds, 32, of Mission Viejo. When asked to describe Johnston, he stated that Johnston was a "cunning determined woman who sought out rich men." He said she contributed to a

$91,000 bankruptcy that occurred while they lived together. "As the relationship started coming apart," Reynolds said, "I began snooping through Johnston's belongings and found a singles' magazine ad Nanette had placed."

"Can you tell us more?"

"It was in a February 1991 *Singles Connection* newspaper and the heading was: 'For Wealthy Men Only.'"

Reynolds went on to say that the ad showed a "boudoir-style portrait" of Johnston and the words: "Single white female who can take care of her men as long as they can take care of her."

He then read them the ad:

"'SWF, twenty-five, five-five, one hundred pounds, classy, well-educated, adventurous, fun, and knows how to take care of her man. Looking for an older man, thirty-plus, who knows how to treat a woman. You take care of me and I'll take care of you. Photo and letter. P.O. Box 544, Balboa, CA 92661.'"

The ad was dated not long before Nanette Johnston and Bill McLaughlin met. Was this how they had been introduced?

With the ad, Nanette appeared to have announced her intentions with a roar. She'd been looking for a sugar daddy. And she'd found him.

Now he was dead.

Later that day, with this new information in hand, detectives called Johnston and mentioned the ad. "I never placed it," she declared emphatically. "It must have been done by a vengeful Reynolds after I left him."

Was Johnston a con artist? At the very least, she appeared to have been living two separate lives—in one she was the penniless but devoted soon-to-be trophy wife of a rich middle-aged man; in the other she was a wealthy self-made entrepreneur with a rough-and-tough young boyfriend by her side. Being a cheat and a liar wasn't something she advertised about herself. It certainly wasn't the image she

*projected to various real estate agents when she was trawl-
ing for expensive homes in the weeks before McLaughlin's
murder.*

At the end of February, Sharon Hedberg, a Realtor, called
detectives because she felt she had important information
she wanted to share concerning the circumstances surrounding McLaughlin's death. She said she had seen pictures of
Naposki and Johnston in the newspaper and wanted to tell
them what she knew of the couple. Hedberg stated that she
had shown Johnston and Naposki a residential lot in an ex-
clusive gated enclave in the Turtle Rock area of Irvine at the
end of July or in early August 1994. According to Hedberg,
the couple stated they had four children and were looking
for a home in the million-dollar range with the hopes of being able to move in during the spring of 1995. The timing
was very important, the pair told Hedberg. "They were looking for [a] spring completion date."

    Hedberg said she had their contact information on a card
that she had filled out during their meeting. It included a
"name, phone number, and the location that the couple were
interested in." In her written notes, Hedberg had jotted down:
"7 Oaks, Number 6."

    Detectives followed up and gathered all the paperwork
from Hedberg. .

    *Were Johnston and Naposki just lookie loos, checking
out real estate and pretending to be serious about buying?
Or was something more sinister afoot?*

As daily newspaper articles focused on Johnston's dubious
financial dealings, reporters were eager to speak with her.
One day, after she dropped off her children at their father's
house in Walnut, a reporter stopped her and asked some
questions.

    "Why do you think the police are focusing on you?"

    "I have no idea," Johnston stated. "It's all garbage. They
[the police] need to find somebody and they're bound and

determined to pin it on somebody. It's been a living nightmare. I'm in limbo. I've lost somebody and now I'm being
pointed at as being involved somehow."

Johnston stated that she wasn't the only one to receive
insurance benefits from McLaughlin's policies—suggesting
that perhaps they should start looking at some of the other
beneficiaries. "It's all so trumped up," she said. "I didn't do
anything."

Asked about why she thought the police were focusing on
Eric, she said, "The police are all wet. Eric was with me
when it happened. I didn't do it and [Naposki] didn't do it. I
don't think they [police] have any real facts. They couldn't,
because I didn't do anything. . . . I stood to gain a lot more by
being with Mr. McLaughlin than [from] an insurance policy."

After being told that the police were looking into the connection between Naposki and the keys left at the scene,
Johnston stated, "He's moved three times in the last three
months. Is making keys unreasonable? And Eric does have
an alibi and police were made aware of that."

As Johnston was getting into her car, she ended the interview by saying, "If I know anything pertinent, I'll be the
first one to blab my mouth to everybody."

Detectives could only hope.

Chapter Seventeen

March–April 1995

Things began taking an even darker turn for Johnston.

On March 15, a letter was sent to Detective Hartford concerning the U.S. Funds account, or W. F. M. Holdings, Ltd. It stated: "McLaughlin was the only authorized signer of the referenced account. In addition, our records do not show that Nanette Johnston had Power of Attorney on the account."

On April 3, a second real estate agent called detectives to offer information on Johnston.

Voth spoke to Betty Comegy, who told the detective that she had shown a property to McLaughlin and Johnston—not *Naposki* and Johnston—on October 27, 1994. Comegy stated that the house she showed the couple was worth approximately $5.5 million.

It seemed that Johnston was looking for million-dollar houses with two different men. Now that's a feat not every woman can pull off!

Naposki was becoming increasingly uncomfortable with the detectives' eyes focused on him. He was hell-bent on getting them off his back and proving his innocence. Certain that McLaughlin's blood was not in his car, on March 7 he provided a blood sample at the law office of his attorney, Julian W. Bailey, in West Orange, California.

Then, in early April, Bailey sent a letter to Debbie Lloyd, deputy district attorney in Santa Ana, forcefully arguing Eric Naposki's innocence.

According to the letter, Naposki had no idea that Johnston was carrying on a relationship with McLaughlin and, therefore, had no motive for killing him. "Not one witness has been found who states otherwise," wrote Bailey.

Further, Bailey claimed, Naposki's alibi could be proved. According to Bailey, McLaughlin was killed at around 9:10 p.m. Naposki left Johnston's son's soccer game at approximately 8:20 p.m. and then drove to his home in Tustin, where he changed his clothes and went to work as a security guard. In the interim, stated Bailey, Naposki's pager went off and Naposki returned the page from a phone in a Denny's at 17th Street and Tustin Avenue in Tustin, at 8:52 p.m. "This was a credit card call," wrote Bailey, "and therefore there is a record of its time and place."

Bailey continued. "He absolutely would not have had time to have driven to the scene of the crime, committed the murder, and fled prior to the time of the 911 call at 9:11 p.m."

Bailey also disagreed with information about the keys supposedly used to enter the complex and house on the night of the murder. Bailey wrote that in the search warrant police stated that Naposki had keys made in November at an Ace Hardware store and that the murderer left a new key in McLaughlin's front door. However, according to Bailey, the police failed to note that the manager of the store in which Naposki supposedly had the keys made told police that one of the keys that was found at the McLaughlin home could *not* have come from his store because the stamp on it was one his store didn't use.

Bailey also included information about firearms. He wrote that McLaughlin had recently "purchased a large number of firearms including assault rifles and handguns. In fact, a number of weapons were taken from the residence including several 9mm pistols. As far as I know, there has been no accurate accounting of the handguns purchased by Mr. McLaughlin to determine if the murder weapon was of a

type he owned or that Mr. Naposki's former handgun has or
has not been eliminated as a possible murder weapon."

Bailey wrote that he was deeply concerned that Naposki
was being singled out in the press on the basis of "false information and innuendo as the sole suspect based upon his
relationship with Nanette Johnston."

Finally, Bailey stated that some of the things the police
stated were "flat out not true. [Naposki] and I both felt he was
unfairly dealt with. I'm taken aback by the whole situation,"
concluded Bailey.

After reviewing the letter and evidence (or lack of it), Deputy District Attorney Debbie Lloyd seemed to agree with
Bailey. Saying that there simply wasn't any proof that Naposki was involved in the murder, she rejected the case and
declined to file charges against Naposki.

Around five months later, Assistant District Attorney
Laurie Hungerford again rejected the case, citing a dearth of
evidence.

The DA's office told Voth that if he wanted this case to go
forward, he would have to bring in the gun used to shoot William McLaughlin, find some new physical evidence, or
come up with a new witness.

This was ecstatic news for Johnston and Naposki. *Two*
different DAs rejected the case for lack of evidence. Now,
maybe, life as it used to be could be the new normal.

Then, there was even more good news for Naposki. Exactly
a month after Naposki had given blood so detectives could
compare it with blood on the towel in his car, the results
came back—and it seemed that Naposki was vindicated.

An April 6 letter from the OC Sheriff Coroner's Department stated that the type of blood found on "six areas of the
towel located in Naposki's car was consistent with Eric Naposki and could not have come from William McLaughlin."

Now, detectives were beginning to have their doubts:
Sure, Eric Naposki had prevaricated. But was he a killer?

Not only that. There even was more good news for

Naposki. In April, Naposki signed a contract with the Balti-
more Stallions, a team in the Canadian Football League,
and returned to Denver to continue his training. Life, it
seemed, just might be sweet once again.

All this time, Jenny McLaughlin had been bothered about
Johnston's keeping her father's Cadillac, which Jenny felt
now belonged to her sister, her brother, and her. In order to
remedy the situation, she asked a friend of hers, Jason Gendon, if he would pick up the car and have it repossessed. He
was in the towing business and Jenny thought it would be
something he could easily do.

On April 14, Gendon and his men followed Johnston from
her Seashore residence to Mission Viejo, then to the school,
located in a church, where she dropped off her daughter, and
finally to a McDonald's in Walnut. While Johnston was inside, Gendon hooked up the Cadillac to his tow truck and
drove off. After Gendon told Jenny, Jenny immediately called
Detective Voth to tell him about the repossession. Voth said,
"Tell Gendon to report it to the Walnut Sheriff's substation
and then call me back."

At around 5 p.m., Jenny called Johnston and recorded the
call. Jenny began by saying, "I understand you guys had a
problem with us taking the car. Is there something I can do
about that?"

In an angry tone, Johnston replied that she was "left up in
Diamond Bar with four kids and all kinds of sports equipment" because someone repossessed her car.

Jenny said, "I understand that you thought we weren't supposed to take the car."

"Well, obviously. I mean it was obviously my car."

"Well, we don't have those records."

"I was the only one who ever drove it," stated Johnston.
"You guys know that it was my car."

"Well, no I don't," said Jenny, "because we all know the
terms of the will. It says you were left the Infiniti."

"[The will] just hadn't been changed yet, and you know
your dad bought that car for me."

"So it was intent—his intention to leave it to you? Is that what you're saying?" asked Jenny.

"I have the title that he signed that you guys were supposedly disputing and saying that I signed it myself."

"Can you show that to my attorney?"

"I did."

"You sent him the original?"

"We sent him a faxed copy."

After the two went back and forth and Nanette gave her reason why McLaughlin hadn't put the car in her name—the insurance would have been too expensive, since she was younger—Jenny then moved on to the checks and asked whether or not Nanette had ever signed her father's name on any of them.

"I've signed his name on many things."

When asked specifically if she signed Jenny's father's name on the $250,000 check, Johnston stated, "No. I did not sign that one. He signed that one."

Things continued to get more uncomfortable for Johnston in the days after the repossession. On April 17, as information continued to pile up concerning Johnston and her check writing, detectives went to the Seashore Drive home with a warrant for her arrest. As soon as she came to the door, detectives told her she was being arrested on a $500,000 grand-theft warrant.

Although surprised, she put up no resistance. However, she made sure the detectives knew how angry she was. She told the officers she would prove her innocence and that this was yet another example of them focusing solely on her and not considering other suspects.

Johnston was taken into custody without incident and booked into the Orange County Jail on fifteen counts of forgery—signing McLaughlin's name on fifteen checks from January 10, 1994, to December 15, 1994—and on one count of grand theft.

The next day, prosecutors revealed to the public why Johnston had been arrested. "Detectives found the alleged

forgeries in January as they were investigating Johnston as
a possible suspect in the murder of McLaughlin," an article
in the *OC Register* by Anne C. Mulkern and Tony Saavedra
stated. "It was the value of the checks—the amounts on
them—that made us investigate whether there was a criminal violation."

Court documents offered specific details about the forgeries. They stated that before McLaughlin's murder—between
January 10 and December 14, 1994—detectives believed
that Johnston forged McLaughlin's name on $355,000 worth
of checks. The latest forgeries, the document detailed, were
dated the day McLaughlin was murdered—December 15,
1994—one for $75,000 and another in the amount of
$250,000.

On Friday, April 21, a bail hearing was held. With TV cameras in the courtroom, Johnston covered her face with her
hand in order to avoid the camera. When asked how she
pleaded, she said, "Not guilty, Your Honor."

Naposki, who was back from Denver to attend the proceedings, mouthed words of encouragement every time Johnston turned around to look at him. It seemed that Naposki
had decided to stand by his woman.

Although Johnston's bail was originally set for $500,000,
Municipal Judge Christopher W. Strople declared: "Because
prosecutors recovered around $250,000 from four of John-
ston's bank accounts, I am reducing the bail accordingly."

Outside the courtroom, Johnston's attorney Barry Bernstein stated that he believed that with the help of family and
friends Johnston could make the bail. However, he added, in
his opinion, the bail was "unusually high for a grand-theft
case" and was "set because of the other publicity and that
there is a certain aspect of anticipatory detention to the current bail."

When Naposki was asked what he felt about Johnston's
arrest, he told reporters, "She should not be in jail. They're
treating her like a criminal. She's done nothing criminal."
He stated that Johnston missed her children, who were now

staying with their father. "I don't think she belongs in jail on
such a high bail. I'm looking forward to her clearing herself.
I know that she's going to get out." He added, "A person is
innocent until proven guilty. I used to believe in the system,
until now."

Naposki stated that he was upset not only about Johnston
but also about himself. Prosecutors, he claimed, would not
clear his name despite his having told them his alibi. He reiterated that he had dated Johnston but did not know that she
was involved with McLaughlin. "Why are they looking at
me?" Naposki asked. "Do I look like the kind of guy who
would need to date someone who already had a boyfriend?"

He told reporters that the investigation was "a destruction
of someone's reputation" and "I was being treated like a
criminal. I think they don't want to admit a mistake. They've
spent a lot of time, a lot of money, looking at me, and they
don't want to admit they came up empty-handed."

Since having been named a suspect in the killing, Naposki stated, "I've lost all privacy. I've been followed by
police and my house has been searched." He said that he
willingly gave investigators blood samples and had offered
an alibi for the night of the murder. "There was no time [for
me] to do something like this."

During the interview, Naposki was told that Johnston was
going to receive an eviction notice, demanding that she move
out of the Seashore Drive home. Although the eviction listed
Naposki on the notice as well, Naposki told reporters that he
never lived in the home. "This is a matter of a mother of two
with her whole life ahead of her, and they're trying to de-
stroy it."

Ending the interview, Naposki declared, "No one is playing by the rules and they don't think there's going to be any
repercussions. They're like vultures."

Julian Bailey, Naposki's lawyer, added that Naposki lost
a chance to play with the World League Barcelona Dragons
due to negative press concerning the murder. "There's no
indication that [Naposki] is involved in this at all. Naposki
can prove he made a credit-card call from Tustin to his

workplace at eighty fifty-two p.m., less than twenty minutes before police were summoned to the crime scene. It would have been impossible for Naposki to have committed the crime."

Even though the phone bill was mentioned several times, as something that, if shown, could clear his name, Naposki never provided it to the police. Nor, for that matter, did detectives ever go after it, as they did phone records from other suspects. It seemed as if each side expected the other to get the bill—and neither ever did.

Johnston remained in jail until April 24, when she put up a $250,000 bond. "The woman's family had put up enough real estate and cash to meet the bail," stated an article in the *OC Register.*

Naposki had vociferously supported Johnston at her hearing, but in the weeks that followed the two were clearly growing apart. During May and June, Naposki was in Denver at the Canadian Football League training camp, hoping to stay healthy and make the cut.

"Nanette and I barely saw each other," Naposki recalled later. "Things had definitely taken a different turn."

Chapter Eighteen

August–December 1995

In August, a preliminary hearing was held in front of Judge Richard F. Toohey, in which Johnston faced forgery allegations. If at the end of the hearing the judge felt that there was enough evidence pointing to Johnston having forged checks, she would then be required to go to trial.

OC Deputy District Attorney Joseph D'Agostino stated that checks amounting to $267,000 were written to Johnston from an account over which he believed McLaughlin had sole control. Further, D'Agostino stated that in the days before McLaughlin's death money totaling at least $130,000 was moved from that same account to an account from which Johnston was entitled to write checks.

McLaughlin's accountant, Brian Ringler, agreed with D'Agostino's interpretation. Furthermore, Ringler testified, only McLaughlin had the power to spend money from the specific account in question.

Charles Beswick, a fraud investigator for Fireman's Fund Insurance Company and a reserve officer in the NBPD, testified that he had compared the handwritings of Johnston and McLaughlin and believed that more than a dozen of the checks had not actually been signed by McLaughlin. "They appeared to have been filled out and signed with McLaughlin's name, only in Johnston's handwriting. I would have to say the defendant penned those numbers."

Johnston's defense attorney, Bernstein, on the other hand, disagreed with Ringler, saying that his client *did* have authorization to sign McLaughlin's name to all his checks and to other documents as well. Further, Bernstein disagreed with the handwriting specialist, citing that the signature on the checks did not match the sample from Johnston, in which she signed McLaughlin's name. "There doesn't seem to be any correlation at all," Bernstein declared.

Under further questioning, Beswick agreed that the signatures were not *identical*. However, he said, it was "highly probable" that one particular check in question, a $250,000 check, was signed by Johnston.

A short time after the end of the hearing, after Judge Toohey had time to go over all the information from the hearing, he told the anxious parties his decision. He declared that Johnston *would* stand trial for forgery and grand theft.

After the hearing, Jenny McLaughlin said that the family was pleased that Johnston would have to account for her actions in court. Kim McLaughlin added that it was her belief that her father had never intended to marry Johnston. "He certainly didn't share that with me," she said. If convicted of the charges, Johnston could face up to ten years in prison. In the meantime, she would remain free on $250,000 bail.

The McLaughlins also told reporters that they were increasing the reward for any information leading to the arrest of the murderer of their father to $100,000, more than double the previous reward. "We are hoping someone will come forward who has information that would lead to the arrest and conviction of whoever killed my father," Jenny said. "It's obviously very frustrating. Number one, it's hard to believe someone could walk into your home and kill you, and number two, that they could get away with it."

Once again, Naposki was not sitting idly by, nor was he continuing to stand by his woman. During July and August, he spent time in New York with his parents and in other places along the East Coast. He was clearly trying to put California behind him.

Then in October, he took a short trip back to California to pick up his truck from Johnston. After that, said Naposki, "I drove home to New York for good. Period."

His tryout for the Canadian Football League had not worked out, but any stigma from being a murder suspect seemed to have worn off, and he signed a contract to play in the 1996 spring season with the WLAF—once again with the Barcelona Dragons. Meanwhile, he picked up some security work for ESPN and other odd jobs, waiting for football season to start. And he had minimal contact with Nanette. For the first time in a long time, Naposki felt cautiously optimistic.

On December 12, nearly a year after the murder, Johnston, now 29, was still awaiting her trial on forgery and grand-theft charges. *But if the McLaughlin clan thought she was just going to sit around and wait for the ax to fall, they had another thing coming.* Johnston was fed up with the direction in which things were going and decided to take matters into her own hands. *After all,* she felt, *if they want to accuse me of stealing money, I could accuse them of not following their father's wishes.*

In court papers, Johnston stated that according to an express oral non-marital support agreement she made with William McLaughlin on August 1, 1991—the day she moved into his house—she was entitled to share *all* of his assets. Therefore, she was suing to that effect.

Specifically, the paper stated, in case McLaughlin passed away before she did, she would be entitled to half of the $9 million in his bank accounts; a $1 million non-marital support agreement; a $5,000 per month stipend, which should be retroactive to the day he was killed; and half of the properties McLaughlin owned: two homes in Newport Beach and two homes in Las Vegas.

The lawsuit alleged: "During the four years they lived together" McLaughlin "had either bought property or shared it with Johnston, including stocks, luxury cars, and bank accounts worth about $9 million." The document alleged that

Johnston and McLaughlin had a verbal agreement to "treat all earnings, income and property acquired or gained by them while they lived together, as joint assets."

It seemed that two could play the *j'accuse* game.

Chapter Nineteen

1996–1997

The end of 1994 and all of 1995 had been a rough time for Nanette Johnston—in her own mind anyway. First her fiancé was murdered, and then she had to endure being pestered by the police and media about her potential involvement in the killing. It was very stressful—and she had thought her other *boyfriend would be 100 percent supportive of her at this difficult time, but no! Eric started bugging her about whether she had been sleeping with Bill McLaughlin all along and then he up and left California. Ugh. Then there was that nasty indictment against her for forging checks and stealing hundreds of thousands of dollars from Bill. But that wasn't the worst of it. She had been booted out of her beloved beach house!*

Fortunately, Orange County was full of red-hot real estate developments. While out on bail, Nanette found herself a new lair in the private, master-planned, guard-gated community of Dove Canyon—a wonderful spot for sun, fun, and a new beginning (and immediately adjacent to Coto de Caza, the current setting for Bravo television's The Real Housewives of Orange County*).*

Despite the indictment looming over her and the fact that she had no significant income, Nanette was hell-bent on maintaining her lifestyle. That's why she had filed the lawsuit against the McLaughlins. If she won, she would once again be sitting pretty. Confident as always, she was waiting patiently to hear the good news.

Meanwhile, she had no intention of going back to living like a mere mortal. And she wasn't going to let a little thing like lack of funds or collateral stop her. Life in sunny Dove Canyon suited her just fine.

But then she hit another snag.

On March 6, 1996, a headline in the *LA Times* read: "Police Allege Nanette Johnston, Girlfriend of a Slain Businessman, Filed False Financial Statements." The article announced that Deputy District Attorney Joseph D'Agostino requested and received a felony arrest warrant accusing Johnston of inflating her income, lying about her tax returns, and using a false Social Security number on several loan documents, specifically: a loan application at California Thrift & Loan in Costa Mesa in May of 1995 to purchase a $20,000 car, a BMW; an October 31, 1995, loan application for $480,000 from BankersWest Funding Corporation for the purpose of purchasing the home she was renting in Dove Canyon; and a November 23, 1995, loan application to lease a new Cadillac.

All told, D'Agostino's warrant included three felony counts and a "crime-bail" enhancement (an enhanced, or additional, charge to already-existing charges), which could add two years to Johnston's sentence if she was convicted of committing further felonies while on bail.

This was the second time in a year that Johnston was being accused of financial improprieties—not a sterling record for the fiancée of a once-prominent businessman. If Johnston was capable of stealing from Bill McLaughlin, forging documents, and filing false financial statements, what else might she be capable of?

The day after the warrant was filed, as Johnston left her home, Newport Beach police officers stopped her in a green GMC Yukon SUV at the intersection of Santa Margarita Parkway and Las Amigas Drive in Trabuco Canyon.

Getting out of their car, the officers approached her vehicle. "You're under arrest."

"For what?" asked a surprised Johnston.

"Suspicion of filing false financial statements in order to buy cars and obtain home loans."

"I don't know what you're talking about," an exasperated Johnston replied. "Why don't you just leave me alone!"

However, the officers made it clear that that wasn't going to happen. In fact, they were going to transport her to the NBPD jail once again. Although clearly angry, Johnston didn't put up any resistance and went quietly into the patrol car.

Once at the jail, Johnston was booked, brought to an interview room, and read her Miranda rights. Two detectives were there to greet her, and they got right to it.

"Mind telling me about the Social Security number you used on your loan applications recently? Was it yours?"

"Of course it was mine," she said adamantly. "I've never used a false Social Security number in my life."

"Oh?" said a skeptical detective. "Well, do you happen to know a Patrick Smith?"

Although seemingly confused by the question, Johnston replied that she did. "I dated him around eight years ago, when I was in Arizona. So?"

"Why is it, then," asked the detective slowly, "that Pat Smith's Social Security number is on several documents you signed as *your* Social Security number?"

Silent for a few moments, Johnston then looked the detective straight in the eye. "I have no idea. I sincerely doubt that's true," she stated.

After showing Johnston the application papers on which Patrick Smith's Social Security number was clearly penned, the detective told Johnston that she had some serious explaining to do. However, Johnston stated that she had nothing more to say until she spoke with her lawyer.

Taken before a judge, Johnston once again proclaimed her innocence. Nonetheless, additional bail was set at $100,000 and Johnston was returned to a group cell in Orange County's

James Musick Facility, a minimum-security jail that housed around twelve hundred inmates.

As the days passed and Johnston remained in jail—unable this time to post bail—she began to stew. This was not her idea of high-class OC living.

In addition to dealing with these new charges, her trial for forgery and grand theft was set to begin in about two weeks, on March 25.

Although Johnston and her lawyer had contended all along that McLaughlin had given Johnston the right to sign McLaughlin's name on checks and other documents, Johnston began to change her tune as the trial neared. After several meetings with her lawyer, Johnston decided to plead guilty to felony charges of forgery along with enhancement—"excessive taking exceeding $150,000." (In many states, an "enhancement" can be tacked onto a felony under certain circumstances. In this case, it was for stealing an excessive amount of money.)

Three days before the trial was set to begin, it seemed that Johnston had finally decided to come clean. She wrote an admission of guilt on March 22: "In O.C. between 1/1/94 and 1/30/95, I willfully and unlawfully embezzled more than $150,000 of the property of W. McLaughlin. On 12/14/94 in O.C., I forged another name on a $250,000 check with the intent to pass the check and defraud." After this admission, she signed her name and wrote the date, 3/22/96.

With this admission, there was no need for Johnston to stand trial on the initial charges. In the plea deal worked out with the district attorney's office, Johnston agreed to turn over the $1 million life insurance policy to the three McLaughlin children. In turn, the McLaughlins agreed that Johnston could retain $385,000 in cash, thereby settling several civil lawsuits. The McLaughlin family also agreed to deliver to Johnston a 1991 Infiniti convertible, along with the title to the car. It was estimated that the wholesale value of the car was $17,500.

Once the agreement was reached, both sides appeared in Judge Richard L. Weatherspoon's courtroom. After the judge went over the specifics of the case, he stated aloud the deal that had been reached. To Johnston, he said, "You will serve one year in county jail to begin in May, plus five years probation."

Johnston remained stone-faced as the pronouncement was read—already aware of what the sentence would be.

According to the terms of her probation, Johnston would be severely limited in her financial dealings. She was to "have no blank checks in possession; nor write any portion of any check; nor was she to have checking accounts or use or possess credit cards or open credit accounts unless approved by probation."

Although Johnston refused to speak to reporters after her sentencing, her lawyer, Barry Bernstein, did make a comment. "All sides, I think, wanted to get past this and go on with their lives," said Bernstein. "These are very difficult things for people. There's a lot of emotion involved."

D'Agostino concurred. "The McLaughlin family seemed to be content with the resolution because they got their money back. And it was very important to them that she went to jail for a year. What [Johnston was] saying was, 'Take the life insurance because I stole it, and I'll take the rest.'" According to D'Agostino, "It's clearly a fair settlement for the estate."

Only two weeks later, on April 3, Johnston was once again in court. This time, she pleaded guilty to falsifying financial statements in October of 1995 in an effort to obtain a $480,000 mortgage loan from BankersWest Funding Corporation in Newport Beach. For this transgression, she was not given additional jail time. "She [will be] serving one year on another case and there was no additional time because the mortgage was not funded," stated the judge.

The next day, a *Daily Pilot* newspaper article reported:

"Nanette Johnston, the 30-year-old [sic] fiancée of slain millionaire William McLaughlin, lost her half of a million dollar home."

She was about to trade in her mini-mansion for a jail cell.

While all this was going on, Naposki was nowhere in sight. He had successfully distanced himself from his former lover and her problems. In fact, his season with the Barcelona Dragons was starting in mid-April and he had once again been training in Denver. It seemed that football would, for now, become the one and *only* love of his life.

As her May prison date neared, Johnston, now 29, made certain that the most important part of her life was taken care of before she was to start her one-year jail sentence. She arranged for her two children to stay with their father, Ross, and his live-in girlfriend.

On May 13, Johnston turned herself over to Judge Weatherspoon to begin her sentence in Orange County Jail. As it turned out, Johnston served only 180 days. Good behavior and time already served brought her sentence to half its original length.

If spending a few months in jail had been difficult for Johnston, one would not have been able to tell based on her actions after her release. Once out, she wasted no time finding herself a new, wealthy man. Naposki, apparently, was history.

Released from jail in November of 1996, Johnston placed an ad in a singles magazine and it took her only six months before she met her new meal ticket—millionaire real estate developer John Packard—and just another five months before they became engaged, in October 1997.

"Nanette did what she always does," Detective Byington explained to eager reporters wanting to know what Johnston had been doing since her release. "She went looking for a new sugar daddy."

During 1997, while Johnston and Packard were canoodling, Naposki was busy, too—playing football for the Barcelona Dragons. He was playing so well and having such a positive effect on the team that not only had he been named team captain, but also his team had won the World Cup Championship.

Late that year, while Naposki was still in Barcelona, a horrific fire engulfed a hotel. As it turned out, Naposki, at great danger to himself, helped evacuate the occupants. For his valiant work he received the Fireman's Helmet Award. According to Naposki, he didn't deserve an award. He was simply doing what was right. His life had taken a decidedly positive turn: He had transformed from being a person regarded with suspicion into someone to look up to.

After the European football season ended, Naposki returned to the States and got a job as a linebackers coach at the University of New Haven under Tony Sparano, now of the Miami Dolphins. According to experts, Naposki was instrumental in having the team go all the way to the 1997 Division II Championship game.

During this time, he was living in Stamford, Connecticut and had reestablished contact with his two children, Krista and Kayla, from his earlier marriage to his high school sweetheart, Kathy O'Connell.

Looking in from the outside, it appeared that Naposki had successfully put the Johnston episode of his life behind him and was carving out a successful future for himself.

By this time, Kevin, Jenny, and Kim McLaughlin had started to lose hope that their father's murder would ever be solved. "We were really low," said Kim. "Having been involved with all this—learning about Nanette and things she had done to my father and the kind of mind she had—it was bringing our morale down, as a family."

The McLaughlins determined that they needed to turn a corner. "My mom was—and is—a very inspirational person and she said we needed to separate ourselves from everything Nanette's done. . . . So we stopped watching TV or getting newspapers. . . . My mom kept encouraging us to stay positive and to surround ourselves with good people whom we could trust. And we followed her advice. We went in a completely different direction and left Nanette and her crap behind. . . . Although there was no resolution to my dad's murder, we were at least trying to move on."

Chapter Twenty

1998–2006

Nanette, too, was moving on. She had worn the diamond engagement ring that Bill McLaughlin had given her for years. This time, she wasn't going to wait to get married. On Valentine's Day, February 14, 1998—four months after announcing their engagement—Johnston and John Packard tied the knot at the Westin Hotel. By all accounts, it was a lavish affair with over a hundred guests enjoying sumptuous food and dancing to a live band. The couple seemed deliriously happy, very much in love.

Although detectives were still checking out new leads on the McLaughlin case, few were coming their way. However, on March 3, 1998—about two weeks after Nanette's wedding—the NBPD received a very interesting phone call.

On that day, a person who identified herself only as "Suzanne" telephoned with information she wanted to share regarding Eric Naposki. She was connected with Detective Tom Fischbacher, and he turned on the tape recorder to document her call.

Suzanne stated she been a neighbor of Naposki's in an apartment complex in Tustin in 1994. She said she had originally called the NBPD back in 1995 to tell them her concerns regarding Naposki, but the detective in charge of the case was not available and she was asked to call back. She hadn't called back until today, she said, because she had been afraid of possible repercussions if Naposki ever found out she'd been talking to the police.

Suzanne told Fischbacher that while she and Naposki were outside by the community pool chatting one day in 1994 Naposki told her he was crazy about his girlfriend, Nanette Johnston, declaring that he had never felt like that about anybody before. Naposki also told Suzanne that it upset him when Johnston told him that the man she was living with had tried to force himself on her in bed.

Continuing, Suzanne said that later that year, in November, Naposki told her that he *hated* the man who was living with his girlfriend. He said that the man owned a house in Las Vegas and would pilot his own plane back and forth between Newport Beach and Las Vegas. Naposki declared that "[he] was going to have the man's plane blown up or something kind of outrageous," Suzanne told Fischbacher.

Then, Suzanne continued, after she not had seen Naposki for around a month, the two once again met in their apartment complex and Naposki told her that the man living with his girlfriend had been killed. Suzanne said she was "shocked and freaked out." She asked Naposki if he had done it, and, according to Suzanne, "Naposki grinned and replied, 'Maybe I did and maybe I didn't.'"

Ending the conversation with Fischbacher, Suzanne said she would not give her last name but would leave her work number and extension in case he wanted to be back in touch. She also said she would *not* be willing to testify about the information she had just given if the case ever went to trial.

Around a week after Suzanne's call to Detective Fischbacher, on March 11, Sergeant Pat O'Sullivan followed up and called Suzanne at her workplace. He wanted to know if she had had any contact with Naposki after December of 1994.

Suzanne admitted that she had. "In a conversation in early January of 1995, before I moved out of the apartment complex," Suzanne recalled, "Naposki told me that if the police came around, I should tell them that I know nothing. Naposki also mentioned that the gun he owned was the same type used to kill the victim, but he continued, 'I don't have the gun anymore because I loaned the gun to a buddy and they are not going to find a murder weapon on me.' "

Suzanne said that was all she knew and hung up.

A witness said Naposki told her that he may or may not have killed McLaughlin. And Naposki had asked this witness not to talk to police if they asked her questions about the McLaughlin murder. Why would a person do that? The detectives already knew Naposki had a big mouth and were growing hopeful that he would finally blab his way into a lifetime prison sentence.

Two months after Johnston married Packard, detectives conducted a court-appointed probation search at their home in Lake Forest, located in South Orange County between the cities of Irvine and Mission Viejo—just to make sure that she wasn't violating any of the stipulations in her probation decree. And to let her know she hadn't been forgotten.

Once inside her home in April 1998, detectives saw two receipts that interested them. One was from Zales and another was from Greenworks for a $400 deposit for wedding flowers. Nanette did, indeed, have a taste for the finer things in life. When detectives asked Johnston if these items had been paid by check, Nanette said yes. When asked if she had written any portion of either check—either the name of the company, the amount, or the signature—Johnston stated that she hadn't. "My husband John Packard did."

It seemed, however, that Johnston was not telling the truth—once again. After the detectives procured the checks and looked at the signatures on them, they realized that Johnston had lied. She had signed her own name. Writing portions of checks was a direct violation of the terms of her probation.

Once again, detectives thought, *lying seems to come naturally to Johnston.*

Despite strong suspicions and some new evidence (Suzanne's phone call), the police still seemed stymied. Although they were pretty sure that Naposki and Johnston were guilty of murder at this point, they had no true smoking gun. Having been rebuffed twice already by the district attorney's office, they didn't think they had enough new evidence to bring charges.

If detectives were frustrated with the progress of the investigation, Johnston and Naposki didn't seem the least bit concerned. Johnston was living in the lap of luxury with her successful new husband. And Naposki was now living in Connecticut and doing quite well. He had joined Guardsmark Inc. Security Company in February 1998, and because his work was superb he was promoted to manager. As such, he was put in charge of his first client account—U.S. Tobacco, in Greenwich, Connecticut.

But that wasn't Naposki's only success. In the spring of 1998, he became engaged to Natalia Algorta, after they had been dating for over a year. It had been love at first sight, and now the two were planning a spectacular wedding—in Barcelona, where Naposki had been a football star during 1996 and 1997.

In June, Naposki and his bride said their vows at the Sitges Hotel, right on the beach, with beautiful gardens and a luxurious pool, in front of over fifty friends and relatives. It was a magical time, stated Naposki later, "being married in the city I had come to love so much."

Later that summer, Naposki received even more good news. He was inducted into the Barcelona Dragons Hall of Fame—the first person ever to receive that honor.

Without question, Naposki's star was shining brightly.

The McLaughlins were also going on with their lives—but it was a bumpy road. In early 1999, Kevin McLaughlin decided to move to Hawaii to be closer to his mother. He had been feeling adrift since his father's murder and wanted the anchor he knew only his mother could supply. Kevin was also trying to deal with his guilt and anger over not having been able to save his father—had he been more able-bodied, he felt, he could have. But he was now ready to try to move

At 18, William (Bill) McLaughlin joined the Marines and served honorably for three years. (Courtesy: The McLaughlin Family)

Bill McLaughlin, ready for an evening out in 1991. (Courtesy: The McLaughlin Family)

(from left) Kevin, Sue, Jenny, Bill, and Kim McLaughlin in 1991 at a Loyola Marymount University fundraiser. (Courtesy: The McLaughlin Family)

McLaughlin and daughter Kim enjoyed many activities together, including scuba diving and flying. (Courtesy: The McLaughlin Family)

Kevin McLaughlin was the only son of Bill and Sue. Kevin's passion was surfing, but he excelled at many other sports as well. He and his father were very close, frequently going on trips together. Kevin found his father dead on December 15, 1994. (Courtesy: The McLaughlin Family)

The McLaughlins lived in the gated community of Balboa Coves, in Newport Beach, CA. (Courtesy: Newport Beach Police Department)

Nanette Johnston was a seductive man-magnet, able to attract any male of her choosing. And she chose many over the years, including Eric Naposki and William McLaughlin. (Courtesy: Newport Beach Police Department)

Nanette Johnston and Eric Naposki attend a friend's wedding. (Courtesy: Newport Beach Police Department)

Eric Naposki had impressive muscles even before he played professional football. (Courtesy: The Naposki Defense Team)

In 1988, Naposki signed on as a linebacker with the New England Patriots, where he played five games in two seasons before being traded to the Indianapolis Colts. (Courtesy: The Naposki Defense Team)

In 2000, Naposki graduated from the University of Connecticut. (Courtesy: The Naposki Defense Team)

Nanette Johnston makes a face during her 1995 arraignment on a grand theft charge of stealing from Bill McLaughlin. (Credit Image: © Ygnacio Nanetti/*The Orange County Register*/ZUMA Press)

Naposki looks on during Johnston's arraignment in 1995. (Credit Image: © Ygnacio Nanetti/*The Orange County Register*/ZUMA Press)

On December 15, 1994, when police responded to a frantic 911 call from Kevin McLaughlin at Balboa Coves, they noticed a key in the front door lock. (Courtesy: Newport Beach Police Department)

Naposki was arrested in 2009 in Connecticut on first-degree murder charges with special circumstances, fifteen years after the death of William McLaughlin. (Credit: Newport Beach Police Department)

Defense attorney Angelo MacDonald addresses the jury during his opening statements in client Naposki's murder trial in Orange County Superior Court in Santa Ana, CA, on June 30, 2011. (Credit Image: © H. Lorren Au Jr/*The Orange County Register*/ ZUMAPRESS.com)

Deputy District Attorney Matt Murphy gives his closing statements during defendant Naposki's murder trial, on July 12, 2011. (Credit Image: © H. Lorren Au Jr/*The Orange County Register*/ ZUMAPRESS.com)

Defense attorney Gary Pohlson gives his closing statements during Naposki's murder trial on July 12, 2011. (Credit image: © H. Lorren Au Jr/*The Orange County Register*/ZUMAPRESS.com)

Naposki speaks to attorney Pohlson at his trial for the murder of William McLaughlin on July 14, 2011. (Credit Image: © H. Lorren Au Jr/*The Orange County Register*/ZUMAPRESS.com)

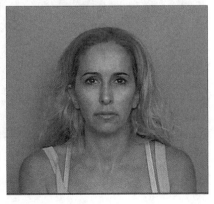

Johnston was arrested in 2009 for the murder of William McLaughlin with special circumstances, fifteen years after the murder. (Credit: Newport Beach Police Department)

Johnston enters the courtroom where she is on trial for the murder of McLaughlin, with special circumstances, on January 23, 2012. (Credit Image: © Pool: Leonard Ortiz/*The Orange County Register*/ZUMAPRESS.com)

Johnston talks to her attorney, Deputy Public Defender Mick Hill, before opening statements in her trial. (Credit Image: © Pool Photo: Paul Bersebach/*The Orange County Register*/ZUMAPRESS.com)

After Johnston's trial, key people in the case congregate for a group photo. From left: Matt Murphy, Susan Frazier, Larry Montgomery, Dena Basham, Tom Voth. (Courtesy: Detective Scott Smith)

on. It was a huge turning point, one that signaled he was determined to get back to a semblance of a life he once knew.

In Hanalei, where he lived in a small house on the beach near his mother, he took long walks along the sand every day. Although his gait was still awkward and it appeared he was staggering rather than walking, Kevin plowed on, convinced that one day he would walk perfectly, swim beautifully, and even surf gracefully and triumphantly, like he used to.

Since he was a child, the ocean had been his second home. Totally at ease in the water, he never felt more alive than when he was swimming or surfing. Every day in Hanalei, he'd paddle on his board in the bay. Before going out to surf, he would say, "I'm going to go out in the water and be humbled now."

"Throughout his whole recovery, what drove him to go on was his goal to surf again," said Kim. Every once in a while, he was able to stand up on a long board, but it was a frustrating process: "His muscles would take a long time to react to what his brain was telling him."

In time, Kevin began to accept his disabilities. He started volunteering at Limahuli Garden, a popular tourist spot, dedicated to Hawaiian plants that were either native or brought there by the first Polynesians. He made speeches at the local high schools, urging students not to drink and drive—and to try to be encouraged by his own story of overcoming adversity. He felt blessed that he was able to give something back and was deeply grateful for the things he had.

He even began writing notes to friends and loved ones. To Kim, he scrawled: "You spend your life giving back to society. You are a special child of God. See you soon. God Bless, Kevin."

Another note, in a childlike print, said, "I am smiling because I have an intelligent, good-looking sister. Actually, I have two. God bless. Kevin."

He also wrote to Kim: "This is a letter to say thank you. Thanks for reading and talking to me while I was in a coma.

I think that is one reason I have come this far. . . . Peace.
God Bless."

Another note stated: "I keep seeing the picture of me and
my family in the different hospitals and want to thank all of
you. I know that one reason I have come as far as I have is
because of the love and patience my family gave to me.
THANK YOU. I know it was not easy, but I am so thankful,
grateful, and happy that I've come this far. PEACE and God
Bless."

At long last, Kevin had reached a place in his life where
each day was a blessing, one he looked forward to and wanted
to fully embrace. That was certainly true, too, for October
23, 1999.

That afternoon, he attended 5 p.m. mass. After he returned, he decided to go for a walk on the beach at sunset, as
usual. After a while, he then decided to go in for a swim. It
was a particularly peaceful time on the beach. Few, if any,
people were there. The water was calm, and the sun was lying low in the sky.

A little while later, two local women walking along the
beach saw something floating in shallow water. Within seconds, they realized it was the body of a man. Panicked, they
ran in and pulled the body to shore. Immediately they recognized the person as Kevin. One began giving mouth-to-
mouth while the other ran up the beach to his mother's house
and, from there, called the paramedics.

In what felt like a terrible dream, a mother's worst nightmare, Sue raced down to where Kevin was lying. Soon after,
the paramedics arrived. For over an hour they tried to revive
Kevin, to breathe life back into a body that had already en-
dured so much, but to no avail. The young man was dead.

Sue sat with her son for three hours under the full moon
and talked to him. She kissed him good-bye. "He looked so
peaceful, so beautiful," she stated later. "There were no signs
of trauma on his face."

No one could figure out exactly what had happened. Had
Kevin lost his balance? Had a huge wave overpowered him?

Had he swallowed some water, been overcome, and been unable to surface?

It was another unfathomable tragedy for the McLaughlin family.

Kevin's sisters immediately flew to Hawaii. Sharing their grief, they told stories of Kevin in happier times, when they were younger and living a carefree life at Balboa Coves. While together, Sue, Kim, and Jenny wrote a letter to their friends to tell them the sad news and to impart some insights and remembrances about Kevin:

> Kevin was at an excellent stage in his life. He was very happy, had finally learned to accept his disabilities, and was so grateful for everything he had. He began yoga classes and became a health fanatic. He grew to love himself again. He wanted to live a long life.

The letter detailed how Kevin had been comforted and inspired by his faith. "His relationship with God grew to be the strongest it had ever been. He said his prayers of thanks many times each day. He reminded our family to say our prayers before meals. He'd kneel down on the sand and make the sign of the cross before surfing."

Crystallizing Sue, Kim, and Jenny's acceptance of Kevin's passing, the letter concluded: "He's free from the physical body that felt like a prison at times, and now he's the new Big Kahuna, riding all the best waves like a pro."

Kevin's death affected not only his immediate family but also the people in the community where he lived. In an article in the local Garden Island paper, beachgoer and friend Evelyn Cook wrote: "When I first saw him walking down the beach, I thought he was drunk, but as I looked more closely, it was obvious that his awkward jerky gait was caused by some sort of serious physical disability."

The two soon became friends, the article stated, and although it was sometimes difficult for Cook to understand Kevin, she learned about his accident and its aftereffects and how he had overcome the seemingly impossible odds against ever being able to walk again and even surf. "By sheer guts, determination, and strength of will, he had forced his shattered body and damaged brain to function again at near normal levels. What an extraordinary human being!" wrote Cook.

Cook went on to write that what endeared Kevin to her was not only his courage, strength, and good looks but also his "willingness to poke fun at himself, his ability to keep laughing despite all the horror and pain he'd been through, and his magnificent lack of self-pity."

Cook ended by stating that she believed Kevin was not "really dead." Rather, she wrote, "he's caught the all-time best wave and is on a ride that will never end. He's stoked right now, and he's going to be stoked forever."

Although life for the dwindling McLaughlin family was difficult at best, the same could not be said for Johnston. She seemed to be riding the waves just fine. Her marriage to Packard was a dream-come-true. He was extremely rich, mostly from real estate investments, and the pair were enthralled with each other. Packard wanted to give Johnston anything she desired, and by the looks of their lifestyle it seemed she was still living the California dream. The couple lived in an expensive home, went on expensive vacations, drove expensive cars, and entertained in an expensive fashion.

In time, the two decided to have a family of their own, and two years after their wedding Johnston gave birth to a baby girl. Now Johnston-Packard was the proud mother of three children.

Although life with Packard was going along just fine, Johnston was not pleased with her ex-husband, Ross. For one thing, he had a habit of telephoning the Packard house and warning her new husband, John, that she was a "murderer." Ross also called several of Packard's friends with the same message. This did not sit well with Johnston or Packard. Packard had his attorney write Ross a letter and tell him to

immediately stop his harassing—or else. Ross seemed to
have gotten the message. The calls stopped.

In March 2001, Nanette filed a declaration against her
ex-husband, stating that she had concerns over her thirteen-
and-a-half-year-old daughter, Lishele, going to Ross's house.
Nanette said that it had come to her attention that, "a fifteen-
and-a-half year old minor who resides with Kevin and his
live-in girlfriend and their two natural children," had been
in Juvenile Hall on charges of sexual assault. Johnston did
not like the idea of a sexual offender being in the same
house as her daughter. Once again, it seemed that Johnston
had no trouble standing up for her rights.

A hearing on the matter took place on April 10, 2001, in
front of Judge Sheila Fell. Based on what she heard, Fell
came to a determination regarding Johnston's allegations.

On June 1, 2001, Fell stated that Johnston and Ross "shall
have joint legal and physical custody of Lishele; that Ross
shall have visitation with Lishele only at those times and
places as agreed to by Lishele—Lishele shall have the right
and option not to visit with her father at her choice; that Ross
shall not go to Lishele's school unless he has cleared the visit
in advance with the vice principal; that there shall be no contact whatsoever between Lishele and the minor for any purpose whatsoever; and that Johnston shall not unreasonably
interfere with Lishele visiting her father."

Obviously, the judge believed that Johnston's concerns
merited some strict guidelines concerning the two youths.

After that, the acrimonious back-and-forth of child custody hearings continued for many years.

While Johnston was enjoying the routine of an OC housewife,
Naposki also continued to live a satisfying life. In January
1999, he moved into a new home in New Milford, Connecticut, to be nearer to his two daughters. In February 1999, as
part of his security work at Guardsmark he served as account manager for ESPN, in Bristol, Connecticut. Later that
year, he opened his first "Youth Concept 2K Gym."

On April 6, things got even better as Naposki welcomed

his first son, Eric John Naposki, into the world. Meanwhile, his gym continued to grow, as did his relationship with his two other children.

Naposki was so successful at his job that in late 2000 he was named Supervisor of the Year for Guardsmark. Not only that. He had gone back to college to finish the degree he had left behind when he was younger. After completing the twelve credits he still needed, in 2000, he became a proud graduate of the University of Connecticut.

That same year, he opened his second gym, in Milford, called The Gym, and closed the YC2K gym. According to Naposki, "It was a great year."

In 2001, things continued to go well for Naposki. He continued to work for Guardsmark and took on his third account manager job, he continued his successful gym, and he continued being "a good daddy." Late that year, after being offered a job as in-house security director/property manager for the real estate company Equity Office, he left Guardsmark. He stayed with Equity for three satisfying years.

However, not everything remained rosy in Naposki's life. For one thing, his younger brother, Frankie, had always wrestled with personal demons. Diagnosed an obsessive-compulsive, Frankie had turned to drugs, gotten clean for several years, and then started using again. Eric had adored his baby brother, but he hadn't heard from him in a while when he received the news in 2001 that Frankie had gone home one day and slit his wrists, leaving detailed notes on his affairs, including what music he wanted played at his funeral. "It was an unbelievable loss," said Naposki. "With Frankie's death, part of me died too."

And things got progressively worse for the Naposki family. His adoptive father, John, whom Eric had also adored, had gone completely off the rails.

Toward the end of their thirty-year marriage in 2003, John and Ronnie Naposki began fighting a great deal. John had gotten into drugs and would become angry, belligerent, and even physical. One day, John hit Ronnie and she ended up in the hospital. When Eric found out, he insisted that his mother come home and live with him—and he banned John from ever coming to see her there.

Subsequently, there was a battle in court over the house John and Ronnie had shared—and it resulted in the judge ordering that John sell the house, so that he and Ronnie could divide the proceeds. John was outraged.

Soon after, John saw Ronnie walking in town and got even angrier. In a rage, he decided to go home and burn down their house—that way, Ronnie would get *nothing*.

"John got a gas can and began spreading the gas over the house," said Eric. Then John realized he had forgotten to turn off the house's fire alarm. The lights were out because John didn't want the neighbors to see what he was up to, so he flicked his lighter to see the alarm more clearly. It was the biggest mistake of his life. The lighter immediately lit the fumes from the gasoline and John Naposki went up in flames, along with the house. Despite his ignoble demise, John was described in his obituary as both a "beloved husband" and "devoted father." And according to Naposki, that was not gratuitous flattery. John had been a great father and a loving husband—until he wasn't.

In 2005, Eric faced more misfortunes. First, his marriage to Natalia Algorta came apart and the couple decided to get divorced; and second, he closed his gym—it simply wasn't doing well enough. But Eric was a fighter. Unwilling to let these two setbacks define him, he began setting up a personal-training business in Chappaqua, New York.

By the end of the year, things were looking up once again. He had become a much-sought-after trainer. Plus, he had met Rosie Macaluso, a pretty blond schoolteacher, and, once again, fallen in love.

Meanwhile, Johnston was continuing her saga of marriage/ child/divorce; marriage/child/divorce. Although Johnston was highly adept at reeling men in, she was less so at sustaining relationships. After nearly five years of marriage, the marital glow between her and Packard seemed to flicker and then it died completely. On March 1, 2003, Packard and

Johnston-Packard separated, and on July 17, 2003, they penned a document declaring the "dissolution of the marriage."

Packard was to pay Nanette $17,000 a month in child support.

Again, acrimonious court proceedings followed, in which Johnston accused Packard of supplying vodka to Lishele, stating that she, Johnston, had to take her daughter to the hospital with alcohol poisoning. Johnston also accused Packard of being a "severe alcoholic" and "very abusive [and] angry when drinking." She demanded that he not have any unsupervised visits with her children.

As dozens of court papers were filed over the next several years—including one in which Packard asked for $332,800 in attorneys' fees and costs, but he was ordered to pay it himself—Johnston was not sitting idly at home. Once again single, she was on the prowl, looking for another man to fulfill her dreams—a wealthy man to be sure. And once again, she seemed to hit pay dirt.

This time, the lucky man was William Wayne McNeal, Jr., an inventor who currently holds three patents. He resembled McLaughlin in that he was wealthy and also owned a new $1.2 million home. His home was in Ladera Ranch, another brand-new OC suburb. Looking at McNeal, one could easily see how women could fall for him. Handsome with dark spiked hair, muscular—a hunk—and eager for fun, he loved to ride motorcycles and was game for just about anything. As was Johnston.

Maybe the third time's the charm. On August 25, 2006, Johnston married McNeal.

It was also in that year she and her ex Ross began a rancorous custody battle, with each side accusing the other of abominable parenting. But this dispute, along with Ross's ongoing worry that his ex-wife had killed Bill McLaughlin— something he did not hide from their daughter, Lishele— was the only thing marring Johnston-Packard-McNeal's sunny horizons. In fact, if you squinted and ignored the fact that she was twice divorced, a gold digger, a convicted felon, and a onetime murder suspect, it might look like she had a storybook life: a sexy husband, loving children, joie de vivre, plenty of friends, and—of course—plenty of money.

That same year, 2006, Detective Voth, after having served for twenty-five years at the NBPD and almost twenty-nine years total in law enforcement, including case agent for the first three years on the McLaughlin case, decided to leave the department to retire. It was his time to pursue other paths. According to Voth, "I chose to retire a year early to travel to New York and follow my oldest daughter's college softball team in her senior year. But I did fish [his passion] my way across country and back after her season."

However, he did have one major regret when leaving the department. The McLaughlin murder. It was one of only a few cases that had not been solved, and that bothered him deeply.

Every Christmas since their father's murder, the McLaughlin daughters had sent the NBPD a lovely gift basket, with a simple note saying: "Happy Holidays." They were still cooperating, still looking for justice—and Voth wished he could have found it for them.

After he retired, he kept in contact with the newer detectives to stay abreast of any developments that might be taking place. And of course, he hoped that somehow something would be uncovered that would bring the McLaughlin case to trial.

Chapter Twenty-One

2007–2008

It had been some thirteen years since the McLaughlin murder occurred and the family had gone on with their lives as best they could. And life at the OC district attorney's office had moved on, too. DAs had come and gone since the murder, and the two DAs who had turned down the case in the nineties, Debbie Lloyd and Laurie Hungerford, had taken new positions. It seemed that the McLaughlin murder had *nearly* been forgotten.

However in mid-2007, things were about to change drastically. Debbie Lloyd was in the courthouse cafeteria when she saw Matt Murphy, a senior deputy district attorney in the homicide unit and one of the most determined—and successful—prosecutors in all of Southern California.

The two struck up a conversation and Lloyd mentioned that she had been haunted all these years by the fact that no one had been arrested in the McLaughlin murder, and she wondered if Murphy might be willing to give it another look. She told him that she had turned down the case years previously, feeling that more evidence needed to be uncovered before it was brought to trial.

Murphy glommed onto the idea immediately—and he knew exactly what to do next. He contacted Larry Montgomery. Murphy had worked closely with DA Investigator Montgomery for years, and Montgomery had recently been transferred to the cold-case unit. Murphy felt that if anyone could open new channels of investigation, it was Montgomery.

Tall, good-looking, rod-straight, and meticulously dressed, Montgomery looked like he could play Gary Cooper in *High Noon*. His mere presence inspired confidence—and when this was coupled with a sharp intelligence, unwavering determination, and meticulous attention to detail, Murphy could do no better than to have him as his right-hand man. Montgomery's reassuring demeanor and casual confidence sprang from years of vast experience and a deep humanity. He knew people's lives rested in his hands, and he didn't take that lightly.

Montgomery started off his career in law enforcement as a reserve officer before becoming a patrol officer, when he worked the streets of Irvine, Orange County, for five years. In 1981, he became an investigator (synonymous with detective), first in crimes against property and then in crimes against persons (rape, robbery, homicide), where he served for twenty-three years. Montgomery loved the variety of cases he received and the ability to use time wisely: "We were not so busy that we were swamped and couldn't work cases diligently. I learned a lot and worked with good people. We were able to solve quite a few difficult cases." All during that time, he said, "I never took the sergeant's exam (a natural next step) because being an investigator was so fascinating that I never wanted to move."

When Montgomery turned 50, he felt he had done just about all he could do in his detail, so he put in an application with the DA's office to become a DA investigator. As he tells it, "I retired from Irvine PD on a Thursday and started work at the DA's office on Friday." And he found the work extremely gratifying. "I had the opportunity to sit as the lead investigator next to a DA in over one hundred trials during my career as a police investigator. While working with Matt Murphy for three years as a DA investigator, I assisted in the investigation and prosecution of over twenty more cases."

While at the DA's office, Montgomery was able to do different things than he could as a police investigator. "I worked closely with the DA to prepare for trial, found witnesses, and reviewed their statements with them to make sure there were no surprises.

"In trials, I usually sat next to the DA and kept notes on what we needed to ask a witness during his or her testimony."

After working for about three years as a DA investigator, Montgomery was approached by the supervisor of TracKRS (Taskforce Review Aimed at Catching Killers, Rapists and Sexual Offenders) and asked if he would be willing to leave Homicide and work cold cases. With little hesitation, he agreed. He still had no thoughts of retiring.

Among the most important tasks of TracKRS is to review old unsolved cases with a fresh set of eyes. Plus, they input all of the county's sexual assault and homicide cases into a computer database; monitor DNA cold hits, which links DNA from crime scenes to DNA belonging to individuals or other crime scenes; and serve as a liaison between foreign nations (mostly Mexico) and OC law enforcement regarding suspects and witnesses who may have crossed borders.

"The most important thing about being here is that I have time to delve deeply into each case," Montgomery said. "I have the opportunity to look at every single detail and every report. Time is not a factor. What I've discovered is that there is a lot to find if you have the time.

"I work solo on a case, although I do ask others for ideas or thoughts. At the end, after I've gone through an entire review, I put a PowerPoint presentation together with all the pertinent information—often with a hundred or more slides that include all the pros and cons—and present it to our unit to see what they think. I want to know if they come up with the same conclusions as I have, or not. Then I reevaluate my presentation and do it again, this time in front of the DA and the agency that asked me to assist them. Once all that is completed, the DA says that he or she would be able to file the case with what I've come up with so far or we need to do more before the case can be taken further."

*　*　*

In mid-2007, Murphy gave Montgomery the McLaughlin case to review. It would be his job to look over all the evidence and determine *if* it pointed to the person or persons responsible. "My goal," said Montgomery, "is to find the truth—whatever it might be."

To that end, Montgomery reviewed fifty-nine interview tapes, thousands of pages of police reports, autopsy reports, crime lab reports, crime scene photos, search warrant affidavits, investigative notes, time lines, phone records, and newspaper articles. He then followed up on details that he felt needed a more in-depth review.

"Sometimes," said Montgomery, "innocent people can look guilty, but there's usually an explanation for it. But with guilty people, there are usually twenty or thirty different things that pop up—and there don't seem to be any explanations for them. In the McLaughlin case, the red flags kept coming fast and furiously."

One day, while researching the case, Montgomery was listening to a tape on which a phone call was recorded from a Realtor, Sharon Hedberg. Hedberg stated that she had information she wanted to share concerning Johnston and Naposki. She told the detective that she had shown the pair a million-dollar home in 1994. The date the call was recorded was February 11, 1995.

"As it turned out," said Montgomery, "the detective who took the call was a weekend detective. He had nothing to do with the McLaughlin murder but was at the desk when the call came in. The call was recorded with other calls that the detective was working on.

"Near the end of side A of the audiotape, as I was jotting down my notes on Realtor Hedberg's phone call," stated Montgomery, "I was listening to the other calls on the tape, which had nothing to do with McLaughlin. Luckily, I kept the tape on in the background, because right near the end of the tape, there was a female voice that said she wished to remain anonymous but that she had information about the McLaughlin murder.

"That really piqued my interest. I had seen nothing in the police reports regarding any written documentation of this call."

The anonymous female stated that she and her fiancé lived in Irvine and that they knew Nanette Johnston from the Sporting Club gym in Irvine, to which they all belonged back in 1994. According to the woman, Johnston approached her fiancé and said she was interested in investing a large sum of money in a computer company that he owned. The detective asked if the informant's fiancé was there, and the female informant gave the phone to a male subject. As Montgomery listened carefully, he thought he heard the woman call her fiancé by name—Robert.

The anonymous male told the detective that he owned a software company when he met Johnston in early 1994 at the Sporting Club gym. He claimed that Johnston said she had worked many years as a sales representative for a manufacturer of medical instruments and was having a hard time selling a particular heart-valve product she had invented. However, she said, she had finally sold the rights to the valve to Baxter Healthcare and was subsequently receiving royalties.

In June of 1994, the informant stated, he had mentioned to Johnston that he was looking for financing for his software business. Johnston told him she was going to be busy all summer, but if he gave her his business plan she would get back to him with feedback by the end of the summer. At the end of August, Johnston told him she wanted to meet to talk about the plan. "Although we did meet right before Thanksgiving, Johnston never got back to me, so I forgot all about it."

Continuing, the caller stated, when he and his fiancée read the news articles about the McLaughlin murder and how Nanette Johnston and Eric Naposki were possible suspects and how William McLaughlin made his fortune, they became suspicious. Since McLaughlin had made his money in almost exactly the same way that Johnston claimed she had made hers, they decided to call the police anonymously to report their suspicions.

After listening to the tape, Montgomery thought: *Johnston was using McLaughlin's rags-to-riches story as her own to explain how she was going to get money to invest in this person's business. If this was true, one way Johnston could get the money was if McLaughlin died.*

Soon after hearing the tape, Montgomery contacted Detective Joseph Cartwright of the NBPD and said he wanted to follow up and see if he could locate this man named "Robert." Of course, it was a long shot, but Montgomery's forte, if one had to state *only* one, was finding a needle in a haystack.

Cartwright was the assigned NBPD investigator for the case at the time. According to Montgomery, "Cartwright checked the gym to see if they had records of clients named Robert in 1994, but those records no longer existed. I checked with the City of Irvine for business license records from 1994 to 1995 for any software companies with an owner named 'Robert.' I found two and contacted them, but neither made the anonymous call."

It looked as if the trail might have gone cold, but Montgomery had another idea. On July 22, 2008, he drove to the Haines Directory headquarters in Fullerton, which had an archive of California crisscross phone directories from 1970 to the present. The documents included all published phone numbers, names, and sometimes addresses associated with those numbers. After photocopying the November 1994 pages of Johnston's car phone records, Montgomery looked up every one of them in the crisscross directory for 1994 to see if any matched to a person named "Robert" or to a company dealing with computer software.

After tirelessly going through each and every number, Montgomery found not a single number matching the desired criteria.

Not willing to give up, Montgomery then researched the 1995 crisscross books for Orange County looking for the same numbers. And bingo! In the 1995 book, one of the numbers not listed in the 1994 directory was listed as belonging to an "R. Cottrill." No address or city was listed for that name in the crisscross directory, although the car phone record indicated the number was from the city of Irvine in California.

Investigator Montgomery then called Detective Cartwright and provided the information he had discovered thus far related to "R. Cottrill." Cartwright immediately checked the name through DMV records and found a match to a "Robert T. Cottrill," currently living in the city of San Clemente in California. Cartwright conducted further law enforcement database searches and learned that Robert Cottrill had been the president of a software company in 1994. During that time, Cartwright discovered, Cottrill had an address in the city of Irvine in California, and he got married in 1995.

Once Montgomery put together all the new information, he had a feeling in his gut that perhaps this new investigation into the murder of McLaughlin might pay off.

On August 4, 2008, Montgomery contacted Cottrill at his home. After identifying himself and saying why he was calling, Montgomery said, "I'd like to play a taped conversation that was made with a detective in 1995. Could you tell me if this is your voice on the tape?"

After listening to the tape, Cottrill said that yes, it was his voice. He continued by saying that he remembered that conversation, as well as the dealings he had with Johnston in 1994. It was his then fiancée, Dori, who had called the NBPD back then and handed him the phone.

"Is there anything more you can remember that is not on the tape?" asked Montgomery.

"When I first met [Johnston] in early 1994, she told me she was single and had just broken up with a bodybuilder boyfriend, who also worked out at the same gym." As the year went on, said Cottrill, Johnston started dating Eric Naposki. "Her ex-boyfriend did not appear to be happy about it."

Cottrill said that Johnston stated she was considering investing $100,000 and maybe up to $200,000. He remembered Johnston saying she had some offshore accounts.

This got the detectives thinking.

Here was another bit of circumstantial evidence. John-

*ston was talking about investing a huge sum of money in
1994, when, by all accounts, she did not have a dime to her
own name.*

Montgomery explained how he approached his work—
particularly the reexamination of suspects' behaviors and
statements. "Every case is unique and you always have to
look at the words and actions of the individuals involved with
an open mind," he said. "I read and listen to every single
thing available. I look at the information through the point
of view of: 'If this person is innocent, what is going through
his or her mind?' Then I listen to the answers and see if
they're consistent with an innocent mind-set: If they are innocent, would they be doing what they did?"

Montgomery went on. "Then I look at the information
through the point of view of: 'If this person is guilty, what is
going through his or her mind?' You listen to the same interview with that thought in your mind and see if it's consistent
with a guilty mind-set: If they are guilty, would they be doing what they did, acting as they did?

"You are looking for things that you would expect to be
there if the people are innocent, and expect to be there if they
are guilty. You have to get into the mind of the person.

"So I say to myself, 'What would any normal person do if
he or she was Nanette or Naposki and you have no idea who
could have killed Nanette's mentor? Would Nanette possibly
feel that she could have been the killer's target . . . but she
just wasn't home that night?' If so, I'm looking for actions
and words either Johnston or Naposki spoke or did that are
consistent with them being scared of the 'real' killers.

"After the murder occurred, I would think an innocent
Naposki would have grabbed Nanette and taken her away
from danger to his apartment or taken her and her children to
a motel or done something, anything at all, to keep her safe.
But that doesn't happen. Neither Naposki nor Nanette seemed
to have been afraid of anything. Nanette went to her other
house, which was only a few blocks away from Balboa Coves.
If the killer had keys to one house, he could have had keys to

that other house as well, but Nanette seemed to have no fear at all. She was observed inside her home with her children standing in front of a picture window in full view of anyone passing.

"Naposki doesn't have his security company do twenty-four-seven protection of her, which he believed she surely could have afforded, nor do they buy a dog, change the locks, or do anything to protect themselves. That's huge in my eyes, and it's not there and should be there if they are innocent."

Montgomery continued, "I also look at details other people might have skimmed over, believing at the time that they might not be important. For example, in this case, I read that the son of the victim said that the dog barked right before the murder. So a dog barked, big deal. But now I ask myself, 'Who could be the killer?'

"One possible killer is Nanette and she lives there, but if she comes through the door, the dog's not going to be barking. He would wag his tail, instead. So the mere fact that there is a dog barking in alarm, then bang bang bang, my thought is that it is likely *not* Nanette who walked through the door that night."

At the end of 2008, Matt Murphy and Larry Montgomery called Jenny and Kim McLaughlin and asked them to come to their office. "They said they needed some facts from us," said Kim. "We answered a bunch of questions and we went away with a slight, very slight, sense of renewed hope. Maybe a 'two' on a scale of one to ten. *Oh gosh, they've never given up,* we thought. *How wonderful! A new DA! How fabulous! They are still working!* But in reality, we were saying to ourselves, *Dream on.*"

As Montgomery was digging into the past—reevaluating *everything* Eric Naposki and Nanette Packard-McNeal had done and said at the time of Bill McLaughlin's murder— Eric and Nanette were going on with their lives, as if nothing had ever happened.

By 2008—some fourteen years after the murder—Eric was firmly established on the East Coast, courting the woman he was about to become engaged to and planning to marry, and Nanette was having another baby, her fourth.

Neither had any idea they were still being investigated for murder.

Chapter Twenty-Two

2009

Time was on Montgomery's side—and he used it doggedly. Continuing to go painstakingly through every report and tape that might lead him in the direction of the murderer, he came upon the recorded conversation between Detective Fischbacher and a "Suzanne" made on March 3, 1998, as well as the follow-up call recorded by Sergeant Pat O'Sullivan on March 11 of the same year. Then, after going through the 1998 file folder with information about "Suzanne," Montgomery called O'Sullivan, who had retired from the NBPD and was working as a DA investigator in Orange County, and asked him to contact Suzanne—with whom he seemed to have had a great rapport in 1998—to see if she would be willing to speak to detectives. Montgomery was hoping Suzanne might change her mind and be willing to testify if enough new information became available to bring suspects to trial.

O'Sullivan contacted Suzanne and soon introduced her to Montgomery. When asked by the investigators if she would be willing to speak with the DA's office now, Suzanne reconsidered and decided that enough time had passed and she *would* be willing. And she told them her full name: Suzanne Cogar.

After ascertaining her address, Montgomery and Deputy District Attorney Matt Murphy met with Cogar at her residence. They asked her if she would listen to the tape recording of the conversation she had had with Detective Fischbacher eleven years ago in order to refresh her memory.

After listening, Cogar remembered something that she neglected to mention to the detectives in 1998. She said that Naposki told her about a key that was left by the killer in the front door or gate area of the victim's house. "He told me that the key had been made at a store near our apartment complex. I remember thinking that Naposki was giving me too many incriminating statements, and I felt very uncomfortable. But since I had not yet heard from any other source that a murder had actually occurred, I didn't even know if Naposki was telling me the truth or not."

Murphy then asked the most important question. "If we have court hearings on the case, would you be willing to testify?"

After taking a moment to think it over, Cogar said she would.

Finally, nearly fifteen years after the crime, we have more evidence and another credible witness who is willing to testify about some incriminating details concerning Naposki.

Detectives and investigators felt they had finally found enough missing puzzle pieces to put together a picture of a murder-for-profit scheme. *Eric Naposki's and Nanette Johnston-Packard-McNeal's days in the sun might just be numbered.*

The district attorney's office agreed.

At 8:15 a.m., on May 20, 2009, a calm, unsuspecting Naposki, 42, left the small country-style home he shared with his fiancée, Rosie Macaluso, turned left out of his driveway, and began traveling northbound on Weaver Street. For him, it was just another day on which he was off to work.

However, the officers at the Greenwich Police Department's Special Response Unit were neither calm nor unsuspecting. In fact, they were poised to coordinate an upcoming high-risk motor stop.

At 6:30 a.m., the detectives who would be involved in the motor stop began arriving at the Greenwich police station. After going over details, mobile units fanned out to the area of Weaver Street and Almira Drive, awaiting instructions from a surveillance unit that was stationed outside Eric Naposki's Greenwich, Connecticut, home.

As soon as the units were notified of Naposki's progress, one car went northbound and "traveled behind the target vehicle and maintained visual contact." Another vehicle pulled up behind it, and a third unit pulled up behind that car.

When all three vehicles were in place, the detectives activated their emergency lights. "As the target vehicle pulled over to the right side of the roadway, one detective pulled around him and continued north on Weaver in order to block southbound traffic and establish a safe perimeter. Three other units blocked northbound traffic on Weaver."

With weapons drawn, they gave the verbal command to order Naposki out of the vehicle. Although shocked, Naposki complied with all commands, "verbally inquiring are we sure we have the right guy." According to a police report, "Naposki was taken into custody without incident. . . . He was placed in handcuffs, utilizing two sets, both double-locked. He did not resist and was helped to his feet and walked to the rear of unit #64. In the car, Lieutenant Mark Marino identified himself and advised Naposki that he had an arrest warrant for him based on a warrant that had been issued in the state of California."

"For a murder that happened over ten years ago?" asked a stunned Naposki.

"Yes. You will get more information when we arrive at police headquarters."

Commenting later, Naposki's attorney, Jeffrey Chartier, said that Naposki was caught totally off guard. "He is perplexed as to why they continue to go after him. He thought this had all been resolved a long time ago, and he maintains now as he did then that he had nothing to do with this."

According to Naposki, "For fourteen years, I had gone on

with my life, establishing a new relationship with a wonderful woman. We planned on getting married and had just sent out invitations the previous day. I couldn't believe what was happening. A SWAT team—men dressed in black with black masks over their faces and guns drawn—tackled me to the ground. They put cuffs on my hands, behind my back, and told me I was under arrest for the murder of William McLaughlin."

At the Greenwich police station, Naposki was taken into an interview room, asked to sit down, and had one arm handcuffed to a railing on the wall next to his chair.

Larry Montgomery and Investigator Joe Cartwright—the assigned NBPD investigator for the McLaughlin murder case—had flown to Connecticut specifically for this interrogation.

When Cartwright set eyes on Naposki, he was struck by how imposing he was. "He was a huge, huge man. And very confident," said Cartwright. "Larry and I had prepared quite a bit because we listened to past interviews and we knew he was a strong personality who liked to take over an interview."

After advising Naposki of his Miranda rights, Montgomery and Cartwright told Naposki he was being charged with murder, along with one felony count of special circumstances murder for financial gain, plus a sentencing enhancement for the use of a firearm. The enhancement charge meant he could have even more time tacked onto whatever sentence he might be given.

Naposki appeared incredulous, maintaining that he thought all this had been settled over a decade ago.

The investigators asked about the alibi he had given fourteen years ago—that he had made a calling-card call from a Denny's, which would have made him unable to commit the crime in the time frame established by the 911 call made when Kevin McLaughlin discovered his father's body. Naposki stated emphatically that he had once possessed the phone records that would substantiate the call, the details of which had also been mentioned in the letter his lawyer,

Julian Bailey, wrote on April 6, 1995, arguing Naposki's innocence.

"Do you still possess the records?" asked Cartwright.

"Who knows? Maybe my lawyer has them. . . . Maybe I gave them to him," answered Naposki.

If I was innocent, thought Cartwright, *I would carry a copy of that phone record in my wallet. I would tattoo it on my back.*

Offering more details, Naposki stated that on the night of the murder Johnston dropped him off at his apartment and, after receiving a page, he drove to Denny's to call his "boss" at the Thunderbird—whose name he gave as "Mike Turismo"—to tell him he was running late.

At one point, Cartwright asked Naposki if he could at least describe what the calling-card phone records had looked like.

Instead of answering, Naposki responded defiantly. He demanded to be taken to California immediately and said he wanted a trial "today." He said he had nothing more to say.

Continuing to investigate Naposki, that same afternoon, Detective Elijah Hayward and Investigator Steve Rasmussen from the NBPD went to the Old Greenwich School in Old Greenwich, Connecticut, to interview Naposki's live-in fiancée, Rosemary (Rosie) Macaluso, where she worked as an elementary school teacher.

Although shocked when the officers told her what had taken place, she agreed to talk with them. Macaluso recounted that she had met Naposki four years before at a bar in Stamford, Connecticut. She said they had moved in together approximately two months before and had gotten engaged three weeks ago. The wedding, she said, was in five weeks. She commented that the "arrest timing was unfortunate in that her wedding invitations went out the day prior." Macaluso said they didn't have any children together but that Naposki had two children, Eric and Suzanna, from a prior marriage—they, too, lived in Connecticut—and two other children, whom she didn't know much about.

When asked what Naposki did for a living, Macaluso said he worked odd jobs, mainly security-type jobs, for short periods. She said they talked a lot about Naposki's past football career but not much about other things in his past. She said Naposki never discussed Nanette Johnston or anything about the homicide.

As the questioning continued, Macaluso's helpful demeanor began to change. She started becoming agitated and curt. At one point, she stated, "I don't feel comfortable answering any other questions about what him and I talked about or what he's done in the last year. I honestly can tell you that I don't see any relevance in that, to this case now." And with that, she abruptly ended the interview.

Meanwhile, activity was picking up in Orange County, California.

At around 2 p.m. California time, Newport Beach detectives walked up to the Ladera Ranch home of Nanette Ann Packard-McNeal, now almost 43, at 3 Illuminata Lane. It was a picture-perfect home—two stories and five bedrooms, with a pool beneath the sun-drenched sky, a "gourmet" kitchen, and a gym. Unfortunately, the picture was about to change for the residents of 3 Illuminata Lane. Detectives had a warrant charging Packard-McNeal "with the death of William Francis McLaughlin, 55, on December 15, 1994."

One of the detectives, Dave Byington, now a sergeant, had been on the case since the very beginning—and he was surprised by how much Packard-McNeal had changed physically in the intervening years. "She was cute," he said, but "no longer the beauty she had been years before." However, he noted, her attitude hadn't changed much.

When she responded to the knock on the door, wearing a "white hoodie, blue tank top, jeans, white sneakers," she initially blocked the door with her knee and said, "What can I do to help you?"

"I have an arrest warrant for murder," Byington told her. She was totally taken aback, and her knees buckled—but then she quickly regrouped. Obviously angry, she quipped, "When will this ever stop? It's been over a decade!"

But it was far from over. In spite of her protestations, Packard-McNeal was arrested. "Why would I want him dead? He was worth more to me alive," she said bitterly.

She put it in perspective for me, thought Byington. *It was all about money, and all this time later, that was the first thing out of her mouth.*

Once at the police station, she was given more information about what exactly she was being charged with: convincing Naposki to murder McLaughlin for financial gain, supplying Naposki with a key to McLaughlin's home, and informing Naposki about McLaughlin's schedule.

Packard-McNeal was told she would remain in custody until a bail review, which was set to take place on May 26.

Finally, fifteen years after the McLaughlin murder, the OC district attorney's office was able to put out the following press release:

> A girlfriend and her former lover have been arrested and charged for the 1994 cold case shooting-murder of her benefactor boyfriend in his Newport Beach home. Nanette Ann Packard McNeal, formerly Nanette Ann Johnston, 43, Ladera Ranch, and Eric Andrew Naposki, 42, Greenwich, CT, are charged with one felony count of special circumstances murder for financial gain. Naposki also faces a sentencing enhancement for the personal use of a firearm. If convicted, the defendants each face a sentence of life without the possibility of parole.
>
> Matt Murphy, who will be prosecuting the case, stated, "We feel strongly that we have enough evidence to proceed with this case and look forward to presenting it to a jury."

Exactly what the new evidence was Murphy would not say publicly.

* * *

When Detective Joe Cartwright called from Connecticut to tell Kimberly McLaughlin, 42, in California, that Naposki had been arrested, she was caught totally off guard. First, she cried out in disbelief. After gathering herself together, she told Cartwright that she had gone on as best she could with her life but always hoped the police would solve the case. She said that other members of her family had also gone on with their lives, too, because "nothing would bring Dad back and he would have wanted us to go on living. We just felt they would get their due when they died and went to hell."

Later, speaking about that day, Kim stated, "I give a lot of credit to the Newport Beach Police Department and the Orange County DA's office. They hung in there for fifteen years because they felt justice needed to be served."

Jenny stated that she was deeply relieved and grateful that the detectives never gave up on the case. "We miss our dad a lot. This should not happen to anyone. My father did not deserve what happened to him."

Summing up, Kim stated, "I was ecstatic. I never thought justice would prevail, but it did."

Both Kim and Jenny stated that when the murder occurred they had no suspicions that their father's then live-in girlfriend might have had anything to do with it. "We didn't particularly like her, and we had told [our father] we didn't like her. We always thought she was a gold digger. But we didn't think she was evil enough to kill someone," Kim was quoted as saying in an article in the *OC Register*. However, after learning that Johnston had embezzled money from their father's bank account "we began to look at her differently."

Once back in Orange County, Cartwright began to check up on Eric Naposki's alibi for the night of the murder. After hours of research, he finally located the person Naposki claimed was his boss, Mike "Turismo," whose name actually turned out to be "Tuomisto." The guy was living in Sweden.

"On 5/24/09," Cartwright wrote in a report, "I called

Michael Dennis Tuomisto at his residence in Sweden. He said that he had been the bar manager at the Thunderbird during December 1994."

Cartwright wrote that he asked, "Has anyone contacted you before concerning Eric Naposki and a murder that took place in December 1994?"

"No. Never."

"What contact did you have with Naposki at the Thunderbird?" asked Cartwright.

"I didn't have much interaction with Thunderbird security," Tuomisto said. "Security guards worked the door and remained outside. I, on the other hand, stayed inside."

"Does security report to you?"

"No."

"Do you remember ever paging Naposki?"

"No, I don't remember even having a conversation with him."

"You sure?"

"I wouldn't have had any reason to page a security guard because that responsibility would fall to the head of security or the club owner," said Tuomisto.

Cartwright thanked Tuomisto for his help and the phone interview ended.

If Tuomisto was telling the truth, Naposki's alibi, claiming that he made a call from Denny's to the Thunderbird on the night of Bill McLaughlin's death, was a pure lie. However, who knew if Tuomisto really even remembered what had happened that night? Fifteen years was a long time.

On May 26, 2009, a confident Nanette entered the Harbor Justice Center courtroom in Newport Beach. The courtroom was jammed with over forty spectators in support of Nanette's lawyer's defense motion to have her released from jail in lieu of bail. But their enthusiasm went beyond mere spectators' support. Around a dozen of them said they would help post her bail by cosigning loans or pledging 401(k) retirement accounts or even their houses. They knew Packard-McNeal as a loving mother who could not be more supportive of her children or a kinder friend. Her husband, Bill McNeal, and her two oldest children, Lishele and Kristopher, were in the courtroom, blowing kissing to Nanette and looking deeply pained.

However, during the five-minute bail hearing all the supporters' enthusiasm was quickly quashed. Superior Court Judge Karen L. Robinson stated that Packard-McNeal was *not* eligible for bail because she had been charged with first-degree murder with the special circumstance of financial gain—which could bring on the death sentence. According to California law, a person charged in this type of capital murder case is not eligible to be released on bail.

The spectators and Nanette's family were visibly upset, unable to comprehend how this charming neighbor and loving wife and mother could even be accused of such a heinous crime.

Outside the courtroom, Matt Murphy said he believed those who "offered to help Nanette out with funds were well-intentioned people." But, he added, "I can't imagine they have any clue about what she is really like."

On Monday, June 1, ten days after his arrest, Naposki was extradited from Connecticut to California to face murder charges. His arraignment was scheduled for June 11. Before he left, he told his girlfriend not to worry. He would be home soon and life would go on as it had been.

On that day, Naposki appeared in court. When asked how he pled, Naposki said, "Not guilty."

Packard-McNeal was also in court that day, but her lawyer, Barry Bernstein, asked that her arraignment be postponed until June 23 so that he could review new evidence. Judge Karen Robinson agreed.

Neither one of the accused looked at or acknowledged the other.

During the proceedings, Jenny and Kim sat in the gallery, focused intently on what was happening. They were bolstered by several friends, all of whom wore badges with their father's photograph on them.

* * *

After the brief hearing, the lawyers offered their differing views on the circumstances.

Murphy stated, "There is no doubt we have the right guys." And he hinted that new evidence would be presented at their trial.

Gary Pohlson, representing Naposki, disagreed vehemently, saying that his client was innocent of all charges.

Angelo MacDonald, a New York attorney also representing Naposki, said his client "is innocent of all charges." MacDonald stated that the NBPD and the prosecutor had "manipulated suppositions, innuendos, and guesses in order to charge their client with murder fifteen years after the slaying."

Packard-McNeal's attorney, Barry Bernstein, agreed with MacDonald, claiming that in his opinion no new evidence had become available. He said he would fight for his client's release so that she could take care of her two youngest children, one an infant boy and the other a girl in elementary school.

Attorneys for both defendants said they would seek bail for their clients, since the prosecutors had tentatively said they would not seek the death penalty for the crime. However, it seemed unlikely that bail would be allowed. According to legal experts following the case, in most circumstances no bail can be posted in cases in which defendants are charged with special circumstances that *could* result in either life without the possibility of parole or the death sentence.

Chapter Twenty-Three

Late 2009—Preliminary Hearing

From the day they were both arrested in mid-2009, Johnston and Naposki remained in separate jail facilities, meeting with lawyers and trying to figure out how to deal with their new dire circumstance. Neither had been permitted to post bail.

And both Johnston and Naposki were enraged. Jail is bad enough for anyone, anytime. But they felt it was especially cruel for them. They believed that being jailed fifteen years after a murder, for a murder they said they didn't commit, based on *no* new DNA or gun evidence, was clearly wrong—a major travesty of justice. But here they were, living in small, confined spaces, without families and friends, just sitting and waiting, sitting and waiting.

It was particularly lonely for Naposki, whose entire family lived on the East Coast. But he did have some visitors. His fiancée, Macaluso, visited him often, flying in and staying for days at a time. His sister, too, who lived in Florida, flew in to visit. He spoke to his mother, who lived with his sister, daily. According to Naposki, their strong bond never wavered. "My mom was my best friend. She was one hundred percent behind me."

As for Johnston, she had family and friends nearby and during this time many came to visit, including her two older children; her husband and their young son; and friends and neighbors.

On Friday, November 6, 2009, a preliminary hearing began in Judge Robert C. Gannon's courtroom at the Harbor Justice Center. Family and friends of Bill McLaughlin were there, as were family and friends of the two defendants. The hearing would determine if there was enough evidence to put Naposki and Johnston on trial for murder. Yes, they had been arrested and charged, but it remained unclear whether the DA could convince a judge that there was enough *new* evidence for this case to go forward.

As soon as he took his seat, Judge Gannon spoke: "Calling the case of People versus Nanette Ann Packard and Eric Andrew Naposki. Appearances please."

"Matt Murphy appearing for the People."

"Good morning. Angelo MacDonald for Mr. Naposki."

"Gary Pohlson for Mr. Naposki, Your Honor."

"Mick Hill, deputy public defender, on behalf of Miss Packard."

The judge stated that the record should show that both defendants were in custody.

Representing the People was lean, chiseled-featured, tanned, and impeccably attired deputy DA Matt Murphy, who had been working the case for over two years. Murphy's soft-spoken, smooth, unruffled manner belied a bulldog ferocity, which had served him well over the years. In fact, it served him so well that of all the homicide cases he had tried, and they numbered over sixty, he had never lost even one.

Murphy grew up in the small West LA residential neighborhood of Cheviot Hills. He attended Loyola High School, where "the Jesuits pounded into our heads that you need to be a man for others." Although a good student, "I was mathematically retarded, which pretty much eliminated medicine [his father's profession] as a career option."

According to Murphy, he discovered a love for surfing. By thirteen, he was totally hooked, surfing every opportunity he had. Today, Murphy stated, "I have as much enthusiasm for surfing as I did when I was a kid."

Currently, Murphy lives in Manhattan Beach because it

allows him to get in the water and then go to work. "I surf several times a week. It gives me perspective and reminds me there is a lot more to life than murders or politics or work in general." Murphy claims he has no real surfing talent but just loves to do it: "I have surfed every ocean," he says proudly.

Murphy began his direct examination with Detective Thomas Allen Voth. Voth, nattily attired, with glasses and a moustache, was well prepared. As the original lead detective on the murder, he had seen the case against Johnston and Naposki rejected by two previous DAs. Like Naposki, Voth had played a little football himself—well, it wasn't in the pros, but playing at Cal State Fresno back in the day had also allowed him to get his degree in criminology. Now that Matt Murphy was quarterbacking, so to speak, Voth didn't want to drop the ball. Even though this was just a preliminary hearing, if they didn't make it through, that was the end of it. Game over. In his carefully outlined testimony, Voth laid out the evidence the police had accumulated in the weeks and months after the murder—the evidence that pointed to a murder-for-profit scheme perpetrated by Johnston and Naposki. Among other information, Voth described how:

- a Realtor said that before the murder she had shown Naposki and Johnston land on which they could build a home and the couple told the Realtor they would be ready to move into the newly constructed home in the spring of 1995;
- Naposki stated after the murder in an interview on December 23, 1994, that he didn't own any firearms; then later in the interview, he stated he had a .380 he had sent to his father; even later, he said he owned a 9mm, which he had given to a friend, Joe David Jiminez;
- after detectives interviewed Jiminez, they came to learn that Naposki had given him a .380, not a 9mm;

• a license plate written in Naposki's notebook came back through the California system as belonging to the victim's Mercedes-Benz.

Representing Naposki, Gary Pohlson, a veteran OC defense attorney, then cross-examined Voth.

To support the defense's view that the case should not be accepted, Pohlson asked Voth to read aloud number 4 of the rules Naposki had written in his notebook, in which he said: "Money is not important. . . . Enjoy the free things life has to offer." Pohlson wanted the judge to see that Naposki did not value money, so he wouldn't have any reason to have been involved in this murder-for-profit scheme.

During questioning, Voth admitted that DA Debbie Lloyd turned down the case, stating that detectives had been told that without a murder weapon the DA could not take the case forward; and that several months later DA Laurie Hungerford also turned down the case for the same reason.

Pohlson asked Voth why he never checked out Naposki's alibi—the telephone call from Denny's—and Voth argued, "I would think that would be important for *him* to bring [the phone bill] to us."

"Okay," said Pohlson clearly miffed, "but you're the one that was trying to prove he did [the murder], right?"

An equally miffed Voth responded, "He's the one that is trying to prove he didn't."

Pohlson also got Voth to admit that neither key found at the residence was made at the Tustin Ace Hardware store, according to Mr. Vandaveer, the manager. Reading from a report that Voth had in his hands, he said, " 'They were the same blanks that they used; however, [Vandaveer told me] their store keys would have had the store name and phone number [on them].' "

Furthermore, under Pohlson's questioning, Voth admitted that after looking at Naposki's finances he noticed that he did not have any "large infusions into his bank accounts or anything like that after Mr. McLaughlin's death," suggesting that Naposki was not receiving any financial gain from the death of Mr. McLaughlin.

Voth also admitted that Naposki had never refused to talk with detectives.

Cross-examination was then picked up by public defender Mick Hill, acting on behalf of Johnston. Although Johnston had been represented by a private attorney at her bail hearing earlier in the year, she had since requested a public defender. Mick Hill, a fifteen-year veteran with the OC public defender's office, had randomly drawn the case.

Representing a defendant on trial for murder was not unusual for Hill. Almost all his cases involved clients facing life sentences or the death penalty. However, defending a woman on trial for murder was not common. Nor was the length of time that had passed before charges were filed— nor all the media attention this case was attracting.

With his booming voice and disarming Irish accent, Hill quickly proceeded in an attempt to discredit Voth—and the work of the NBPD in general.

Hill stated that he was incredulous that anyone was now accepting as true that the pair had killed McLaughlin, since they had been "forty miles away attending a youth-soccer match in Diamond Bar."

Giving details about exactly where his client was on the evening of the murder, Hill spoke so quickly that the judge asked him to slow down so the stenographer could catch up. In one round of rapid-fire questions, Hill asked Voth if the time line of the murder "to the minute" was crucial.

"Yes," admitted Voth.

"Did you interview any of the referees at the game to determine when the game and trophy ceremony ended?"

"I did not."

"Do you know, in fact, if there even was a referee refereeing that game?"

"I don't know."

"Do you know what the name of the team was that her son played for?"

"I don't think it's in my notes."

"Do you know the name of the team that her son's team played against?"

"Not offhand."

"Do you know the name of all of the other players who were on her son's soccer team?"

"No."

"The only person you interviewed about this at all is Mr. Johnston, correct?"

"And his current, I believe, wife."

"Did you interview any of the kids or other parents, besides one adult couple, at the soccer match to confirm or challenge when Naposki and McNeal claimed they left on the night of the murder?"

"No."

"Did you find out from Mr. Johnston the names of the other parents that may have been at the game?"

"No, I didn't."

"Did you search to see if any parents videotaped the game and possibly captured images of those watching?"

"No."

Switching for a moment to shine a light on a different possible murderer, Hill asked, "Did you think a man who'd lost a bitter, multimillion-dollar business litigation with the victim could be involved in the killing?" He was referring to Hal Fischel, McLaughlin's former business partner, who indeed had been a suspect in the early days of the case.

"Slow down," said the judge.

"I get excited," replied Hill with a smile on his face. Continuing, Hill asked, "At any time, did detectives do a search of Fischel's home to see if he had any guns?"

"No, sir."

"At some stage, I'm assuming that you subpoenaed Mr. Fischel's telephone records to determine whether or not he was making any calls to any interested parties around this time period?"

"No, sir."

Hill stated, "So it seems to me about two days after this

killing, you decided my client was guilty and you stopped all other avenues of investigation to any other people. Would that be fair to say?"

"No."

Hill pointed out that not long after the murder Naposki told the police that he was on the phone with his place of employment less than twenty minutes before McLaughlin was shot. "Did anyone check his employers' phone records?"

"No," responded Voth.

Hill also got Voth to admit that the NBPD never checked how many cars were in the soccer game's parking lot, in order to ascertain how long it might have taken someone to leave the area once they got in their car, nor had the police checked the traffic conditions on the night of the murder, to ascertain how long it might have taken someone to drive from the game to Balboa Coves. Furthermore, Voth admitted that no one checked what time Johnston had arrived at the South Coast Plaza mall to see if it was even possible for her to have had time to commit a murder before shopping.

By the end of the day, Hill was not the only person in the courtroom who was exhausted. Everyone who was following his questioning was breathing quickly, having tried hard to keep up with him during his breakneck-speed questioning.

Voth, in particular, was worn out. The defense had put him through his paces—asking numerous unanticipated questions—and he had been on the stand for a day and a half. From his and the McLaughlins' point of view, things were looking a bit shaky for them.

After the weekend, the hearing continued, with Investigator Laurence Allen Montgomery called to testify.

Under Murphy's questioning, Montgomery described the tape he had listened to of "Suzanne" talking to an NBPD detective in 1998 and the subsequent interviews he had with her, in which she expressed her willingness, now, to testify against Naposki. Montgomery also gave details about Robert Cottrill and how Montgomery felt that Johnston's lying about her profession and income—and passing herself off as a clone of McLaughlin—could be incriminating.

Then it was Angelo MacDonald's turn to ask questions.

The New York lawyer was representing Naposki under an arrangement between California and New York that allowed MacDonald to serve as co-counsel even though he had not taken the bar in that state. This is referred to as being given permission to represent a specific client under a grant of Pro Mac Vice. It is a courtesy granted to non-admitted attorneys if they can show that they have the requisite knowledge and experience to handle that type of matter.

MacDonald had known Naposki back east, through their mutual friend, John Pappalardo. Eric and John had gone to high school together and the two were friends then and remained so. Pappalardo had stayed in New York, becoming a successful defense attorney. MacDonald was Pappalardo's mentor—"I second-sat him on his first case"—when both were serving as DAs in the Bronx. Now MacDonald was working the other side of the aisle, as a defense attorney. And he was intent on showing that sloppy police work had compromised the investigation of the McLaughlin case from the beginning.

MacDonald grew up dirt poor on the bad side of town, in Detroit. Generations of his family had worked the assembly line—and that was about as good as it got. However, there was one ticket out of his dingy lower-class predominantly Catholic neighborhood, and that was the seminary in the local parish. After graduating at the top of his seminary high school class, he attended the University of Michigan on a scholarship and then went to Villanova University Law School. In his third year, he applied to be a prosecutor and New York City was his first choice. The Bronx DA's office grabbed him up and he worked there for thirteen years, the last nine in the Homicide Unit, before leaving the profession briefly before returning, as a defense attorney.

A big man—over six feet tall—he has a big neck, a big chest, a big watch, big glasses, and big hands. He has a big smile and a big laugh. In court, MacDonald has a big voice and an even bigger swagger.

Under MacDonald's questioning, Montgomery admitted that in 1998 detectives had all the information he had today on Suzanne Cogar, but no one ever followed up. According to Montgomery, that was because Cogar said she wouldn't testify and wished to remain anonymous—and, therefore, whatever she said couldn't be used in court.

An incredulous MacDonald asked Montgomery if he had ever heard of a "material witness," a person who is "ordered to testify or at least appear in court. The court," stated MacDonald forcefully, "*can* force a witness to testify in a criminal matter, but you never did that."

Montgomery concurred.

MacDonald asked "Is it fair to say . . . that we have no murder weapon? . . . No DNA evidence connecting this crime in any way whatsoever to Mr. Naposki?"

"Yes."

"In fact," stated MacDonald, "some of the weapons recovered from McLaughlin were not registered and some even had no serial numbers on them."

Montgomery agreed.

MacDonald asked, "In your opinion, did the Newport Beach police adequately follow up in investigating the alibi given by Naposki and Johnston back in 1994 and 1995, when memories were still fresh?"

When Montgomery did not immediately answer, Judge Gannon said, "The record should note a pause."

Finally, Montgomery spoke. "I think that more could have been done. However, not enough information was available [at the time] to determine if that was a valid alibi or not."

Once again, MacDonald appeared incredulous. He went over the fact that there was a letter from Naposki's attorney back in 1995 in which it was stated that Naposki got a page and he returned it from a Denny's.

"Did you go get the telephone records?"

"No, they don't exist now."

"Would they have been available to detectives back in 1994, 1995?"

"If they existed, they should have been available."

"Did the police ever speak to Mr. Bailey about his letter?"

"No," responded Montgomery.

Seemingly satisfied MacDonald ended his questioning. Now Hill took his turn.

After getting Montgomery to agree that the "time line is the very basis of this case," Hill asked Montgomery, "If Packard and Naposki were at this game until eight forty-five . . . there is no way they could have made it at night from Diamond Bar down to Balboa to commit a crime, correct?"

"Absolutely."

"And do you agree with me that it would have been helpful to talk to some of the other parents . . . and to determine traffic conditions then . . . or the time they left?"

"Yes."

And with that, Hill took his seat, pleased that he had done his very best.

After a day and a half of this, onlookers in the court began to wonder if the defendants might walk before even facing a jury. *Would Judge Gannon believe there was enough probable cause to allow the case to proceed?*

When the testimony ended, the judge asked Murphy if he had a motion.

"Move the defendants be bound over [held] on all charges and enhancements."

"Mr. Pohlson, would you like to be heard?" asked the judge.

"I would," he responded. This gave Pohlson his last chance to convince the judge that this case was a non-starter.

Pohlson stated that in this particular case, more "than any serious case I have probably had," what was surprising was "the lack of evidence. There was a lack of evidence way back then and they have no more now."

Furthermore, the case had been rejected twice before by the DA's office—with good reason. "The only difference in this case from where it was back in 1995 is that Matt Murphy has the case," said Pohlson. "But his *perception* is not what wins the day here. The *evidence* is what has to win the day."

Pohlson portrayed the prosecutor's case as not just circumstantial but weak: "A woman out to find a rich man, that's not evidence of anything. . . . You know, going to look at rich houses, when I was a poor DA, my wife and I did that every Sunday because that's what we liked to do. . . . Naposki's statements to Suzanne Cogar [that he would like to see McLaughlin's plane blown up] are very equivocal. . . . Nanette stealing from McLaughlin, there is no evidence that Eric Naposki knew anything about any of that, nor that he got any benefit from any of that. . . . And the fact that Eric Naposki worked two hundred fifty yards from the scene, I don't know what that proves other than he would really have to be a really dumb criminal to go commit a murder right where he was working."

Pohlson concluded, "I just think it doesn't add up, Your Honor . . . the case itself fails for the same reason it failed years and years ago with the other DAs."

After Pohlson finished, Hill began his final statement. The Newport Beach police, said Hill, had focused on Johnston from the get-go and failed to properly scrutinize other suspects and scenarios. "I can go into all of the mudslinging, character assassination the district attorney has done to my client . . . but just because you are cheating on your boyfriend does not mean you are out to kill him. . . .

"What happened in this case . . . is that two or three days after this investigation [started], the police found out that my client was cheating on Mr. McLaughlin with Mr. Naposki. That was the end of their investigation. The only thing they cared about was proving that the two of these people did it."

Hill said that "Hal Fischel lawyered up on his first interview and he had been mentioned as a suspect by five different people . . . and they did not investigate him."

In conclusion, Hill stated, "There is not enough evidence to bind my client over at all and I would ask the court to dismiss the case."

In spite of being told he didn't "have a scintilla of evidence" by the defense attorneys, Matt Murphy remained unflappable during his final statement, methodically ticking off numerous points, including the following:

- Nanette started stealing from McLaughlin in early 1994, and the amount of money kept going up. "There are tens of thousands of dollars stolen four or five days apart as we start getting closer and closer to the murder," and "as soon as Bill McLaughlin realizes that Nanette Johnston is stealing from him, I'm going to go out on a limb and bet that relationship is not going to be very healthy."
- When police interviewed Naposki after the murder, he initially concealed the information that he owned a 9mm. Later, he stated that he did own one, but he claimed he had given it to a friend—which turned out to be a lie. At the time those statements were made, "no word had leaked out as to what kind of gun was used in the killing of McLaughlin, so why was Naposki hiding the fact that he owned a 9mm?"
- Naposki had written down McLaughlin's license plate number in his notebook and "I can't wait to hear the explanation when we get to trial for that one and what interpretation of that evidence points toward innocence."
- Packard-McNeal had instructed her ex-husband that if police asked he wasn't to say anything about her relationship with Naposki.

In conclusion, Murphy told the judge, "When the court examines the information in this case before the murder, the night of the murder, and after the murder . . . the evidence is overwhelming that these two people conspired and murdered Bill McLaughlin."

After the judge had listened to the strongly opinionated

lawyers, it was now up to him to decide whether or not there was enough evidence to merit taking the case before a jury. Certainly, the case remained circumstantial. There was still no murder weapon, no eyewitness to the killing, and no physical proof linking either of the accused to the crime. How would the judge rule? To many courtroom observers, it seemed like a toss-up.

But not to Kim McLaughlin. Later, when she was interviewed, she stated that on that day she barely knew Matt Murphy. They had met only once or twice. But when she observed Murphy in court, her spirits soared. She thought she had finally witnessed the man who could bring the killers to justice.

Later that afternoon, on November 9, 2009, Judge Gannon entered the hushed courtroom, a solemn look on his face. He had reviewed the statements over and over again and had come to a conclusion. After taking his seat, he stated his opinion. There *would* be a trial. The prosecution had convinced him.

So finally a decade and a half after the murder, Eric Naposki and Nanette Packard-McNeal would stand trial for the death of William McLaughlin.

Chapter Twenty-Four

2010

Although Bill McNeal had, at first, stood by his woman, he had decidedly had a change of heart after attending the preliminary hearing. As more and more incontrovertible facts emerged about his wife, he realized he did not know who or what she was. It was like he had been living with a stranger—or worse.

On May 24, 2010, a disgusted McNeal filed for "dissolution of marriage," citing "irreconcilable differences."

This did not sit well with Nanette. Not one to sit idly by, on June, 25, Nanette responded by writing: "I am currently incarcerated in OC County Jail but once released I want custody of my child back in full."

In a July court order, a judge gave sole legal and physical custody to the boy's father and basically dismissed her request. "The court finds that it is not appropriate to address visitation at this time."

So not only was Johnston-Packard-McNeal incarcerated and set to go to trial for murder; she also was a thrice-divorced woman who didn't have custody of any of her four children. Certainly, that was not how she envisioned her life when she was living high in Balboa Coves.

During 2010, while Johnston and Naposki remained in jail, the prosecution and the defense spent a great deal of time honing their cases. To that end, Murphy contacted Detective Voth and asked him if he would be willing to come out of retirement and go back on the case. Without a second's pause, Voth agreed.

In a letter several months later to city officials, the DA's office wrote: "Thus far, Mr. Voth has spent a large number of uncompensated hours assisting DDA Murphy on the pre-trial preparation for this case. As the trial draws near, he will be required to perform additional pre-trial preparation and be present during the entire trial." The prosecution then asked that Voth be paid $48.83 per hour, or $46,876.80 altogether, the same pay as a part-time police officer.

Detective Voth was thrilled to once again be involved in the "case that got away." He planned on making sure that the people of Orange County got their money's worth.

Chapter Twenty-Five

2011 Pretrial Hearing

It is a common procedure before a trial begins for the defense to seek dismissal in front of the judge who is scheduled to try the case, and it is just as common for the judge to deny the request.

In late March 2011, a pretrial hearing began on just that—whether or not the trial should come to pass—in Orange County's Central Courthouse in the Santa Ana courtroom of Judge William R. Froeberg.

One of the county's most senior judges, Froeberg had been sitting on the superior court bench for more than twenty years. Although he looked strikingly similar to Mr. Burns, the crafty and unscrupulous owner of Springfield's nuclear power plant in *The Simpsons,* Froeberg displayed none of Burns's evil intent. Instead, the judge was measured, serious, and deeply involved in the proceedings, often closing his eyes and listening intently before uttering an insightful and carefully worded statement.

Speaking for the defense and representing Naposki, Angelo MacDonald and Gary Pohlson argued that law enforcement had *purposefully* stalled in arresting the two suspects for fifteen long years, and, as a result, lost key exculpatory evidence. Further, they stated, key witnesses either had died or could not be located. In addition, back in the day the

NBPD detectives missed opportunities to follow up on leads and alibis that could have cleared the defense's clients.

Denise Gragg, Johnston's public defender for the hearing and a powerful courtroom advocate, also spoke in favor of immediate dismissal: "They [police] deliberately let this [pay-phone-call] evidence disappear. There was an alibi that we can't put in front of a jury anymore. That's prejudice." Evidence of the phone call, Gragg said, would have proved that Naposki did not commit the crime, and if Naposki had a solid alibi that meant Packard-McNeal was not guilty, either. "To allow the case to proceed to trial would be the height of unfairness," stated Gragg. "All the records that would support their alibis were not kept by police."

Prosecutor Murphy, assisted by prosecutor Keith Bogardus, begged to differ.

Bogardus argued that the 8:52 p.m. phone-call alibi was "speculative" and implored Judge Froeberg not to "whack prosecutors with the ultimate punishment—dismissal—based on claims that although they might sound forceful" are no more than "paper tigers." He added, "Why should prosecutors be blamed after the defense lost its copies of the supposedly exculpatory records?"

Murphy concurred and argued that Naposki never even made the call—no records were ever located to show as much—and even if he had, "he still could have gone to McLaughlin's home on the Fifty-Five Freeway, used a key that Packard-McNeal gave him, opened the door, committed the murder, and then gone to work, only a few hundred feet from McLaughlin's home."

"All the relevant evidence gathered and preserved points squarely at Mr. Naposki and Mrs. Packard," added Bogardus.

After listening attentively to both sides, Froeberg said that he would have an opinion in a few days.

On April 1, Judge Froeberg came down with his ruling—the most important one so far in the long-ago murder of William McLaughlin—on the defense's request for dismissal.

The McLaughlins were as nervous as they'd ever been. This seemed to be their last—and best—chance. If Froeberg ruled in favor of dismissal, they feared their father would never receive the justice he deserved.

After taking into consideration the many excellent points that the defense made, the judge stated that he nevertheless sided with the prosecutors. Explaining his opinion, Froeberg ruled that the delay in filing charges had to do with the ongoing investigation rather than being a tactic to hurt the accused. The judge did not think that the defendants' rights were prejudiced enough to call for a dismissal.

This was the news that the McLaughlins had prayed for.

Only a week before the trial was slated to begin, Judge Froeberg issued an important statement. On Monday, June 13, 2011, he ordered that Eric Naposki and Nanette Packard-McNeal were to be tried separately. Their case was being severed, and there would be two different trials.

According to most lawyers, the order made sense. In a single trial, the attorneys for the two former lovebirds would most likely try to push responsibility for the murder off on each other's clients. That would not be in the best interest of a defendant, especially if one of the co-defendants has significant evidence against him or her.

Naposki's defense team wanted his case to go forward as soon as possible and requested as much. Their pleas were heard and Naposki's trial was slated to begin in mid-June—about a year away. In legal time, that is "as soon as possible."

Chapter Twenty-Six

2011 Opening Statements Murphy

Opening statements in Eric Naposki's trial were set to begin on Monday, June 20, 2011, sixteen and a half years after William McLaughlin died of six bullet wounds to his body. It was expected to be a headline-grabbing trial, one that included the murder of a man of enormous wealth in a home only steps from the Pacific Ocean; a successful and prolific gold digger; an ex–pro football player; and plenty of sex.

It was standing-room only in Judge Froeberg's courtroom. Visitors lined the back and side walls of the room, which held approximately a hundred people. Crews from *Dateline NBC* and CBS's *48 Hours Mystery* were poised with their cameras directed toward the defendant after they had been given permission to film opening statements.

The trial pitted one accomplished prosecutor against two veteran defense attorneys, with three wildly differing styles.

On one side was the handsome, lanky, smooth-talking, and sincere Matt Murphy, Orange County's senior DA, whose sterling record preceded him.

On the other side was Gary Pohlson, who had litigated death-penalty cases since 1983, had been voted "Criminal Trial Lawyer of the Year" by the Orange County Trial Lawyers Association, and called a "Super Lawyer" by *Los Angeles Magazine*. His avuncular looks, often-bumbling style, and sharp wit and humor endeared him to jurors and court watchers.

Also appearing for the defense was Angelo MacDonald, a fast-talking, hard-driving veteran, with a brash Bronx courtroom manner. A big, expansive man who liked to take over the courtroom, MacDonald had known Naposki as an acquaintance for many years, and he truly didn't believe Naposki had committed the crime of which he was accused.

After thanking the judge and welcoming the jurors, Matt Murphy began. He said that his opening statement would provide "a road map of where I expect the evidence to go." Then, with his customary engaging manner, Murphy began what became a two-and-a-half-hour, finely crafted PowerPoint presentation—expertly prepared with photographs and text. First, he told the jurors about the McLaughlin family while projecting a photograph of "some of the players."

"This is Kevin McLaughlin," Murphy said pointing to a handsome blond-haired young man. "This is Kim, this is Bill McLaughlin, our victim, and this is Jenny."

Everyone in the courtroom looked intently at the slide showing what seemed to be a picture-perfect family—arms on one another's shoulders and smiling broadly: a good-looking, tanned father; two blond-haired pretty daughters; a photogenic Hollywood-handsome son.

After giving a few details about the children's idyllic lives, Murphy mentioned McLaughlin's marriage: "There was a divorce, like a lot of families, in 1990." And after the divorce, Murphy stated, Bill's wife moved to Hawaii.

"Now one of the things about Bill McLaughlin," continued Murphy, was that "Bill was a very successful businessman. Back in the eighties, he got together with some guys and they figured out a way to separate plasma from blood . . . he sold this company . . . he made a lot of money, but he wasn't mega wealthy. He wasn't like Bill Gates wealthy, not so wealthy he wouldn't notice a bunch of money if it was missing."

Murphy pointed out that two significant events took place

in 1991. Bill's son, Kevin, was hit by a drunk driver while skateboarding, and as a result Kevin suffered a severe brain injury. "He was in a coma for about three and a half months." After projecting four photographs of a happy, healthy Kevin, Murphy went on to describe Kevin's love of surfing: "He was the real deal, loved to surf." Murphy continued, "The evidence is going to be very clear that Kevin's disability was never going to go away. It was a real bad head injury. He had problems speaking, and he walked with a severe limp and probably would have for the rest of his life.

"Tragically," Murphy stated, "several years after the murder, Kevin was at his mom's in Hawaii, and he went out for a swim and he drowned." After pausing for a moment, he continued. "So Kevin is not going to be testifying in the case."

The jurors were clearly surprised—even stunned—by this news: a son with a permanent disability; a father dead; then the son dead.

The second significant event that took place in 1991, stated Murphy, was that Bill began dating Nanette Johnston. "He had been married for twenty-five years. He is kind of back on the scene, you know, he liked having a woman in his life, and he dated Nanette."

Murphy pointed out that there was a significant age difference between Bill and Nanette. Johnston was 25 when the two began dating. Bill was almost 52. Johnston, Murphy stated, had also been divorced, and she had two children, whom her husband had custody of. In spite of that, Murphy said, "she was a devoted mother. And, she was a devoted health enthusiast. She *said* she was a graduate of Arizona State."

He paused to clarify this last point. "It turns out, however, it is *not* true. She never went to Arizona State," Murphy revealed. "And for a lot of people who know Nanette, that is sort of her current theme—lying."

Murphy then put up a photograph of Nanette, showing an attractive woman wearing sunglasses and a sun hat.

He then moved on to offer details about Nanette and Bill as a couple.

"Now, Nanette moved in very quickly. At first it seemed like a pretty good arrangement. Bill was kind of lonely, and she was very eager to move in. She moved her kids into Jenny and Kim's bedrooms." Since the McLaughlin girls were already grown and no longer living at home, they agreed to the arrangement. "It appeared like their dad was really happy with her, so they didn't put up too much of a fight.

"One of the interesting parts of their arrangement," Murphy continued, "is she decided to keep a bedroom for herself separately downstairs. So Bill's master bedroom is upstairs and she kept another bedroom for herself downstairs."

Murphy then projected four photographs, each showing a happy Bill with Nanette's children, everyone smiling, everyone having a great time together.

Murphy described the financial arrangement between Bill and Nanette: "She and Bill had a joint checking account for her to pay household bills. It had no more than around ten thousand in it.

"Bill also had a main bank account where the royalties were distributed for his invention. That account could have over seven million in it at any given time. For that account," stated Murphy, "Johnston was not a signatory.

"Like a lot of people with a lot of money," continued Murphy, "McLaughlin was in the process of establishing his residency in Nevada." Doing this, said Murphy, would allow McLaughlin to avoid paying California's relatively high state income taxes. "The law requires you spend at least fifty-one percent of your time there to get no state income tax. So what he would do is fly back and forth on his plane. . . . Week to week, very few people knew when Bill was going to be home on any given night. Kevin was always in the loop. Bill would always let Nanette know. Other than that, it would be kind of tough to predict when Bill was going to be around."

Murphy also laid out what kind of lifestyle Nanette enjoyed while she was living with Bill. She didn't have to work. They went on exotic vacations and ski trips. Bill paid her credit card bills and for cosmetic surgery. He bought her a convertible Infiniti, loaned her money to get out of debt, and bought a house by the beach where she spent much of her time. He was kind to her children, and Nanette didn't have to worry about earning money to pay rent, taxes, insurance, or bills. Although there was no engagement party or wedding date set, Murphy said, Bill had given Nanette an expensive ring. He trusted her.

Murphy then spoke about the night of the murder, December 15, 1994, and projected the following series of events as bullet points:

- Bill returned from Nevada
- Ate dinner with Kevin
- Kevin almost always gone on Thursday nights
- Didn't go out and was listening to music upstairs
- Bill was in the kitchen in his robe
- Murderer walked into the house and shot Bill 6 times
- One of the bullets tore through Bill's heart
- Kevin heard the shots
- Immediately came downstairs and dialed 911
- Distraught and difficult to understand
- Time of the call was 9:11
- Police soon arrived and the investigation began

The next photograph Murphy projected showed the kitchen of the McLaughlin home. A man lay on the floor, apparently dead, with blood clearly visible on the white floor tiles. Murphy then projected this time line of the night of the murder:

Nanette arrived a little after 10:00
Interviewed by detectives outside
Police were very careful about information
Asked her to recount her activities
She went to her son's soccer game
Went shopping at South Coast Plaza
Receipt from Crate & Barrel at 9:29
Said she had no idea who would want to kill Bill

Asked to go to Beach house for the night
Kevin also went
Nanette asks very few questions of officers at the
scene
Didn't ask to see Bill
Didn't cry

After describing Nanette's non-reaction to the news of
the murder, Murphy paused and looked at each of the jurors.
Then he stunned the courtroom with these words:
"At nine ten and one second, when Mr. McLaughlin's
heart stopped beating, Nanette became a millionaire."

Murphy then moved on: "Now, one of the most interesting
things that the police discovered when they got there was
that the killer had left a key stuck in the door. Living next to
the ocean, everything corrodes very quickly, including
anything metal. And this key got stuck in the door. The police officers really had to work it to get it out. So the killer
had a key that he left and right below it there was a pedestrian access key."
Murphy projected the names of the people who had keys:

Mr. Kennedy: Elderly, liked Bill, no issues, noth-
ing to gain
Mary Berg: Housekeeper for decades, loved Bill,
no issues, a lot to lose
Kim: Loved her father, was living in Japan
Jenny: Loved her father, living in Dana Point
Kevin: Loved his father, handicapped, didn't need
a key, no GSR [gunshot residue]
No gun found by Police divers behind house
Nanette: Had keys; Also had a big secret

After reading aloud the last line of the projection, Murphy paused before laying another bombshell on the jurors.
"Nanette's secret," he stated softly so everyone had to be

ultra-attentive to hear, "was Eric Naposki." Murphy paused again to let that detail sink in.

"So, as she's living with Bill and spending time with Bill and meeting Bill's family and doing all that kind of stuff and saying how she wants to marry Bill, behind Bill's back for about a year, Nanette had been sleeping with Eric Naposki."

Murphy then introduced Naposki to the jurors as he projected a round-faced, good-looking man smiling at the camera, followed by a photo of Nanette sitting on Naposki's lap, his arm around her as they are kissing.

Murphy filled in some information about Naposki's brief NFL career and then went on to state that whatever money he had made playing back then was long gone by the time he met Nanette. "The evidence is going to be crystal clear [that] in 1994, he was actually in debt," said Murphy.

Murphy then projected the following details about Naposki:

> Grew up in New York
> Played football in the NFL before moving to OC
> Worked as a personal trainer at Sporting Club Irvine
> Had a small security company
> Worked as a body guard
> Started sleeping with Nanette around January of '94

Murphy also projected a slide about Naposki's "Money Problems":

> In debt
> Owed ex-wife thousands of dollars
> Bad credit
> Driving his father's car
> Didn't have a pot to piss in

And then Murphy projected a list of Naposki's work problems:

Lost Job at Sports Club Irvine
Lost Job at Metropolis Nightclub
Lost Job at Roxbury South
Lost account in Lake Elsinore

Murphy described Naposki as a "desperately broke former athlete who couldn't hold down a job. He was beyond broke and deeply in debt." In spite of Naposki's work issues, said Murphy, "on the good side of things for Mr. Naposki, his relationship with Nanette was progressing nicely. She bought him nice clothes. She paid for an expensive gym membership at the Sporting Club.

"In May," continued Murphy, "things were progressing so nicely that she actually took him to Chicago to meet her grandmother. After that, they went to Jamaica. All paid. In July, they went house hunting, but they told the broker that they wouldn't have the money to buy the home until sometime in the spring."

Murphy summarized: "Two people. Zero assets." Then Murphy wondered out loud, "How could Naposki and Johnston with zero assets be able to buy a house or invest in anything?" Murphy gave the answer.

"She had a one-million-dollar life insurance policy on Bill, which, of course, only pays out if he dies. She had a hundred-and-fifty-thousand-dollar provision in his will, which would pay out upon his death. She had the provision to live in the beach house for one year upon his death. She's got the title to the Infiniti convertible upon his death. And at some point before the murder, Nanette convinced Bill to make her the first trustee of his estate, which means she would have control over all of Bill's assets and all of Bill's financial bank accounts and everything else during disbursement to his heirs."

That, said Murphy forcefully, was the motive for murder: Johnston needed McLaughlin dead to live the life she wanted with her rugged, young, secret boyfriend.

Continuing to describe Johnston, Murphy stated that it

appeared that not only did she want McLaughlin dead, but she also wanted to use his money while he was alive.

Murphy let this piece of information settle in before continuing. As the day of the murder neared, Murphy stated, "her thefts kind of picked up a bit. She steals forty thousand in the month of October. She steals another twenty thousand in the month of November. Then we get into December where we go from stealing four grand every six weeks, she starts ripping off money every other day in December. And it's not four grand. It's eleven thousand here, five thousand there, as we get closer and closer, culminating with this. This is the fifteenth of December. There's a check dated December fourteen, the day before the murder, for two hundred and fifty thousand dollars. Another one for seventy-five thousand dollars also dated the day before the murder, and another one for thirty thousand dollars dated the day of the murder."

Walking back and forth in front of the jury, Murphy remained quiet for a few moments, seemingly pondering the weight of these deceitful actions. Then, speaking again, he began to focus on Naposki. "On August 2, 1994, three months before the murder, Mr. Naposki purchased a very expensive Beretta 9mm model 92F. His bank account, like a lot of people who have been struggling, would fluctuate from a thousand bucks to no money at all." Then making his point clearer, Murphy said, "It's about a six- or seven-hundred-dollar gun."

Continuing to lean on Naposki, Murphy said, "Naposki had keys made—once in November, once in December, at Ace Hardware in Tustin." Plus, added Murphy, Michael Rivers, who worked at the store, stated that Naposki wanted a silencer to fit his 9mm Beretta. He claimed he was going to be in a movie and needed a prop.

Murphy then got to the night of the murder. "As for the evening of the murder, where exactly were Johnston and Naposki?" Murphy stated that Nanette picked up Naposki and drove him up to her kid's soccer game. "The two attend the game and then after it was over, before the trophies were handed out, they left. The time is estimated by several people to be eight twenty p.m."

Murphy continued. "Kevin Ross Johnston, Nanette's ex-husband, was there. As they're leaving, she goes, 'Yeah, Eric's got someplace he's got to be at eight.' Ross Johnston looked at his watch, saw eight twenty, thought to himself, he's already late."

Continuing, Murphy stated, "Even more important than that, she has a car phone, and it's early nineties, right? Early, mid-, so we had car phones back then instead of all of our cell phones, so this is a phone that is actually attached to a car. She checked her messages at eight twenty-four. It takes a couple of minutes to walk off the field, so they left at eight twenty."

After projecting an image of the soccer field and a high-lighted route of how one might drive from the soccer field to the McLaughlin house, Murphy put up a slide labeled "Plenty of Time":

> 35 minutes straight (15 minutes to spare)
> 40 minutes with stop (10 minutes to spare)
> Easy drive back to Crate & Barrel (15 minutes to spare)

Continuing with the time line, Murphy stated, "So around nine-oh-nine, the killer used the original pedestrian access key to enter Balboa Coves. At nine ten, the killer used an Ace Hardware key to enter the gate—in the front door. We know the key got stuck. The evidence is going to show that he dropped the pedestrian access key. Nine ten, the killer murdered Bill McLaughlin. The reason we know that is because Kim actually timed Kevin walking down the stairs to see how long—given his handicap—how long would it take him to get down the stairs. She timed it at fifty-two seconds. The murder happened right about nine ten.

"At nine eleven," Murphy continued, "Kevin dialed nine-one-one. Every police car in Newport sped to the scene. The evidence, ladies and gentlemen, is going to be crystal clear that during the time of the murder, nobody at the Thunderbird Nightclub [where Naposki worked as a security guard] is going to say Eric Naposki is there. Nobody anywhere is going to come in and say, 'Eric Naposki was here with me at this time.'

"Nine twenty-nine, she [Nanette] bought the vase.

"Nine fifty-two, Nanette Johnston got a two-minute phone call on her car phone. Unknown number. And she failed to mention that to the police when they interviewed her.

"At ten o'clock, Nanette arrived at the murder scene. Didn't mention Eric Naposki or being with Eric Naposki. And in her initial interview, she left the detectives very distinctly with the impression she was by herself. '*I* went to my son's soccer game. *I* went shopping.' She doesn't mention anything about picking up Eric Naposki.

"The police then, as we know, escorted Nanette to the beach house. When we look at those phone records, what do we discover? Pretty much as soon as the police leave— there's an active landline in that beach house—what does Nanette do? The evidence shows that Nanette goes back down to her car and checks her messages on her car phone.

"At one thirty-six a.m., she paged Eric Naposki. She received a four-minute incoming phone call immediately thereafter."

After giving jurors a moment to digest this sequence of events, Murphy went right back at it, relentlessly describing Nanette's suspicious behavior.

"Morning after the murder. Now, Nanette did not call any family members. Kim is in Japan; Jenny is in Dana Point. Bill McLaughlin had an extended family. He's got a brother in Chicago. There's a ton of family members. You've got the ex-wife. Kevin can barely talk. Nanette leaves it up to Kevin to notify people. Nanette doesn't call a soul.

"At ten o'clock the next morning, thereabouts, Kevin gets ahold of Jenny at her job and gives her the horrible news. Jenny immediately gets in her car. She also had a car phone and she calls the beach house on her way up. Nanette answers, and Jenny says, 'Oh, my god, Nanette, is it true? Is it true?' And Nanette says, 'Yeah. It sucks.'"

Hysterical, Jenny tells Nanette that she is coming up there to try to figure out what's going on.

"When Jenny arrives, Nanette is inside the house. Kevin is waiting outside by himself. Jenny observes Nanette peeking out through the front door, and watches her as she closes the door. The evidence is going to show, no shared hugs; no tears; nothing like that. Just closed the door."

Summing up what he had just recounted, Murphy reprojected the image of McLaughlin lying on the kitchen floor, stating the time as 9:10.

> 9:10:01 Nanette Johnston became a millionaire
> 9:11 Kevin called 911
> 9:12 Every police car in Newport sped to scene
> 9:00–9:15 No one will put Naposki at Thunderbird
> 9:29 Nanette bought a vase at Crate & Barrel
> 9:52 Nanette got a two-minute phone call
> Unknown number
> Failed to mention that to police
> 10:00 Nanette arrived at murder scene
> Didn't mention Naposki
> Asked no questions
> Police escort Nanette (and Kevin) to Beach House
> Police leave
> Nanette went back to her car
> Checked her messages from car phone
> Paged Naposki (1:36)
> Received a 4-minute incoming call

Murphy then projected what took place "On the morning after the murder":

> Nanette did NOT call any family members
> But did call Naposki again . . .
> Kevin called Jenny at work
> Jenny called Nanette: "Yeah, it sucks."

Nanette let Kevin wait outside alone
Peeked outside when Jenny arrived

Several days later, continued Murphy, on Sunday, December 18, police talked to Nanette's ex-husband [Ross Johnston]. Johnston told them that a day or two after the murder Nanette called him and said, "Bill was murdered, but I have an alibi." Murphy continued, "Johnston is going to testify that in that same telephone conversation, Nanette told her ex-husband, 'And when the police talk to you, if they do, don't tell them I was at the game with Eric. Don't tell the police anything about Eric.' Now, given that, the police are obviously very concerned. They want to know who is this Eric guy.

"Detectives decide to watch the Balboa Coves residence," continued Murphy. "And then what did Nanette do on Monday December nineteen?"

"The evidence is going to show Nanette didn't change the locks on the Balboa Coves house. The locks had not yet been changed on the beach house. She's sleeping there every night. The killer had not been caught."

Furthermore, continued Murphy, when Detective Voth checked Nanette's keys he found that Nanette had her key to the front door of the house in Balboa Coves, but "lo and behold, she was missing her pedestrian access key."

The aftermath for the family was horrible, stated Murphy. "They were dealing with their grief, and at the same time, had to figure out all of the financial dealings, taxes, mortgages, investments, who would care for Kevin, and so on."

After projecting a photograph of Bill's funeral, which took place on Wednesday, December 21, Murphy projected a photograph of a store called Champion Motorcycles and the date of December 21 and then a shot of a Wells Fargo.

"After Nanette leaves the funeral," said Murphy, "the first thing she does is page Eric Naposki. From there, Nanette went to Champion Motorcycles on old Newport Road, put down Bill's credit card, and bought ten thousand dollars' worth of off-road dirt bikes. From there she went to her Wells Fargo bank and cashed one of her checks for three thousand dollars.

"That day, Mr. Naposki is moving out of his four-hundred-forty-five-square-foot studio apartment. He moved out into the Ramada Inn.

"The next day, Mr. Naposki went Christmas shopping for Nanette. He bought . . ." Then Murphy paused for effect. "He had less than a thousand dollars in his bank account that day—he bought her a six-hundred-dollar Movado watch.

"The police then see Mr. Naposki for the first time. He's at the beach house. This is seven days after the murder. . . .

"After detectives ran the license plate number on the car," Murphy told the jurors, "they discovered that [Naposki] had an outstanding traffic warrant." Murphy stated that the detectives stopped Naposki as he left the Thunderbird Nightclub in the early hours of December 23 and soon after impounded the car, asking if they could search it to see if there is "anything that can clear him or implicate him, anything that might be able to help." They also searched his hotel room and found no weapons. They photocopied his keys and a notebook from his car.

Later that day, December 23, Murphy stated, the police had their first interview with Naposki. A month later, they had their second interview.

In the first interview, Murphy stated, Naposki was "polite, cordial, and there was a professional tone. He was even-keeled." During the second one, his demeanor changed dramatically.

Highlighting the differences between the two interviews, Murphy first projected the differences in how Naposki described his relationship with Nanette:

1st Interview—December 23, 1994

Nanette and I are pretty good friends
Not totally solo relationship
Girlfriend like I would call someone I hugged in the club

2nd Interview—January 18, 1995

Nanette is my girl, she's the greatest thing ever, I love her, and the relationship may last forever

Then, highlighting differences in details given about the time of the murder, Murphy projected the following from Naposki's interviews:

1st interview

Left soccer game at *** [Naposki didn't give a specific time]
Got home around 9:00
Got situated
Left and went straight to work. "I was in a hurry to get to work, she was in a hurry to get to the mall."

2nd interview

Moseyed to car at 8:35
Nanette dropped me off between 9 and 9:15
Drove to Leonard's house
Got a page, stopped at Denny's, called Bar Manager
Went to work

Finally, Murphy highlighted the differences in Naposki's two interviews regarding details about the guns Naposki owned:

1st interview

I don't do **any** armed security work
I don't even have a sidearm
Oh, "I had one gun," a .380 I gave to my dad
Oh . . . I also had a 9mm I loaned to Joe Jiminez

2nd interview

I had 3 guns

I used my 9mm in Mexico doing armed security
work

I don't want to talk about my 9mm, it doesn't matter, it's irrelevant

I lied because I was scared

(2 months before info went public) [Murphy explained that Naposki was hiding the fact that he had
owned a 9mm two months before anyone outside the
police force even knew that a 9mm was used in the
killing.]

I lied because I was playing the old "mind fuck
game" about the gun

Wrapping up his opening argument, Murphy promised
the jurors that he would unequivocally prove to them that
when these facts were taken all together, they would show
that Naposki was responsible for the murder of William
McLaughlin—and here's why:

The killer wanted to kill Bill. Naposki said he wanted to
kill Bill.

The killer planned a murder. Naposki had a silencer
made for a 9mm gun.

The killer knew how to shoot. Naposki knew how to
shoot.

The killer used a Beretta F-series 9mm. Naposki owned
a Beretta F-series 9mm.

The killer used Federal Hydra-Shok ammunition. Naposki used Federal Hydra-Shok ammo.

When the killer was traveling toward the murder scene,
Naposki was traveling toward the murder scene.

Naposki was not buying cars and Bill [the victim] was
not selling his car, but Naposki had Bill's license plate number written in his notebook.

Naposki lied about his relationship with Nanette.

Naposki lied about where he was during the murder.

Naposki lied about owning a Beretta 9mm.

He was lying about not having a 9mm when nobody but the police and the killer knew that the murder weapon was a 9mm.

The final words Murphy spoke to a hushed courtroom, as he turned to point directly at Eric Naposki, were these: "Thank you for your attention. At the end of this case . . . you are going to hold this guy accountable for what he did, I guarantee it."

As Murphy said those words, Naposki stared straight at him, a smirk on his face.

Chapter Twenty-Seven

2011 Trial

In most criminal trials, the prosecution's opening statement is then followed by the defense's. So when Murphy concluded his opening remarks, the judge, following protocol, asked the defense, "Will there be an opening statement from the defense at this time?"

Pohlson responded, "No, Your Honor. We're going to waive opening statement at this time and reserve it for the beginning."

"The beginning" meant immediately before the defense began its direct questioning. In many trials, the defense chooses to postpone, or reserve, its opening statement until the beginning of its presentation of evidence. One reason for this is so that the defense has the jury's fresh attention. If the defense follows the prosecution's opening, some defense attorneys argue, the jurors suffer from information overload and can't concentrate on this second argument.

The judge then said, "Reserved. First witness."

"Your Honor," stated Murphy, "at this time the people would call Kimberly McLaughlin."

The jury of seven women and five men sat watching and listening attentively.

Petite, with long dirty-blond hair, Kim walked slowly to the stand. This was a difficult moment for her. The surviving McLaughlins had been waiting for justice for such a long

time. Now, they would have to see it through, however pain-
ful the process. Choking back tears, she began by stating her
full, married name: Kimberly McLaughlin Bayless. When
asked how she would describe the McLaughlin family, she
stated, "I had a very special family. We were really close.
There was my mom and my dad, and I'm the oldest daughter, and my sister Jenny is two years younger than myself,
and Kevin is four years younger than myself. And we were
very close and we did a lot of activities together. There was
lots of love, and we had a very special childhood."

Murphy then said, "Why don't we start with Kevin's relationship with your dad. What can you tell us about that?"

"First and foremost," said Kim, "my dad was a family
man, and he loved each and every one of us a lot. And we
were everything to him, including Kevin. And so my dad
loved family time. . . . We'd have long family dinners so we
could have discussions. And after church on Sunday, Dad
would arrange Sunday brunches because you can eat a lot
and we could sit around and communicate. He and Kevin
had a very tight relationship, so they were kind of silly and
wacky together."

Murphy then asked Kim to recount an incident involving
her father discovering that Kevin was smoking marijuana.
The incident took place after Kevin's skateboarding accident, when he was living at home with his father.

"That was a real hard time in our family," said Kim
softly, "because smoking pot was a big, huge no-no in our
McLaughlin family. . . . Kevin was smoking pot and my dad
was devastated. He was really hurt and very angry at Kevin
for doing that and making those choices. So he tried putting
him on restrictions and giving him some boundaries and
taking some things away, and Kevin didn't like that, either."

Murphy asked, "Was that the undoing of their relationship or was that a problem? In other words, did they remain
close?"

"Yes, of course. My dad loved his son unconditionally,
but it hurt him to know that his own son was smoking pot.
And, Kevin knew that Dad loved him, and he was putting

these restrictions on him because he loved him, but yet Kevin didn't want to stop. So it was tension between them, definitely, between our whole family, you can imagine."

Murphy then asked Kim about Kevin's injury.

"One night, at [the] end of October 1991, he was skateboarding from a bar down on Newport Boulevard to his apartment, and he was hit from behind by a drunk driver in a car going sixty-five miles per hour and he hit the windshield and went over the top of the car and landed. And he had multiple internal injuries and traumatic head injury. The two sides of his brain sheared.

"He was Life-Flighted to the hospital intensive care, [he] almost died. And he was in a coma. There's many different stages of coma, we came to find out, but [he was in a] deep coma for a month, and then it lingered—it went on for three or four months. Then he was in hospitals, different hospitals rehabbing, waking up and relearning skills for a year and a half, and he had to relearn to talk again, walk again.

"At first he couldn't even hold his head up, and eventually he learned to do that, then sit up in a wheelchair, then he graduated from a wheelchair, then a walker, then he learned how to walk, but it was still a little wobbly. He was still a little uncoordinated, but he tried to relearn how to drive eventually again, take care of himself eventually. And he went to Orange Coast College brain injury program to learn cognition skills."

Homing in on the night of the murder, Murphy asked, "At the point of your father's murder, what was Kevin doing back then?"

"Kevin had been hit in 1991, so this was three years after that. And, he was in hospitals, like I said, for a year and a half. So then I think he moved right into my dad's house, our house we grew up in. . . . And my dad was in charge of continuing with the rehab and making sure Kevin's paperwork was all filled out for Social Security services and making sure Kevin was getting to his appointments in Orange Coast College. My dad was his primary caretaker at that point because Jenny and myself had moved on to different places and were working and living somewhere else."

"In mid-December 1994," asked Murphy, "had Kevin made significant progress as far as recovery?"

"Yes. His cognition was enough that he could understand that he had been hit in an accident and that he was permanently damaged, and he wasn't happy about that. Like I said, his walk was a little uncoordinated and wobbly. A lot of other people had a hard time understanding him. He kind of mumbled. A lot of brain-injury patients do. So he'd have to repeat himself, and he got frustrated about that. He could write again, but it was very shaky. He could read again, but he now needed glasses and some other special things to read. He was just taking driving lessons again at the time of my dad's death. And he was trying to learn how to surf again, how to swim again. And my dad had arranged for teachers and lessons and therapists for all of this for him."

"Jump ahead here quickly," said Murphy. "At some point after the murder you became aware that your brother actually called nine-one-one, right? There was an experiment that you conducted with Kevin to figure out how long it would take him to get from the bedroom he was staying in down to the phone in order to do that. Is that right?"

Kim responded, "The detectives asked me to time him from his bedroom to the kitchen, and so you have to understand, Kevin was sleeping in one of my dad's upstairs guest bedrooms because when he moved back in the downstairs bedrooms had already been taken by Nanette and her kids."

"How long did it take Kevin to do that?"

"Going as fast as he could, fifty-two seconds."

Murphy asked, "What can you tell us about Kevin's schedule at the time of the murder? Specifically what about Thursday nights?"

After thinking for a moment, Kim stated, "He went to a meeting every Thursday night. He was very proud because he was elected secretary at that meeting."

"What kind of meeting was that?"

"It was an AA meeting, because our family got on him when he started smoking pot really hard-core. We said, 'You need to do something about this. We won't allow it anymore,' so we encouraged him to go to Alcoholics Anonymous and Narcotics Anonymous meetings."

Continuing to offer details about Kevin, Kim said, "So after my dad was killed, Kevin lived with us for a while in the beach house while our whole family came together again, including my mom, who lived in Hawaii, and we all lived for two years in Balboa Coves trying to piece together our lives again. And then Kevin spent a few years on his own in Newport; then he decided to move to Hawaii to be close to my mom and because he said Newport was getting to be 'zoo port.' He was getting too old for the rat race in Newport."

"Okay. Now, Kevin at some point passed away. When was that in relation to the murder?" asked Murphy.

"Kevin passed away one Saturday evening [at the] end of October, 1999."

"So eight years after his accident?"

Kim began to explain. "[My mom and Kevin] had gone to church on a Saturday evening and then they came home together and they gave each other a hug. Kevin went into his own home. My mom went into her home. Then Kevin must have changed, got his suit on, and gone out to the water to take a dip in the ocean like he had done so many times before. And it was probably about sunset at this point. We're not really sure what happened, but there was a rip current out there that night or that evening, and what happened they think is that Kevin had gone to take a dip in the ocean in shallow water. And oftentimes, when he was relearning how to swim again, if he got water in his mouth, he would have to stand up to cough it out because when he was in the hospital he had a tracheotomy in his throat, a breathing tube, and so he had scar tissue in there still. And it really affected him when he swam. So I think what happened is he got a little carried out by the ocean a little too deep and probably couldn't cough it out and drown[ed]."

After taking a few moments to collect herself, Kim continued. "That evening two hours later a couple walking by in the full moon had the courage to pull him out."

After Kim finished describing Kevin's death, the judge suggested that this would be a good time for everyone to take a break and court was adjourned.

An emotional Kim left the stand and was immediately surrounded by a group of loving friends and family members.

When the trial recommenced the next morning, Kim once again took the stand. Murphy decided that it was time to delineate the motive behind the murder. He began by asking Kim about the kind of person Nanette was in relation to the kind of person Kim's father was.

Kim stated that her father was an affectionate man who "loved challenges and learning new things." Johnston, however, was "cold and unintelligent."

Murphy asked Kim if Johnston had been pilfering money from her father. Kim responded that she had had absolutely no idea anything nefarious was going on until after the murder, when it was discovered that Johnston had been stealing money.

The first inkling that Nanette Johnston was not just coldhearted but criminal came when the McLaughlins suggested that Nanette could take her belongings from the Balboa Coves house and bring them to the Seashore Drive house in the weeks after the murder. Nanette took them up on this—and then some. When the family returned to Balboa Coves, Kim said, they were startled because her father's office "had been cleared out, basically." Computers gone. Fax machine gone. Taxes gone. Favorite baseball gone. "Interestingly enough," said Kim, "photos of my dad and Nanette were not gone."

This invasion was alarming, hurtful, and dubious all at once, and Nanette's behavior went on to become even more suspicious, Kim told the court. When Kim or her sister asked

Nanette about their dad's finances—because they needed to pay bills and settle his affairs—Nanette was weirdly unco-operative. Why exactly had she taken their father's papers and computer if she wasn't planning on helping?

However, Kim testified, at that time she had no idea Nanette was up to anything sinister. Kim only realized that huge sums of money were missing from her father's bank accounts *after* her father's accountant spoke to her about some highly irregular withdrawals.

And these weren't the only nasty surprises Nanette had in store for the McLaughlins. Kim stated that she had no clue Nanette had a boyfriend, besides her father, until after her dad's death.

Leaving that cold fact in the jurors' minds, Murphy ended his questioning and a clearly distraught Kim took her seat.

It was now the defense's turn to cross-examine the witness. Defense attorneys usually walk a tightrope when it comes to questioning sympathetic witnesses. They know they can't be too antagonistic for fear that the jury might become angry and turn against them.

Angelo MacDonald began his cross-examination by extending his condolences for the loss of Kim's father and brother. It appeared as if he might go easy on her. But when he moved on to the subject of Nanette he didn't exactly handle Kim with kid gloves.

In direct contrast to Murphy's calm, soft-spoken manner, MacDonald began pacing back and forth, taking his glasses on and off, and speaking loudly and quickly.

"Fair to say that you and the family discovered, along with the accountant, that Miss Johnston had systematically stolen from your father, correct?"

"Yes."

"Over a period of time, right?"

"Yes."

"Months and months and months, correct?"

"Yes."

"Hundreds of thousands of dollars, correct?"

"Yes."

"You discovered that she was a cheat, right?"

"Yes."

"A forger, correct?"

"Yes."

"A thief, yes?"

"Yes."

"A liar?"

"Yes."

"Very deceptive?"

"Yes."

"Devious?"

"Yes."

"Pathological?"

"Yes."

Finally, MacDonald paused for a second to catch his breath. Then he started right up again.

"Fair to say that, and this is no insult, she took your father for a fool, right?"

"No."

"Your father bought her a ring, right?"

"Yes."

"You described it as a big rock. How big was that ring? How many carats?"

"I have no idea. I don't pay attention to those things."

"Fair to say it was a big ring, though, right?"

"Yes."

"He paid for all of her expenses?"

"Yes."

"Gave her a car?"

"Yes."

"Let her use that home on the beach, right?"

"Yes."

"Fair to say that was a million-dollar home."

"Yes."

"She stayed for free in Balboa Coves of all places, correct?"

"Yes."

"He put her on various boards of different charities—excuse me, of different trusts that he had set up, correct?"

"Well, she was a trustee of one trust."

"He entrusted her with his financial affairs, for the most part, correct?"

"The everyday bill paying, yes."

"She was in his will, correct?"

"Yes."

"As a matter of fact, after all of this, she had the audacity to sue the family for a part of his estate, correct?"

"Yes."

"And, unfortunately, the family had to settle for hundreds of thousands of dollars?"

"Yes."

"Did she, in fact, wear the diamond engagement [ring for] people to see on her finger?"

"Yes."

Once again, taking only a second to catch his breath, he started again, changing the subject to *his* client: "Did you ever know Naposki, or had ever even met him?"

Kim replied, "No."

MacDonald paused very pointedly. He wanted the jurors to note that, despite all the damning testimony about Nanette, Kim had not said a single negative word about Naposki.

MacDonald then asked Kim about Kevin. "He had gone with your father and practiced shooting guns, correct?"

Kim said that was true.

"Your father has a lot of guns in the house, doesn't he?"

"Yes," replied Kim.

"Was your father angry over Kevin's pot smoking?"

"I suppose he was."

"Nothing more," stated MacDonald as he returned to the defense table, satisfied that he had planted the notion of an alternative scenario in the jurors' minds. *Could Bill and Kevin McLaughlin have argued? Could Kevin have had a motive? Could he have been the shooter?*

Now it was the prosecution's turn to try to diffuse any

advantage MacDonald might have gained in his questioning concerning Kevin. Murphy asked Kim what Kevin's demeanor was at the funeral of her father.

"A mess, angry, crying."

Pointing the finger once again at Johnston, Murphy asked Kim to describe how Johnston reacted at the funeral. "She didn't shed a tear and seemed detached."

Following up on Kim's testimony, Murphy then called two witnesses who spoke further about Johnston's stealing money and forging checks.

Brian Ringler, McLaughlin's accountant, stated that he noticed "around six hundred and ten thousand dollars was missing during the month McLaughlin was killed." And Charles Beswick, a Newport Beach detective trained in discovering forgeries, testified that in his opinion Johnston not only signed checks with McLaughlin's name but also made out several checks to herself.

Murphy then called two people to the stand, who both testified to Johnston's portraying herself as a millionaire—or a soon-to-be one—and that Naposki had been right alongside her while this was going on.

Realtor Sharon Hedberg testified that Johnston and Naposki shopped for a home in the Turtle Rock area of Irvine before McLaughlin's death; that the couple had stated that they "expected a future financial windfall"; and that they wanted a home that would be ready in spring of 1995. The homes they were looking at were in the $900,000 range.

Robert Cottrill, whom Investigator Larry Montgomery had painstakingly located more than a decade after he was recorded in 1995 giving an "anonymous" tip to detectives, testified about Johnston passing herself off as a wealthy businessperson. Cottrill, a software developer, stated that in 1994 Johnston told him she wanted to invest a lot of money in his company; that it was money Johnston said she had gotten when she sold her company, which had to do with separating blood, to Baxter Industries; and that Naposki and Johnston "talked about getting married."

Murphy was attempting to show that in the months before

the murder Naposki and Johnston were planning a life together—a life of luxury—and that they were working together to get McLaughlin's money.

On the third day of the trial, Suzanne Cogar, 46, took the stand. The same woman who had told the police in the early days of the case that she was too frightened to give them her full name or testify in court now gave the most telling evidence yet against Naposki.

Describing her first aborted phone call to the police, made in 1995, Cogar said, "I guess I was still afraid of Eric or of what could happen, you know, if my name got out there that I had told this information, and I was just afraid for my safety."

Not anymore.

Cogar testified that, prior to the murder, she and Naposki were neighbors in the Archstone apartment complex in Tustin. There Naposki told Cogar that McLaughlin was making sexual advances toward Nanette. Naposki was angry about this. He told Cogar that he knew McLaughlin often flew his plane to Las Vegas, and said he "was going to have his plane blown up. I know how I could have it done."

Cogar then recalled how Naposki had returned to the complex after Christmas of 1994, after having moved away, and told her that the man he had told her about previously had been shot to death. She told him she didn't want to hear about it.

But Naposki told her anyway. "Maybe I did and maybe I didn't, and maybe I had someone do it," he replied cryptically. Cogar said Naposki's demeanor at the time was "creepy, serious, with a half smile and very unnerving."

Cogar also testified that Naposki told her the killer used the same kind of gun that he owned, but that Naposki said he had loaned his gun to a friend before the murder took place.

Cogar also stated that Naposki told her that the police thought the key that was left in the front door by the killer had been made at the nearby Tustin hardware store.

Murphy said that the information about the gun and the

key was crucial and that the jury should remember it, because at the time Cogar and Naposki had their conversation the police had not revealed *any* information about the kind of gun that was used in the murder or where the key was made.

The defense then cross-examined Cogar, but they were unable to shake her or her story. Nonetheless, Pohlson tried to show the jurors that, although Naposki might have said something like, "I wish he were dead," he did not mean it literally. Saying such a thing in anger, Pohlson pointed out, is not the same thing as acting on it.

Pohlson then asked Cogar a series of questions, the answers to which portrayed Naposki in a positive, non-threatening light.

Asked if Eric Naposki ever threatened her, she responded that he hadn't.

"So let me just put this in perspective, okay?" said Pohlson. "Always a nice guy. Then all of a sudden he comes to you and he says, 'I want to have Bill McLaughlin's plane blown up,' and you take him seriously right from the start, right?"

"I took him seriously to a point. It was hard to believe, and I wasn't sure whether to believe it or not. But he seemed serious, and it unnerved me, and I just wasn't sure what to think. I didn't like what I was hearing, so I just wanted to disassociate myself from him, so I didn't talk to him very many times after that."

"But you still never warned Bill McLaughlin?"

"I didn't, no."

Continuing, Pohlson gave Cogar a transcript of the conversation she had in 1998 with Detective O'Sullivan and asked her to look it over. After she had read it, Pohlson asked her if she remembered telling O'Sullivan that "the first thing that Naposki said about [the murder] was that he didn't do it?"

"I see that that's the statement that I made. It's just hard to remember this long later exactly how the conversation went. Certain phrases stand out in my mind, but I wasn't sure exactly what order."

"Okay," said Pohlson gravely. "This is rather important,

as you can imagine. The first thing it says on here is, 'Nap
did say he didn't do it.' Do you remember that?"

"I don't remember exactly. I see that it's in my statement.
I [am] just having a hard time remembering whether he said
that or not."

"Back in 1998, you were trying to tell the truth to Detective O'Sullivan, right?"

"Yes."

After feeling he had made his point, Pohlson said he had
no more questions.

Glen Garrity then took the stand. Now a private investigator,
he stated that on December 15, 1994, he was on bicycle patrol for the NBPD and was among the first to arrive at the
crime scene. He detailed the difficulty Kevin McLaughlin
had speaking and walking—the implication being that Kevin
was a highly unlikely candidate for being the perpetrator.

On cross, MacDonald once again tried to show his client's innocence. MacDonald pointed out that Garrity would
have ridden up to the crime scene from the exact same direction that Naposki would have used to get to his job at the
Thunderbird Nightclub—or that he would have used *if* he
had committed the murder.

"Did you see Naposki?"

"No," replied Garrity.

Murphy then called Detective Thomas Voth to testify. Recounting his involvement in the case, Voth recalled how the
detectives had bagged Kevin's hands after the murder to test
them for gunshot residue—but that none had been found.
Voth went on to describe Kevin's manner immediately after
the killing.

"You could see he was confused. It was really hard for us
to understand what he was saying, not having known him
prior. Once we knew him for a while, you could kind of pick
words out of his sentences that would help you understand. . . . Demeanor-wise, he was cooperative. He did everything we asked him to do, sat down, stood there. He must

have had the bags on his hands for an hour and a half. Didn't say anything to us about wanting them off or anything like that."

Murphy stated, "Since we are on the topic of Kevin's speech, this might be time to play the nine-one-one tape."

A transcript of the tape was handed out to each juror "as an aid to help you understand what is said on the recording."

As they listened to the 911 tape, several of the jurors were visibly upset. The desperate sound of Kevin's attempts to make himself understood by a patient operator were anguishing to hear. They listened as Kevin struggled to say what had happened: "Shahht," and to whom: "Daaad."

As the tape dragged on, it was impossible not to wonder if Bill McLaughlin's life had slipped away during this frustrating exchange. Certainly that's what Kevin must have been thinking. What was the defendant's response to this heart-wrenching recording? One reporter in the courtroom with a view of Eric Naposki's face noted that Naposki smirked during the playing of the tape and that he "smiled and snorted throughout his trial."

After a bit more testimony from Voth, the judge decided to call it quits for the day. It had been a rough one—for the jury and the McLaughlin family members who were in court every day.

As Naposki was exiting the courtroom, he winked at his fiancée, Rosie Macaluso, who smiled a lovely wide smile in return. Macaluso had attended every single day of the trial, even bringing Naposki clean, ironed pastel-colored shirts to wear.

As day four of the trial began on Thursday, June 23, Murphy began calling witnesses to testify to the close ties between Naposki and Nanette—some of which went beyond ties of affection and reached directly into Bill McLaughlin's wallet. Bill had trusted Nanette to handle everyday bill paying—but he had no idea that in addition to paying for their housekeeper, gas, and groceries he was also buying expensive gifts for Nanette's hunky man on the side. To clarify this, Murphy called Christopher Todd Griffiths, a former salesman for Thieves Market, a shoe store in nearby Costa Mesa. He testified that in late 1994 he had sold Nanette alligator cowboy boots for her boyfriend, who she said played for the NFL. About two weeks later, Griffiths stated, she exchanged the boots.

The receipt was entered into evidence and Murphy said, "All right. So that happened on December 15, 1994, at what looks like five fifty?"

"Correct."

"That's four hundred and twenty-nine dollars, so we're talking about a pretty nice pair of boots?"

"The nicest in the store."

It seemed from the receipt that Nanette was exchanging a pair of boots less than four hours before Bill's murder.

Gary Rorden, a Costa Mesa businessman, stated that he often saw Nanette and Naposki together and that they never hid their relationship. They would come to sports events in which his kids, too, played. "They made no secret that they were romantically involved. They weren't trying to hide it." He went on to say they weren't hugging or smooching, but they were "friendly, very friendly."

Labeling Naposki "a very nice gentleman," Rorden continued. "I was in an awkward situation back then because I knew both men"—he knew McLaughlin from a church in Newport—but Rorden had made a decision not to tell McLaughlin about Nanette and Naposki.

Upon questioning from defense attorney Pohlson, Rorden admitted, "I didn't ever like Bill McLaughlin."

Later that day, Voth was called back to the stand. He testified about Johnston going to the motorcycle dealership right after Bill McLaughlin's funeral. She bought three new motorbikes using his credit card, then went to a Wells Fargo bank and cashed a presumably forged check for $3,000.

Voth was then asked to elaborate about one of the keys found at the murder scene. The one found on the mat outside the door was a key to the pedestrian access gate to Balboa

Coves. *Where might it have come from?* the police had wondered. A few days after the murder, they had asked to look at Nanette Johnston's key chain.

Murphy asked Voth, "So on Nanette's key ring there was no key to that pedestrian access gate?"

"That's correct."

The implication was clear: Nanette had given away her key to the pedestrian access gate—and to whom might she have given it? The answer, to Murphy, was obvious.

Murphy moved on to the gun used to pump six deadly bullets into Bill McLaughlin. "When was the first information released in the media about a 9mm?"

"I believe it was mid-February '95," said Voth.

Again, Murphy was driving home the fact that Naposki could not have known, when he talked to Suzanne Cogar in January of 1995, about the type of gun used in the murder—unless he had been involved in the crime.

If Voth's testimony thus far had seemed smooth, he was in for rougher treatment from Naposki's defense team. On Monday, June 27, MacDonald began a tough line of questioning. Time and again, when MacDonald asked if Voth followed up on this lead, on that lead, on this bit of evidence, on that bit, to each, Voth answered, "No."

Referring to the store where Nanette had made a purchase not long after the murder, MacDonald asked, "Did you test the drain of the woman's bathroom at Crate and Barrel for gunshot residue?"

"No."

Referring to the children's soccer game that Nanette and Naposki had left about an hour before the murder, MacDonald asked Voth, "Did you get the name of all of the kids who played in this particular game?"

"No."

"Did you speak to any of the other parents besides Mr. Johnston with respect to seeing if anyone had any information?"

"No."

"Ground crew?"

"No."

Referring to the location where Naposki claimed he was just twenty minutes before the killing, MacDonald asked, "You knew there was a Denny's there, but that was never included in any of the time trials, just so we're a hundred percent clear, correct?"

"Not that I know of," said Voth.

"Now, during the course of the investigation, sir, did you or anyone go to the Thunderbird Nightclub and try to interview people?"

"Yes."

"Well, we certainly know, because you have already testified, no one interviewed Mr. Tuomisto, but who did you speak to, to the best of your recollection?"

"During that time no one interviewed Mr. Tuomisto. He was interviewed later."

"That was years later, correct?"

"Correct."

"Like fifteen years later, right?"

"Not fifteen. I think it was fourteen."

"And isn't it a fact that [Naposki] mentioned to you that he was in his truck and he had to stop and place the call, correct?"

"That's what he said, yes, sir."

"And do you recall asking him what pay phone he called from? . . . Did he tell you that he believed that he made it from a Denny's on Seventeenth Street, correct?"

"Yes, sir, that's there."

"And the name Mike Tuomisto. At any time after speaking to Mr. Naposki approximately a month and a half after this murder, did you go and speak to Mike Tuomisto to determine whether or not he worked there that night?"

"No."

"Did you order the telephone records of Mr. Naposki after this interview, that second interview?"

"No. We were hoping he was going to bring them."

"Did you ever order them?"

"I did not, no, sir."

"Did anyone in the police department ever order them?"

"Not to my knowledge."

"Like, for example . . . the phone records that you ordered for Ms. Johnston for her car phone, do you remember her records?"

"Sure. We just put them into evidence. Yes."

"Those ones you did order, but Mr. Naposki's you did not, correct?"

"That's correct."

"Did you ever order the records from the two phones that were in the Denny's restaurant?"

"No, sir."

"Isn't it a fact that not only did Mr. Naposki give you the name of Mike Tuomisto, he actually gave you the phone number, correct?"

"There's a phone number there, yes."

"Phone number two-one-seven-two-three-one-six, that's in your writing."

"Yes."

"And he even indicated to you that he had made the call at approximately nine o'clock, correct?"

"Yes, sir."

Voth further admitted that back in 1995 Naposki's lawyer, Julian Bailey, drafted a letter in which he discussed the call: the time it was made, to whom it was made, and from where it was made.

If MacDonald was trying to show that the NBPD engaged in slipshod police work, he seemed to be succeeding.

"Just so it's one hundred percent clear," said MacDonald, "at the scene of the crime, there was no physical evidence whatsoever indicating that my client, Mr. Naposki, was there, correct? In other words, no DNA, fingerprints, fibers, like that? Anything found to be connected to him?"

"No, sir."

"And did you find that Eric had anything at all to do with Nanette's forgeries?"

"No."

In speaking about McLaughlin's guns, MacDonald asked if the detectives had gone to Las Vegas to retrieve a number of his guns.

"We didn't retrieve them. We categorized them," responded Voth.

"Is it fair to say you found a whole cache of guns in Las Vegas."

Voth agreed.

In that last question before dismissing the witness, MacDonald was clearly implying that with so many guns, surely it was *possible* that one of them was used in the murder—and it certainly wasn't in the hands of Naposki, who had no access to them.

In response to this rapid-fire questioning, Murphy calmly resumed calling new witnesses. He first questioned K. Ross Johnston. A white-bearded, jolly-looking man with a quick laugh and a jovial manner, Ross stated that he had been married to Nanette for five years and that he was the father of two of her children. Ross said they separated in 1988 and he had gotten sole custody then of their kids. Nanette, Ross said, had visitation rights.

Speaking about the night of the murder, Ross stated that at the soccer game Nanette and Naposki came up to him. Nanette said that Naposki had an eight o'clock appointment.

"So I looked at my watch," said Ross, and I said, 'Well, it's eight twenty right now. There's no way he can make it to an eight o'clock appointment. Just stay for the ceremony.' She said, 'No. That's okay. We got to go. We'll see you later,' and they took off running."

The next day or the day after that, Nanette called him and said that Bill McLaughlin "had been shot there at their home . . . that she was shopping . . . that the police were going to contact me to validate her alibi, where she was before. And I said, 'Oh, okay.' And she said, 'When they do, you don't need to tell anything about Eric because he's not involved. It's just that I was there at the game.' I said, 'Okay.'"

"Did Mr. Naposki come to a lot of soccer games?" asked Murphy.

"Yeah. He was great. And baseball, too, yeah, and bas-ketball. He was there. He coached my son in all of them, you know, helping him out. They had a great relationship in that way."

While this implied that Naposki was quite serious about his relationship with Nanette, Ross described his ex-wife as an operator when it came to men. He recalled one time that Nanette showed up at a soccer game with yet *another* boy-friend, but then Eric had turned up, too. "She came with one and left with Eric," Ross said.

Due to the lack of physical evidence directly tying Naposki to the murder, Murphy was working hard to make the cir-cumstantial links stronger. For example, he wanted to prove to the jury that Naposki had owned the exact same type of gun that was used to kill Bill McLaughlin.

Testifying for the prosecution, Thomas Matsudaira, a bal-listics expert at the OC Sheriff's Department Crime Lab, told the jury that he wouldn't consider any of the guns owned by McLaughlin as being a candidate for the murder weapon. He testified that he had narrowed down the murder weapons to only one that could have ejected the 9mm casings and spent bullets found at the scene. "It was a 92F 9mm."

"And isn't that the model that Naposki owned?" asked Murphy.

"Yes, I believe so."

On cross, however, under sharp questioning by MacDon-ald, Matsudaira admitted that he had not looked at *all* types of 9mm pistols but only the many popular brands he was familiar with. Moreover, he was forced to concede that the 92F 9mm was a very popular gun. Naposki was hardly unique in owning one. When asked, Matsudaira said that he believed "Beretta has at least two million 9mm 92s out there . . . as of 2004."

Murphy's final witness, Jenny McLaughlin, was called to testify on June 29. Jenny was a soft-spoken witness, whose pain at having to testify was obvious.

The first part of Murphy's questioning seemed designed to diffuse the notion that Kevin would have been very slow to respond to the sounds of gunshots and to dial 911 on the night of the murder.

"Did [Kevin] have any trouble dialing a phone?" asked Murphy.

"No," Jenny responded. "He called people regularly and had no problem dialing the phone."

"And how would you describe Kevin's walking? We've heard some testimony about that. What can you tell us about that?"

"Kevin's impairments, his gait was stilted. His balance wasn't a hundred percent, so you could get him off balance with some, you know, work, but he could sort of run. It wasn't great, like he couldn't be a runner and go jogging, but he could run, you know. . . ."

"Did you ever see your brother sitting on a couch, lying on a bed, and get up for any reason?"

"Yes."

"Okay. And, ma'am, was there any problem with Kevin like was it labored? Would it take him minutes to do that? How would you describe that for us?"

"That was not a skill that was really impaired. He could get up and down just fine."

Murphy then asked how she had learned her father had been murdered.

"Kevin called me at work in the morning and told me that our father had been shot, and . . . I asked him, 'Is he in the hospital or has he passed away?' He said, 'He's no longer with us.' So at that point I said, 'Okay. Where are you? I'm going to come get you. We're going to figure out what's going on.'"

Murphy asked, "What happened next?"

"I got in my car. He told me he was at the Seashore house, so I got in my car and I headed straight there. On my way there, I called that house and Nanette answered, and I—"

"Tell us about that," said Murphy.

"I said, 'Is it true? Kevin called me and said our dad's been shot.' And she said, 'Yeah. Yeah, it's true.'"

"Did she say anything else other than 'Yeah, it's true'?"

"I think she said, 'It sucks. It really sucks.'"

Jenny went on to describe how she and her sister were attempting to get their father's financial affairs in order, pay essential bills, and follow the wishes in his will. But whenever they tried to enlist Nanette's help, Nanette would dodge them.

"As things would come up," testified Jenny, "we would ask her questions about 'do you know this person or do you know about this situation? Can you enlighten us?'"

"How did that go?"

"She would not return phone calls. She was evasive and very uncooperative."

"All right. Tell us what you did . . . as far as the beach house goes and Nanette living in it," said Murphy.

"I think in the beginning we were all on board of supporting my dad's wishes that she be taken care of, and we tried to be respectful and treat her well. . . ." But as Nanette's lack of cooperation with settling the estate and her lies began to build up, the family became less sympathetic.

Murphy then asked what happened when Nanette was arrested for stealing money from Jenny's father's bank accounts. "Did you receive a phone call from Mr. Naposki?"

"Yes. I received I believe two to three phone [calls at] least. . . . I was very surprised that he was calling us. He was calling the house, my dad's house where we were staying. . . ." Jenny stated that after the first call she called the Newport Beach police and they suggested that she try to record Naposki if he called again—which he did, wanting to discuss the lawsuit that Nanette had by then filed for "palimony."

Jenny explained, "She filed what was called a palimony suit where she alleged that, because she had been living with my dad, she was entitled to half of his assets. I suppose it was supposed to be like a sort of an implied marriage. And what she asked for in that lawsuit was half of all of his assets. . . . And she asked for ongoing support. The number she came up with was five thousand dollars a month. And there's a million dollars asked for in there."

Murphy then played a tape of Naposki speaking to Jenny in 1995—soon after Johnston was arrested for forgery. In the conversation, in which Naposki stated he was calling on behalf of Johnston, he first asked the McLaughlins to return the Infiniti that McLaughlin had given to Johnston in his will. Then Naposki went on to describe how the NBPD had wronged *him* and stated that it would be a good idea if the McLaughlins and Johnston would work out their differences with lawyers instead of bringing all this to a criminal trial.

Naposki followed up by advising Jenny that it would be in her family's interest to settle with Johnston out of court. "You know", he said cryptically, "she has things that can hurt you guys. You have things that can hurt her."

Although Jenny pointed out that Johnston had not told her the truth time and time again and had also implicated Naposki, Naposki still defended Johnston: "It doesn't matter, because I'm her friend," he said.

Jenny's testimony extended into a second day. And on June 30 Murphy began his questioning of Jenny by stating that he wanted to pick up on something. "In any of the trusts in your father's will, was there any legal right bestowed upon Eric Naposki to live in your beach house?"

"No."

"Okay. Eventually did you have to make efforts to essentially get them out of the beach house?"

"Yes . . . we filed paperwork that would enable us to evict them."

Going back to Kevin, Murphy asked again about the relationship between Kevin and his father.

"They had a very good relationship," Jenny reiterated. "I mean, my dad's a very warm guy, and we all loved him dearly . . . they'd kiss all the time and hug. . . . They had no embarrassment about that."

After Jenny completed her testimony, Murphy said, "Your Honor, at this time subject to the admission of exhibits, the People rest."

The prosecution felt that they had done an excellent job of showing the jurors who, they felt, was the murderer. And so did the McLaughlins. They believed the trial had gotten off to a great start.

Chapter Twenty-Eight

MacDonald Opening and More Trial

Thus far, the prosecution had done a thorough job of excoriating Naposki, supplying motive and opportunity in a clear and logical fashion. Now it was the defense's turn to convince the jury to see all the prosecution's so-called facts from an entirely different viewpoint.

On Thursday afternoon, June 30, Angelo MacDonald, wearing a dark suit and a blue striped tie, began what turned out to be a sixty-four-minute opening statement. "Good afternoon, ladies and gentlemen," he said, speaking quickly. "I'm sensing there's a perception that I have a penchant for talking a lot," he said loudly. "Maybe even gesticulating every now and again," he said as he took his glasses off and let them swing from his hand, then let them dangle from his mouth. "But despite that, I'm going to try to be as brief and succinct and direct as possible with respect to my opening statement. It may not be as smooth as the prosecutor, but we're going to do our best. . . . So, at the end of this case, after the defense's case, if you find that Mr. Naposki had an alibi, you must find him not guilty. . . .

"The defense is going to prove . . . that Eric Naposki did not commit and could not logically and reasonably have committed this crime because he was somewhere else at the time of the murder. . . . Mr. Naposki could never have gotten into that house and done the murder, not even if he were superhuman," MacDonald argued.

"Eric Naposki told the police everything they needed to know about his whereabouts at the time of the murder. He gave the date and the time and the name of the person he talked to on the phone on the night of the murder. He even gave the police that man's [Tuomisto's] telephone number. . . ." But, continued MacDonald, "sloppy, lazy Newport Beach police detective work ignored critical exculpatory evidence to make Naposki a prime suspect. They never investigated this, and now all phone records are destroyed. Somebody dropped the ball here. . . . Somebody dropped the ball big and now Eric Naposki is on trial for murder."

MacDonald then gave the jury an alternative theory of the crime—one in which there was a different killer and Naposki's arrest was collateral damage or even part of a well-designed scheme to make him a patsy. "The evidence in this case, and at this trial, shows that Nanette Johnston is the person most likely to have committed this murder. . . . Nanette Johnston is an accomplished liar, thief, manipulator, con woman, and promiscuous gold digger. Combine those qualities with the fact that she's pretty good-looking, is in great shape, is young, and has the ability to literally charm the pants off men. She is the only person in the world with the motive, means, and opportunity—and callousness—to pull off this murder."

After allowing his words to sink in, MacDonald then projected a photograph of a "neat" crime scene, in which there was obviously no struggle. The photo showed McLaughlin on the floor, as well as a tidy kitchen counter and table and chair.

Pointing to the photo, MacDonald claimed that McLaughlin was sitting in the chair when someone entered his house. He argued that McLaughlin, an ex-marine who was in great shape, would have knocked the chair over and gotten physical with a stranger who walked in and threatened him. "The reason the killer got close was because the killer was someone he knew."

MacDonald then discussed Johnston's "alibi." He theorized that she shot Bill McLaughlin, then jumped into her car and drove to the mall where she bought a vase at 9:29, according to her receipt. "Rushing to the Crate and Barrel and supplying the police with a receipt is a classic example of trying to create an alibi," he noted. "However, there was a fatal mistake [in her plot]. She never counted on Eric Naposki getting that [phone page]."

MacDonald ended his delayed opening statement with this promise to the jury: "The evidence is overwhelming that Nanette Johnston both independently and exclusively committed this crime, that reasonable doubt exists as to whether Eric Naposki is guilty of the charged crimes. The defense is going to prove that he is not guilty of these charged crimes."

If the defense had originally intended to throw suspicion on Kevin, they had clearly rearranged their tactics. They were now completely focused on bolstering Naposki's alibi and showing that Nanette—and Nanette alone—was the killer.

After the opening statement, the defense team got down to business and called its first witness. Pohlson called Jim Box to the stand. Box had been hired by Naposki's lawyer in 1995, Julian Bailey, to serve as his private investigator.

Pohlson asked Box about Naposki's alibi—the call from Denny's. Box testified that in 1995 he saw "eight fifty-two p.m." on a Naposki phone bill. Box said that he had done a test drive of the route between the Denny's restaurant and the McLaughlin home in 1995 and it took him twenty-one minutes and forty-seven seconds—obviously making it impossible for Naposki to have committed a murder before 9:11 p.m., when the 911 call was made.

Asking for more details about the phone bill he saw, Box stated that he discovered that the phone in Denny's matched the number on [Naposki's] bill.

Furthermore, Box continued, the night of the murder, December 15, was the first night of the Newport Beach Boat Parade, "so traffic in that area would have been heavy." Due to those factors, stated Box, Naposki could not have committed the crime.

Then, speaking of Tuomisto, Box said that he interviewed the manager not long after the crime and wrote up the interview in a memo to Julian Bailey, on February 18. Pohlson entered the memo into evidence.

In the memo, Box wrote that Tuomisto told him that when he arrived at work, which normally was between eight thirty and nine o'clock, he noticed that there was a lot of traffic, more than normal traffic. He noticed when he got to work one or more employees weren't there yet who would normally be there, so he thought it was the first night of the boat parade and assumed that excessive traffic was associated with that.

"So he called our client's pager and our client called him back. He told our client that he ought to leave a little bit early because there was heavy traffic and he may need some extra time."

Pohlson asked, "Did he tell you at what time he paged Mr. Naposki?"

"Shortly before nine p.m."

"Okay. Now, was this a telephone interview of Mr. Tuomisto or was this an in-person interview?"

"It was an in-person interview," stated Box. Continuing to describe what happened during the interview, he said that Tuomisto stated, "Sometime around nine thirty, he [Tuomisto] comes out and checks the restaurant and talks to the staff and that kind of thing. He came out that night. He saw our client there. Didn't see anything unusual about him."

Switching to the subject of the keys used to enter the McLaughlin house, Pohlson asked Box about his interview with the manager of the Ace Hardware store in Tustin. "On February 20, '95, you go and you talk with Mr. Vandaveer," said Pohlson. "What does Mr. Vandaveer tell you with regard to whether he made these particular keys in question?"

"He said, 'There were two keys, one silver, one gold.' He told the officers that the silver key could have been made at his store or another one of several Ace stores, either in

Orange County or in the nation. He said that the gold key
with the letters—it was not cut at his store . . . because of
the way the letters *A-C-E* were put on the key."

After Box's testimony, the defense felt confident they had
planted seeds of doubt in the jurors' minds. On cross, however, Murphy felt that he had scored several points: Box admitted that although he had written up a memo detailing his
interview with Vandaveer, he had never given the memo to
Vandaveer to read over and sign and therefore its accuracy
had never been authenticated; Murphy established that Box
used a circuitous route during his trial run and *not* one a
killer would be likely to use *and* that in 1994 the boat parade didn't begin until several days after December 15, so
that Box's statements and Tuomisto's reported statements
that traffic was heavy due to the boat parade were incorrect
at best, outright lies at worst.

Furthermore, Murphy got Box to admit some uncertainty
about the phone call from Denny's. "So it sounds based on
that testimony, sir," said Murphy, "that there's some ambi-
guity in your mind whether you actually saw a phone bill at
all. Am I right?"

"Well, I don't know if it was a bill or if it were documents
from the phone company about the bill that I was looking at
positively. I know it was from a phone company. I know it
had credit card calls on it. I know it had dates and times."

When court adjourned for the day, Murphy had already
put Box through the wringer—and he would be in for more
when the cross-examination continued after the long weekend.

After a break for the July Fourth holiday, the ninth day of
the trial resumed on Tuesday, July 5, and Murphy got right
to it—again. He called into question Box's "circuitous" route
from Denny's to Balboa Coves; Box's remembering more today about what he did seventeen years ago than he did then;
and why Box didn't write up reports for some of the "new"
information Box was giving the court today. Murphy also
became quite insistent in asking Box if he had, in fact, seen

a phone bill with the 8:52 time on it why he didn't make a copy of it.

Box stated that he most likely scanned the bill and saved it to his computer, but one day his computer crashed and everything on it was lost.

Pohlson called Julian Bailey next. When asked what he saw and what he remembered about the phone call from Denny's, Bailey stated, "I believe I saw the [phone] bill." He added that at that time the phone bill was extremely important to the defense's case, so he included it in a letter he wrote to the OC DA's office on Naposki's behalf, in attempting to have prosecutors not file charges.

He stated that "if my memory serves me correct, I ended up writing a letter to the district attorney's office in I think June of . . . 1995. We just never heard anything more." In the letter, Bailey said, "I did record the contents of a phone bill."

"As you sit here right now, what is your belief with regard to whether you saw that phone bill or not?"

"I believe I saw the phone bill."

"Now, do you recall if you had the bill, the bill with the eight fifty-two on December 15, in your file?"

"I don't believe I ever had it in my file. I believe I gave it to James Box."

"Now, you, of course, had a copy machine in your office back then, right?"

"I did."

"Do you have any recollection of making copies of it?"

"No."

"But the eight fifty-two, that time on December 15, you concentrated on that for your investigation?"

"It was very significant."

"Okay. And you included this in a letter to the DA?"

"I did."

And with that, Pohlson stated, "I don't have anything further."

* * *

On cross, Murphy said to Bailey that he seemed somewhat tentative about whether or not he saw the bill.

"No, I believe I saw that bill," said Bailey.

"And there's that word. You *believe* it."

"Yes, sir."

Bailey then explained that he had a belief that he saw a bill, "but to say that I remember seeing something seventeen years ago . . . it would not be fair to say that I remember seeing it."

Murphy continued by saying that such a fine lawyer as he, with decades of experience, and with "your level of professionalism and your reputation, what I'm trying to understand is if you've got that document, that's golden, right? For lack of a better term, that is pure gold, right?"

"Absolutely."

"You had a copy machine in your office, right? . . . Given your level of experience and all that and everything I know about you, I just don't understand if you saw that phone bill why you wouldn't make a copy of it, if, in fact, you saw it?"

And Bailey responded, "And, you know, sitting here all these years later, I wish that I had, but I didn't."

"If you had this document in your hand and you made a copy of it or maybe even stapled the original, you could have sent that to Debbie Lloyd [then DA] and put this entire matter to rest, right?"

"Well, there's an answer to that, and I'd like to give it with your permission. . . . At that point we had been, in my opinion, extremely cooperative with the district attorney and the police. There was a towel that was found in Mr. Naposki's vehicle that had some blood on it and there was some thought in the prosecution that the blood was somehow related to this homicide. And I told Ms. Lloyd . . . that we would produce Mr. Naposki so they could do a blood draw without a warrant and they could get all the DNA and blood evidence from him. So I felt as if I had extended a considerable amount of cooperation to them, and yet the only way I was finding out about the prosecution side of the case was what I was reading in the newspaper. And I felt as if the police department in Newport Beach was feeding selective information to the police and press.

"Mr. Naposki was suffering significant harm to his reputation and, you know, I was hoping that that would stop . . . and with regard to sticking a phone bill on there, one more thing, Mr. Murphy, a phone bill, you know, as close as I can say that I remember it, a phone bill, it didn't just have a single phone call on it. There were a lot of numbers on there and there were things that could well have been further investigated and would have been further investigated if the prosecution had gone on at that time. But you know, I wrote this letter and then the case kind of died. And, you know, maybe I did a great job, maybe I didn't."

On redirect, Pohlson got Bailey to admit that at the time he didn't know that the phone bill would absolutely clear Naposki. When Bailey wrote the letter to the DA, he said he laid out a series of facts and suggested that the right thing to do would be not to prosecute Naposki, including talking about a credit card call and saying based on that information of the call being made at 8:52, Naposki would not have been able to have committed the crime.

"Would you have written a letter like this simply based on your client telling you, without you verifying it?"

"Absolutely not."

It now appeared that the defense's case was relying strongly on proving that the 8:52 call had been made. *But what exactly did that mean in relation to the crime itself?* The murder may have taken place anywhere from 9:08 to 9:10, depending on how long it took Kevin to get downstairs to call 911 after he heard the gunshots. If you accepted the truth of both the alibi and the possibility that Kevin was significantly slowed down by his disability, that left just sixteen minutes for Naposki to get from Denny's to Balboa Coves. *So how long did that drive really take?*

On July 6, to counter the previous day's testimony, which suggested Naposki could not possibly have made it to Balboa

Coves in time to commit the murder, Murphy invoked his right to call rebuttal witnesses.

Investigator Larry Montgomery and Detectives Scott Smith and Garrett Fitzgerald, who had performed timed test drives on December 14, 15, and 16 of 2010, were called to the stand. Each drive had been videotaped and was projected on the screen in real time, so the jurors and audience could watch.

The length of the timed drives varied, as did the places between which the drives were taken: between the soccer field where Naposki and Nanette had been on the night of the murder and the bridge on Newport Boulevard that led down to the pedestrian gate into Balboa Coves; between the soccer field and Denny's; between Denny's and the bridge. But at the end of the day, after all the trials had been projected, discussed, and dissected, the consensus was that even *if* there had been a phone call at Denny's, there was still enough time for a killing to occur at around 9:10, 9:09, or even 9:08. In all the timed trials, the "perp" could have arrived at the bridge anywhere between 9:04 and 9:07 and 46 seconds.

MacDonald asked if any of the tests were done from the bridge to the gate to the house, into the house, and then back out without a key to unlock the pedestrian gate. Investigator Montgomery admitted that although he did *part* of that run in the daylight the previous evening, he had never gone from the pedestrian gate to the home and into the house and back out.

MacDonald then cast another doubt on the trial runs citing the minute the officers began them, at 8:52. He stated that their timing didn't leave any time for anyone to actually speak on the phone. MacDonald also brought into question the fact that the trial runs took place recently and did not take into consideration any changes between 1994 and today in regard to traffic lanes, traffic conditions, speed limits, traffic lights, and lighting in the area.

At one point, MacDonald's questions were becoming louder and louder and coming so quickly that Murphy interrupted. "Your Honor," he said. "I'm going to object. Counsel is not letting the witness answer his question."

The judge agreed. "Could you take the decibel level down a few notches?"

MacDonald responded, "I want to make sure Jay [the court reporter] hears me."

The judge stated, "They heard you three courtrooms away."

MacDonald responded, "Okay, let me rephrase the question. The time trial you had in your report started at eight fifty-two-point-twenty-four seconds, correct?"

"Yes."

"And you have no idea how long the phone call lasted at eight fifty-two back in 1994, right? Just so it's clear, did I ask you to actually go out last night and do all this stuff?"

"No, sir."

"Someone else asked you because I was asking some very important, probing questions [yesterday] that you didn't have an answer to, correct?" asked MacDonald.

"Oh, my god," shouted Murphy. "Objection. Where am I going to start?"

The judge responded, "We deal without the 'oh, my gods' and just make the objections."

"Yes, sir," stated a non-contrite Murphy. "It is argumentative, assumes facts not in evidence, grandstanding, badgering, and I'll leave it at that for now."

The judge ruled, "Sustained."

Later in the afternoon, after Murphy objected for the third time to excessively aggressive courtroom tactics and grandstanding, Judge Froeberg stated, "Grandstanding is not a legally recognized objection in the state of California . . . but [the question] does call for speculation . . . Sustained."

The timing question was so central to the case that reporters Frank Mickadeit and Larry Welborn, who were covering the case for the *OC Register,* had decided to do some fact-checking on their own the previous week.

In an *OC Register* article published on July 5, 2011, Mickadeit wrote that he and Welborn went to the Denny's off the 55 freeway in Santa Ana during the long weekend recess.

He then gave a detailed description of how they stood where the pay phones used to be at exactly 8:52 p.m. and chatted a short while—as if they were making a call and listening to the person's responses. Then, they went to their car and drove on the Pacific Coast Highway to near the Hoag Hospital in Newport Beach. Mickadeit said they never drove above 70 mph. When they arrived there, it was 9:05:12. After that, they parked the car, talked some more, got out of the car, walked to the path under Newport Boulevard, and finally arrived at the pedestrian-only gate into Balboa Coves. The time, stated Mickadeit, was 9:07:44. The McLaughlin home was approximately 120 feet away.

According to Mickadeit, it *was* possible that even if Naposki had made the phone call from Denny's, he still would have had time to commit the murder.

Their test was not admissible in court, but it did cause a bit of a stir. Judge Froeberg acknowledged the reporters for their amateur sleuthing and called them "the Hardy Boys." And he reminded the jurors not to try anything similar or do any investigations on their own.

On Thursday, July 7, the defense called Leonard J. Jomsky, longtime friend and a former housemate of Naposki's, who also worked security with Naposki. Jomsky testified that in the summer of 1994 he, Naposki, and Johnston went target practicing. He believed that they used two guns: a .380 handgun and a 9mm semiautomatic. "[Johnston] made a point of that once we returned back to the house, she let everybody know that she shot better than I did."

MacDonald asked, "How long did the group fire?"

"We fired guns into paper targets for about an hour."

Jomsky also testified that on January 19, 1995, he remembered clearly that Detective Byington and six or seven officers came to his apartment and "kind of sequestered me in my room" and asked me many questions about Eric. "It was not fun."

After Jomsky's testimony, the judge asked if the defense had any more witnesses.

Pohlson replied, "No, Your Honor. The defense rests subject to the admission of the evidence."

Many in the courtroom were clearly disappointed that they would not be hearing directly from Eric Naposki.

He was not going to be testifying in his own defense. Nor was he going to be doing any finger-pointing. Apparently Naposki had decided he would let his attorneys take care of that.

The judge then said, "Mr. Murphy, further rebuttal?"

Murphy then called on private investigator Joseph Stoltman, who was also a firearms and combat expert. He testified that around three months before the killing he held a one-day training session for Naposki and other security people, focusing on SWAT techniques, including something known as the "double-tap" method of shooting. (In the double-tap, one fires two quick rounds, assesses the victim's condition, and continues firing bursts until he drops.) Stoltman claimed that trainees in the double-tap method are taught to aim for the lower chest or stomach area. "The stomach shot is a very lethal shot," he added.

Murphy wanted the jury to know that Johnston may have been a better shot than Jomsky, but there was no arguing that Naposki had been trained to kill.

Murphy then recalled Jenny McLaughlin to the stand to testify about the lighting conditions around the pedestrian gate outside her Balboa Coves home. She said she never had trouble seeing the lock in the gate.

MacDonald argued that because she had used the gate so often over so many years, of course she wouldn't have any trouble seeing the lock where the key would go. Jenny agreed that there were a lot of trees and shrubs around the gate—implying that it might be difficult for someone who was not familiar with the gate to be as facile with the key as she was. MacDonald was intent on adding seconds and minutes to the timing to help show his client could not have had time to commit a murder.

Murphy then recalled Detective Voth. "Did Eric Naposki ever approach you and ask you any questions like, 'Can we get extra patrols? I'm concerned about my girlfriend. There's a killer on the loose'? Anything like that?"

"No, sir."

"To your knowledge, did you ever read any reports in your involvement in the investigation where a similar request was made of anybody else at the Newport Beach Police Department?"

"None."

When MacDonald questioned Voth, he got him to admit that, in many ways, Naposki had been very cooperative with the police, never hesitating in allowing the police to search his apartment, his hotel room, and his car; nor did Naposki object to having his blood taken.

On Monday, July 11, Voth was called back to the stand for more cross-examination. After being asked by Pohlson about Johnston's résumé, which he admitted he had seen, Voth stated that many items on it were simply not true: for example, that she was a travel agent, that she graduated from Arizona State, that she had a BS in Business Administration, that she had a life insurance license.

It appeared that Pohlson was attempting to defame Johnston's character, once again. If she was such an accomplished liar, Pohlson was implying, why wasn't it conceivable that she lied to Naposki and was lying to everyone about not having killed McLaughlin?

Murphy then called Larry Montgomery to testify. After giving details about his credentials and his duties in the TracKRS unit, Montgomery stated that he was asked by Murphy in 2007 to look into the McLaughlin case and in doing so he had reviewed fifty-nine tape recordings and some two thousand pages of documents. He stated that he also located two of the earlier witnesses, who did not make themselves known in 1994 and 1995. Montgomery gave details about exactly how he went about finding Robert Cottrill and Susan Cogar.

Murphy then said, "All right. Now, over the course of your investigation, you became aware of this letter from Julian Bailey, where there was this eight fifty-two time that was thrown out. Is that right?"

"That's true."

"In your review of all the documents, including the defense file that was provided, Mr. Box's file, all that stuff, did you ever locate a copy of that phone bill?"

"No."

In discussing the timed trial Montgomery took, Murphy asked, "Was there ever a time that you couldn't make it there by nine zero nine, nine ten?"

Montgomery replied, "There was never a time that I couldn't make it there by that time."

Montgomery was then cross-examined by MacDonald regarding the phone bills from Denny's and the Thunderbird. "You couldn't get any of those things because they no longer existed, correct?"

"Yes."

MacDonald then wondered why, if Montgomery was assigned the case in 2007, he didn't do any trial runs until 2010—a little over three years later. MacDonald stated that the road conditions were so different between 2007 and 2010 and between 2010 and 1994 that it was irrelevant what timed trials he did do.

Montgomery stated that his main reason for not doing the test drive earlier was because there was no actual proof of an 8:52 p.m. phone call, so there would be no reason to do test drives based on that time frame. Furthermore, Montgomery stated, because Naposki had changed his stories multiple times about what he actually did that evening it was nearly impossible to do trial runs for each of the various scenarios.

However, continued Montgomery, when the prosecution

learned that the cornerstone of the defense's case was going to be to *prove* that Naposki would not have been able to drive to Balboa Coves and commit the crime *since* he had made the 8:52 p.m. phone call, Montgomery then felt it was necessary to do trial runs.

Under further defense questioning, Montgomery also admitted that he never did a test drive between the South Coast Plaza and Balboa Coves to see if Johnston could have made it there in time to commit the murder. MacDonald was clearly suggesting that the police glommed onto Naposki from the get-go and didn't even bother checking out any other suspects or investigating the possibility that Nanette might have done the murder on her own.

After that, the judge asked both sides if they had any more witnesses to call to the stand. They each said no.

So finally, after thirty-seven witnesses and some 240 exhibits, the prosecution and defense both rested their cases. Naposki hadn't said a word at the trial. He did manage, however, to make his presence known. Often, he would chuckle, shake his head, speak to his attorneys, or scowl and smirk.

Only the closing arguments remained.

Chapter Twenty-Nine

Closings and Verdict

On Monday, July 11, 2010, around one hundred spectators once again filled Judge Froeberg's court to overflowing as Murphy began his closing arguments. He spoke for about an hour before court closed for the day.

On a screen aimed at the jury, Murphy projected an image with the title "Totality of the Evidence," in which he showed a pointillistic painting, *A Sunday Afternoon on La Grande Jatte—1884*.

Murphy began, "You've all seen this before; at least I'm sure most of you have. This is a technique called pointillism. It came around in like the late eighteen-hundreds. I think the French invented it or French artists. This is a painting from a French artist named Seurat. We've all seen this because it was in *Ferris Bueller's Day Off*, one of my favorite movies.

"You create these images with small little dots of color. . . . And when you look at it up close, you look at one dot at a time or a few dozen dots at a time, it might not mean anything. And it's only when you step back and look at everything in relation to everything else that the picture becomes clear.

"This case is one of those. Now, what are the parts of our picture? Let's go through this like the detectives did. . . . When you look at those things all together—motive, keys, and everything else—you start out with the population of the Earth and we wind up with two people, two people that fit those categories. . . . So the whole question, this whole case, boils down to one thing: Did Nanette do it herself or did she get Eric to do it? That's it. Did she do it alone or did they do it together?

"Because if they did it together, with our law of aiding and abetting . . . he's on the hook if he just helps her, more than just encourages her on this one, but the whole case boils down to that.

"Is Nanette our shooter? Because if Nanette is *not* our shooter, ladies and gentlemen, and she got somebody to do it, based on this evidence and your common sense, there is that list of potential suspects that Nanette got to do it and there is one, and he's sitting right there. One person." Murphy raised his arm and pointed his finger to Naposki.

Murphy continued. "Now, I want to quote Mr. MacDonald on this because I could not agree more. 'This woman is an accomplished liar, thief, devious cheat, con woman, manipulator, selfish, promiscuous gold digger.' " Murphy added, "And then some . . .

"Now, Nanette is one in a million, probably one in a hundred million as far as she's got one gift. She is better at this than anybody I've ever encountered. She's good at the manipulation of men to do her bidding. That's Nanette's deal. She's not trained in firearms. She's not trained in tactical shooting. Nanette is good about wrapping men around her little finger and making them do what she wants. Better at that than any of us, I would imagine, has ever encountered in our lives." And then he paused before offering his summary of Nanette: "If diabolical behavior was an Olympic sport, she would be a gold medalist every year."

Pausing for a moment to let those words sink in, he continued, "It doesn't end with this case, either. Her behavior like that goes on and on and on until she's arrested. She's incredible. But her gift, her power, is the power that she exerts over men."

After going into specific details about what Johnston and

Naposki did leading up to the murder, the day of the murder, and the days and weeks following the murder, Murphy said, "So if Eric Naposki's innocent, ladies and gentlemen, Eric Naposki, like any of us in that circumstance, if we're innocent, is thinking: 'Oh my goodness. A killer is on the loose.' So what does he do? He went shopping. They are seen together at South Coast Plaza between the shooting and Christmas. He buys a Movado watch for Nanette. Breaks his bank to do that, six hundred bucks. Christmas shopping with the kids . . . They spend New Year's in San Francisco. They do more house hunting. . . . Is that consistent with innocence?

"A man in his situation that knows nothing. All he knows is somebody was murdered in his soon-to-be fiancée's kitchen. What does he know that he doesn't post guards outside the beach house? He doesn't get a guard dog. He does not insist the kids stay in Walnut. He doesn't insist Nanette leave until the killer's caught. He doesn't offer any help to the family and, interestingly, he doesn't change the locks on the beach house. What does Eric Naposki do? Totally innocent, two days later, killer still on the loose. Everybody else is scared. The community is freaked out. The family is grief stricken. And what does he do? He rolls up to the beach house, took the kids Christmas shopping with Bill's money. This is from the check that she cashed, a three-thousand-dollar check the day before at Wells Fargo. . . . This is right after the funeral, same period of time. It's less than two days after police see her pretty much from that spot decorating the tree inside that house. Eric Naposki rolls up with that little girl and her brother and walks into the beach house without a care in the world. Two bags of presents, walks right in."

After going into details about the arrest of Naposki and the taking of his notebook, in which McLaughlin's license plate number was found, Murphy wondered what possible reason there could be that could point to innocence in having that number in Naposki's notebook.

Winding up for the day, Murphy stated, "I am asking you folks, I'm going to address you again, listen very carefully

to Mr. Pohlson. He's a fine attorney. You know what I think
of him. I will rebut every single thing that he says."

And with that, Murphy took his seat.

The next day, Pohlson began the defense's closing argument
as MacDonald sat quietly by. "How are you doing?" Pohlson
began. "I told you back in voir dire [the preliminary examination of prospective jurors under oath to determine their
competence or suitability] when we talked about the kind of
things you'd see and feel throughout the case that Matt Murphy is a really good lawyer and he was going to do excel-
lently throughout the trial. And he just gave an amazing
argument, okay? But what was probably the most amazing
thing to me about his argument is he talked almost two hours
and forty minutes without mentioning one thing that he actually *proved* that meant anything.

"In a criminal prosecution, in order to be successful, the
prosecution has to have proof. They have to have evidence.
They have to have something that actually shows that the
person committed the crime.

"Now, at the end of the day yesterday Mr. Murphy said in
a very dramatic fashion, pointing at the exhibit that has the
notebook and the license plate on the top of it, he said, 'If
you believe that he had this, then there's no other explanation
than that he's guilty.' He goes on to say something like 'that
cannot be explained in any innocent way. And I can tell you
nine different ways that it proves he's guilty.'

"Now, he didn't," stated Pohlson definitively. "He didn't
say anything about why he was guilty based on that, but
what I'm asking you to think about is what does that license
plate number being on the top of a notebook page show about
anything with regard to proof in this particular case? It doesn't
show anything. Was Mr. McLaughlin ever hurt while he was
driving the car? Was the car damaged? Was the car stolen?
Anything that we know about in this case happened because
of the license plate being in the notebook?

"Murphy didn't link the plate number to anything that

Naposki or anyone else did. The car never entered the equation."

Pohlson then moved on to Nanette, calling her a master manipulator and a "heartless, cruel person," who was more likely than Naposki to be the shooter. Furthermore, Pohlson stated, according to Murphy, if Naposki aided and abetted Nanette, he was also guilty. However, stated Pohlson, according to the law, one can *only* aid and abet if Nanette was *convicted* of being the killer, and she was not, stated Pohlson, so "aiding and abetting does not come into play in this case at all."

Pohlson stated that the defense didn't have to prove that Nanette committed the crime. "We just have to convince the jurors that it is *possible* that she did it. That qualifies as reasonable doubt." Pohlson stated that there was no reason Johnston needed Naposki to commit the murder. The motive for Nanette, according to Pohlson, is that she was the one who would be in serious trouble when McLaughlin found out she was embezzling and had taken up with Naposki.

And although Naposki might gain from McLaughlin's death, stated Pohlson, if he were in cahoots and could presumably share in proceeds, he wouldn't actually lose anything that "he already had if McLaughlin lived to uncover Nanette's deeds."

Nanette, Pohlson stated, "could have swiped Naposki's 9mm or gotten one another way. She knew how to fire a gun.

"Nanette would have had a much easier time getting in and out of Balboa than Naposki. Driven through, parked car, entered home through front door, easily gotten close enough to shoot him. She might have even left the keys behind to set up Naposki."

Pohlson stated that Naposki was a "nice guy"—by accounts from many witnesses—who had an alibi for the time of the shooting and always acted the way an innocent man would.

"He didn't have time to do it," stated Pohlson. "The person who most likely committed this crime is Nanette. . . .

[Naposki] was a patsy and the patsy maker was Nanette."
Pohlson labeled Murphy's recounting of the evidence as a
case of "misdirection."

Pohlson stated time and again that Murphy did not prove
his case and that Pohlson's client was driving his car to his
place of work at the time McLaughlin died. After rebutting
each one of Murphy's arguments, Pohlson stated, "You take
all these things, and nothing points to Eric having done it
other than he was at the soccer field with Nanette. He's guilty
of being at the soccer field; that's all he's guilty of."

And then in a dramatic moment, Pohlson went close to
the jury and scanned each and every juror. Then, in a soft
voice, he pleaded, "Please, as much as I wanted anything in
my life, I want you to find him not guilty. Because this man
is not guilty. This is an innocent man. Thank you."

Emotionally spent, Pohlson walked slowly to his seat.

Now it was Murphy's final opportunity to have the jurors
see things his way. Without a second's hesitation he began:
"Ladies and gentlemen. Mr. Pohlson is a very fine attorney.
You know, I really like the guy, but when a man gets up and
says, 'I want this as much as I've wanted anything in my life,'
it's moving when you hear that, and he's one of the best attorneys I've ever dealt with. . . ." And then Murphy paused
before continuing. "It was moving the first time I heard it. It
was moving the second time I heard it, and it was moving
today . . . but, ladies and gentlemen, I want you to see that
for what it is. That's an attorney making a very good argument pitching his case to you on behalf of his client."

According to Murphy, there was only one person who
could be the shooter of Bill McLaughlin. Pointing again at
Naposki, he said, "And he's sitting right there.

"Only Naposki could have done the deed. Why? Because
McLaughlin needed to be killed before he found out that
Johnston was not only embezzling from him, but was also
involved in a romantic relationship with Naposki."

Murphy labeled Naposki's behavior after the crime as
"outrageous, arrogant, astounding" and the work of a "bully,"

whose acts made "perfect sense" for someone who was guilty of murder. As for Naposki's alibi, Murphy called it "garbage."

Murphy added, "Who did Johnston talk to before and after the murder? The evidence shows it was Naposki. They're inseparable." And besides, if a killer was on the loose, Murphy said to the jurors, "Why did both Johnston and Naposki take no safety precautions in the aftermath of the December 15 murder even though they were occupying the dead man's beach house? A killer is loose and they didn't have a fear in the world. Why . . . didn't they ask the NBPD for protection?"

Murphy told the jurors that Johnston and Naposki waited until thirteen days after the murder to change the locks.

Furthermore, even though Murphy said he did not believe in the defense's argument that Naposki made an 8:52 p.m. phone call, Murphy stated that even *if* Naposki made that call, he *still* would have had time to commit the crime.

Murphy then defended the NBPD against the sloppy police work accusations leveled by MacDonald. "They were not perfect. They absolutely made mistakes. But I'll stack their work up against anybody in New York."

At that, Naposki laughed. In fact, all during the time Murphy gave his closing Naposki smiled, laughed, and shook his head.

Speaking about his opposing attorney from New York, MacDonald, Murphy stated, "He's got the suit. He's got the hair. He's got the watch and the shoes. He's a master in his style. . . . [He] sounds great, but there's absolutely no substance. . . . Maybe that works in New York."

While Naposki's response was to scoff at Murphy's words, MacDonald sat stone-faced throughout, brimming with anger, scribbling notes. At one point, it looked as if MacDonald were going to wrestle Murphy to the floor, after Murphy accused the defense of inflating times it took to get from the soccer field to the McLaughlin home.

But Murphy urged jurors not to be fooled by MacDonald's aggressive style or the humor of Pohlson. "I hope you folks are way too smart for that. There are great sounds [coming from the defense]. But it's incredibly misleading, and it means absolutely nothing."

According to Murphy, Naposki was greedy and wanted to share in the goodies that would be coming Johnston's way after McLaughlin was dead. Mentioning McLaughlin's son, Kevin, Murphy said, "What that young man went through was a nightmare, and he went through that because of the greed of that man right there, because he was too stupid to realize that the woman that he was with was making him do something horrible."

Ending his argument, Murphy stated, "Every one of you right now, when you go back there, you have an opportunity to make that right. It's going to take you awhile to get through this stuff. There's plenty of evidence. You stick with each other. You talk about this. You go through it. Take all the time you need. But when you're done, ladies and gentlemen, I'm going to ask you, you make sure there is justice for that moment. The evidence is all there. You make sure there is justice."

Murphy's dramatic ending echoed in the courtroom long after the jurors left to begin their deliberations. The McLaughlin family, in attendance every day, huddled together and spoke softly. Naposki's girlfriend, also in attendance every day, spoke to Naposki's lawyers. For both sides, hope was in the air.

Jurors, stone-faced as they had been throughout the trial, filed out of the courtroom. By late afternoon, they had deliberated for three hours before being sent home. Early the next morning, they returned to the courthouse and continued deliberating. It was now July 14.

All during the deliberations, those involved with the trial stayed close by, hoping a verdict would be reached soon. And they weren't disappointed. After four hours, the five-man, seven-woman jury filed solemnly back into the courtroom. Most kept their heads down, seemingly determined not to give away a hint of their verdict.

Then Judge Froeberg entered the courtroom and sat down

on his raised chair. His eyes took a fast sweep of the now hushed gallery before asking the jurors if they had reached a verdict. The foreperson responded that they had.

Froeberg then asked the clerk, Laura Hoyle, to read it aloud. "We the jury," she began, "find the defendant Eric Naposki guilty. . . ."

As soon as the word "guilty" was spoken, the McLaughlin children, their spouses, relatives, and friends let out a collective sigh of relief, as tears streamed down their faces. Jenny, Kim, and Kim's husband Smoky joined together in an emotional group hug. Murphy, too, was obviously elated, high-fiving his assistants and others who had worked so hard on the case.

Naposki, on the other hand, seemed shocked, shaking his head in disbelief. MacDonald and Pohlson were clearly upset.

Naposki's fiancée, Rosie Macaluso, broke down, her shoulders shaking.

Judge Froeberg polled the jurors individually. As each of the jurors said the word "guilty" to special circumstances murder Macaluso became visibly more upset.

A few moments later Naposki was taken away in handcuffs. As he left the courtroom, he smiled at Macaluso and said to her, "Don't worry, babe, everyone makes mistakes, including those twelve."

Then, as the courtroom began to empty, in a remarkable gesture of kindness, Kimberly McLaughlin Bayless walked over to Macaluso and began to console her.

It had been a long time coming, but finally someone was being held accountable for the murder of William McLaughlin.

When reporters approached, asking the McLaughlin daughters for their response to the verdict, their reaction was poignant.

Kim said, "My dad is honored today," tears welling in her eyes.

Jenny said, "We're very happy that justice has been served on [my dad's] behalf."

The sisters thanked the jurors, who mostly left without speaking to reporters, and hugged and thanked the prosecutors and detectives for their work.

Later, one female juror remarked soberly, "We thought the prosecution proved its case. We discussed the things we needed to discuss. We're really here for the family because they spent seventeen years waiting for this."

Chapter Thirty

Nanette's Trial

Eric Naposki had been convicted of first-degree murder with special circumstances—murder for financial gain—which brought with it a possible sentence of life without parole. Now, he had to sit in a small cell and pass his days contemplating this new reality, while talking about his innocence to anyone who would listen.

While awaiting his sentencing hearing, Naposki was the subject of an hour-long *48 Hours Mystery*. Wearing a crisp, light-blue button-down shirt, he appeared well-spoken and intelligent on camera. Although Naposki did not testify at his trial, he wanted to tell the world that he was an innocent man.

"I thought you had to be convicted on evidence, not suspicion, not lies that you told the police, not Matt Murphy's closing statement," Naposki told CBS news correspondent Troy Roberts. "I thought it was going to come down to evidence, which they don't have . . . not one bit of what you call hard evidence. They built a case on cards, and . . . it'll come down. It'll come down eventually."

When Roberts asked Naposki why he had lied to the police about his 9mm Beretta, Naposki replied, "I think I was just scared, because I didn't buy that 9mm for myself. That was Nanette's 9mm Beretta. . . . I was scared to start throwin' around, 'That's Nanette's gun. You know, go look

at Nanette.' . . . That would have been really like pointing
the finger." Although Naposki said he didn't believe Nanette
was involved in the murder at the time, he was convinced of
her complicity now.

The *48 Hours* episode, titled "Murder in the O.C.," aired
in October 2011, drawing 5.5 million viewers, just six days
before the trial of Nanette Johnston Parkard McNeal, 45,
was slated to begin. She, too, faced a life sentence without
parole if convicted of special circumstances murder.

However, on November 4 Johnston's lawyers asked for a
postponement. At the hearing Matt Murphy argued vehemently against the delay. He also told the court that Eric Naposki had spoken to law enforcement officials since his
conviction—and spun a slightly different tale from the one
he had provided to the television cameras. According to
Murphy, Naposki still claimed he was not the shooter and
that he never set foot in McLaughlin's home. However, Naposki told officials that he had introduced Johnston to a potential hit man and he was sure that the 9mm Beretta he had
purchased was used in the murder.

*A hit man? Now this was certainly a new spin on how
McLaughlin was murdered. But the detectives and investigators weren't buying it—except for the part about his being
sure that his gun had been used in the killing.*

In spite of Murphy's objections, Nanette's trial was
postponed until the new year. On Monday, January 9,
2012, the much anticipated trial got underway. The packed
courtroom was filled with approximately one hundred spectators who included many print reporters, two TV crews,
each making a documentary on the case, and friends and
relatives of Bill McLaughlin, including his two daughters.
Once again, as in the Naposki trial, the proceedings were
taking place in Judge William Froeberg's tenth-floor courtroom.

Johnston, sitting next to her lawyer, Mick Hill, appeared
much aged from the images displayed to the jury at Naposki's trial. She was no longer a stunningly attractive, skimpily
clad, flowing-blond-haired sex bomb. Now, she wore her long

hair pulled tightly back in a ponytail and was dressed in a conservative beige suit. However, hints of the siren she once was were apparent in the alluring smile she flashed from time to time—the same smile that she once used to lure many men.

Mick Hill began his opening by painting a decidedly un-lovely picture of his client. Yes, he said, she was totally motivated by money. Yes, she stole from Bill McLaughlin. Yes, she cheated on him many times while they were to-gether. "She always had a lover on the side. Does that mean she's a killer? No," stated Hill emphatically. "She was not involved in the December 1994 murder." Continuing, he ar-gued that she was *so* greedy and *so* money hungry that it simply didn't make sense for her to kill off her benefactor.

Just as Naposki's attorneys had tried to convince the jury at Naposki's trial that Nanette was the killer and that she had acted alone, Hill pointed the finger away from Nanette and straight back at Naposki. In Hill's version of events, Eric Naposki was a wildly jealous man who acted on his own in killing the man his girlfriend was living with. Naposki had a key made to gain entrance to McLaughlin's home, and he killed McLaughlin while Nanette was Christmas shopping at South Coast Plaza.

Even if Johnston was cheating on McLaughlin, Hill ar-gued, she was also a mother who loved her children and the children loved McLaughlin, who doted on them. "She would not have done this to her kids," said Hill. "This murder takes place less than two weeks before Christmas."

All Nanette wanted was "a rich man to take care of her," continued Hill. "Eric Naposki had none [money]. He was a deadbeat dad. She would never, ever leave Bill McLaughlin for someone with no money—never, ever. . . . Money is the driving force behind her. Nanette liked the high life. . . . If you are motivated by money, you aren't going to kill the golden goose to be with the pauper. . . . She had the perfect life."

Hill told the jurors that they might not like his client but that not liking her would not be reason enough to find her

guilty of murder. And with that, Hill took his seat, hoping
that his logic would resonate with the jurors.

In Murphy's opening statement, delivered in his charac-
teristic calm manner, he agreed with Hill. Yes, Johnston was
a liar. Yes, she was a thief. And yes, she was a cheater.

But, added Murphy, she was one more thing as well. "She
is also a murderer who conspired with Naposki to murder
McLaughlin." Detailing the motive, Murphy told the jury
about the $1 million life insurance policy of which Johnston
was the beneficiary and the hundreds of thousands of dollars
she had stolen from McLaughlin's bank accounts. Describing the means, Murphy said Johnston supplied the house key
for Naposki to copy and also gave him her pedestrian gate
key from her key ring. Using the keys, said Murphy, "the
killer then walked into his house and shot Bill six times."

Before trial began the next day, the prosecution scored a
significant point. They asked the judge that Suzanne Cogar
be allowed to testify. For them, she was a key witness who
had helped convict Naposki in his trial—and they felt that
her testimony would be key in Johnston's case as well.

Murphy argued that Cogar's role would not be the same
as it was in the Naposki case, because now Naposki *was convicted* of having been the killer. Instead, in this trial, Murphy
would be attempting to prove that Johnston conspired with
Naposki—and was therefore also guilty of murder—and
that Cogar's testimony was key to proving this.

Murphy stated that he wanted the jury to hear Cogar's
testimony about what Naposki told her—that Johnston told
him that McLaughlin sexually assaulted her. Murphy contended that Johnston told Naposki that in order to enrage him
and cause him to become so jealous that he would join in
her scheme to murder McLaughlin.

If Cogar's testimony along these lines was not permitted,
argued Murphy, then the defense could simply argue that
Naposki did the deed alone: He was a jealous lover who didn't
need any prompting by Johnston to commit the murder.

The defense strongly disagreed, arguing that Cogar's

statements were hearsay. Hill argued that since Cogar *never* spoke to Johnston, anything Cogar stated that Naposki told her that Johnston said was hearsay. Hill argued further that if he couldn't cross-examine Naposki—and he couldn't because a person cannot be made to testify against himself—then allowing Cogar to testify violated Johnston's constitutional rights.

After listening to both sides, Judge Froeberg ruled in favor of the prosecution because, he said, the evidence from Cogar showed Naposki's state of mind. According to the judge, it didn't matter whether or not McLaughlin ever *truly* assaulted Johnston. What did matter was that Johnston tried to make Naposki believe it. "Naposki's state of mind is not considered hearsay," said the judge.

The prosecution began its case just as it had at the Naposki trial—by playing the 911 tape. The jurors were grave as they listened to Kevin desperately trying to get the operator to understand him. During the playing of the tape, Johnston looked pained, lowering her head, rocking back and forth in her seat, and wiping away tears with a tissue. But after that, she showed little emotion.

The testimony for the prosecution repeated much of the information that was given during Naposki's trial. But unlike Naposki, who was very animated and engaged during his three weeks in court, Johnston sat quietly and stoically, rarely revealing her feelings.

On the third day of the trial, Murphy mentioned that Johnston had been married three times "that we know of." He then called Kevin Ross Johnston, her first husband, to the stand. In addition to testifying about the soccer game and Nanette's asking him not to tell the police that Eric Naposki had been with her at the game, Ross gave some background on his and Nanette's relationship.

They were married, he said, when she was 18 and he 23 in Arizona, where they both were working. Neither had much money. After five years, Ross said, the marriage fell apart and Ross had to pay the divorce lawyer's $500 fee in installments, since he didn't have the money to pay it off in one payment. Speaking about why they divorced, Ross stated that it was because he found a note Nanette had left on a "very nice" car of a guy. It asked him to meet her for a date. Ross stated, "I couldn't afford the nicer things."

Ross also said that he later discovered that Johnston had been cheating on him all during the marriage. He said that a person named "Ted" had given her the new BMW she brought home one day while they were still married.

Hill asked, "Did the relationship [between Ted and Nanette] last long?"

"Well, she was cheating on him with another guy," said Ross. Snickers could be heard in the courtroom.

Talking about some of the lies Johnston told over the years, Ross mentioned that she told people she graduated from Arizona State. "To my knowledge," said Ross, "she never even graduated high school."

On day four of the trial, Detective Tom Voth testified that six days after the murder, on December 21, 1994, detectives looking at Johnston's key ring noted that the pedestrian access key was missing. Murphy contended that Naposki was unable to return Johnston's key to her because he had dropped it on the mat as he hurriedly escaped from the Balboa Coves home. Further, Murphy contended, if she did not conspire with Naposki, when the detectives pointed out that her pedestrian access key was missing she would have told detectives, "I guess the killer stole the key from my ring!" And who, wondered Murphy aloud, was the most likely person to take something from her ring? Her lover, Naposki. Yet, contended Murphy, Johnston continued seeing Naposki.

Continuing with testimony, Detective Randall Parker testified that while he was surveiling Johnston the day after the key ring discovery Naposki arrived at Nanette's home with her two children. Nanette was not there.

Murphy wondered aloud, if Nanette was innocent, why had she just allowed a man who might be a murderer to baby-sit her kids?

That afternoon, William Wayne McNeal, MBA graduate from USC and Johnston's third husband and the father of

Johnston's young son, took the stand. Murphy asked him only one question: "When Nanette was arrested, did she have many photos in her possession?"

"Maybe a couple," McNeal responded. Although it wasn't clear exactly what Murphy was getting at, one court reporter surmised that perhaps Murphy was attempting to show that Nanette was trying to erase her past.

Under cross-examination, McNeal stated that in 2009, after he had been married to Johnston for three years, Johnston was arrested for special circumstances murder and he was taken completely by surprise. "I was completely blown apart. I never even knew she was a suspect in a murder case." Furthermore, he stated, she had never even mentioned living with William McLaughlin or the fact that he had been murdered in 1994 or the fact that she was a suspect. All of that, McNeal said, came to light when she was arrested.

McNeal stated that in May 2009 he, along with forty of their neighbors, had supported Johnston unconditionally in the courtroom while she was being arraigned on murder. Many at that time were willing to co-sign loans for their houses to help post bail. No one had the slightest idea that Nanette was anything but a perfect mother and neighbor.

McNeal pointed out that he continued to support his wife until facts started emerging that showed she had lied to him—specifically about her background, about her finances, and about the fact that she had never told him she had been a suspect in a murder.

McNeal told the jury that in March of 2010 he stopped bringing their son to the jail to visit Johnston and that he started divorce proceedings. He was raising the boy alone—and he now faced lawsuits by people alleging his wife bilked them out of money while they were married.

On redirect, McNeal came out with a bombshell. He said that in 2008 Nanette ripped off $8,000 from friends in their Ladera Ranch neighborhood by using her own eight-year-old daughter. The scheme? Nanette set up an auction for clothing her talented daughter *supposedly* created. The proceeds were said to be going to orphans in Africa.

McNeal stated that after the clothes were auctioned he learned that some of these so-called original designs were on racks in local department stores. Plus, continued McNeal, the $8,000 profit never went to any orphans anywhere. Instead, Nanette pocketed the loot.

Now, no longer was Nanette just a cheater, a liar, a forger, and a thief. She was also someone who used her own daughter to commit a crime.

If Nanette's being a good mom was part of the defense's strategy, the façade was starting to crack.

When the trial recommenced on Tuesday, January 17, Murphy played a tape recording of Johnston being interviewed on January 19, 1995, a little over a month after the murder. On the recording, two detectives were interviewing Nanette and she sounded affable and accommodating. Nonetheless, she coyly tried to play down her involvement with Naposki.

"Did you [ever] stay the night [with Naposki]?" one of the detectives asked.

"Never the whole night," Johnston responded.

"What is the *whole* night?" asked one detective.

"I only stayed until six or seven in the morning."

Seems like the definition of whole *might be taken into question.*

Also on the tape, Johnston was heard saying that she never saw any of Naposki's guns. When asked if she had ever gone to a shooting range, she said that Naposki "mentioned going to a gun range. . . . He mentioned he wanted to teach me to shoot." She added that she never saw Naposki with ammunition, nor did she ever see his roommate, Leonard Jomsky, with a gun.

On the recording, the detectives could be heard cautioning Johnston that if she was lying, they would catch her out. But she calmly informed them that they wouldn't be able to catch her in a lie because she "didn't do anything."

Clearly relishing the next moment, Murphy called Leonard Jomsky to the stand. Jomsky testified, as he had during Naposki's trial, that he, Johnston, Naposki, and another man went to a local range. "Eric was showing both Nanette and I how to operate the gun and how to shoot," he said.

This was as close to a smoking gun as Matt Murphy was going to get. He rested his case.

On Wednesday, Hill began what appeared to be a continuation of his "good mom" defense by calling Lishele Wigand to the stand as a character witness. Now 24, Lishele was Johnston's first daughter, from her marriage to Ross Johnston. Tanned, pretty, and dark-haired, Lishele testified that her mother was a great mom, who baked cupcakes for her even when she was in college. However, she also mentioned that for her mother having money "means you are important." Describing her love of shopping, Lishele stated that Nanette's closet was bigger than most clothing stores; her shoe closet was almost as big as the jury box. Lishele also testified that Ross, her father, had a "disturbing obsession with the murder case."

That day, Johnston's second husband, John Packard, took the stand. Handsome and now in his late fifties, he stated that as a real estate developer he had taken a beating in the recession. However, he had once been wealthy enough to pay a $17,000 monthly child support payment to Nanette.

Unlike Nanette's first husband, Ross, and her third husband, McNeal, Packard had only kind things to say about what a wonderful mother Nanette had been. He painted Ross Johnston as a crank, who had constantly called him and said Nanette was a murderer.

Packard also testified, in direct contrast to McNeal, that Nanette told him *all* about the murder. When he was asked by Hill to tell specifically what she said, Murphy objected, saying it was hearsay. *If Nanette had something to say about the murder, she could say it on the stand and be cross-examined.*

Ending the day's witnesses was Mary Berg, the former housekeeper at the McLaughlin home. While Hill got her to cast some light on McLaughlin and Johnston's relationship (that it had seemed like a good one) and say that Nanette appeared to be a caring parent, Berg ended up throwing the

jury for a loop with her oddball testimony. After telling the
judge that he was "cute," she said that "Mr. Bill didn't like
me vacuuming." When asked about whether she thought Mr.
Bill was happy, she responded, "I'm not an expert on happy."
When asked about the day of the murder, she stated that she
remembered it well. In fact, she was furious when she found
out Mr. Bill had been killed in the kitchen. *Why?* Because
she had just given it a good cleaning.

As she left the stand, she turned to Hill and said, "You're
cute."

"Cuter than the judge?" quipped Hill.

Berg took a long moment to stare at Froeberg and then
said, "No." And with that, she exited.

Closing arguments began Wednesday afternoon, after just
six and a half days of testimony. Murphy rose and walked
right up to the jury and began his unequivocal malignment
of Nanette. He told them that Nanette Johnston had a gift.
It was her power to manipulate men. "It was her talent on
earth," Murphy said, "Johnston wanted McLaughlin's
money—but without Bill. She is the person who put all this
in motion."

Continuing, Murphy stated that Johnston was the su-
preme manipulator who persuaded her boyfriend, Eric Naposki, to kill McLaughlin for two reasons: so he wouldn't
discover the fact that she had been stealing thousands from
him, and so she could collect millions of dollars from his
will and life insurance policy. Murphy said that if McLaughlin discovered she was stealing from him, he would have
kicked her out and then she would have had nothing. To help
Naposki achieve *her* goal, she had keys made for him to let
him enter the house.

Murphy said that although his case was circumstantial,
there was overwhelming evidence that Nanette orchestrated
the murder. Ending, he urged the jurors to think long and
hard about everything they saw and heard, and then come to
the only logical conclusion—guilty.

* * *

On Thursday, January 19, Hill began his closing statement. He acknowledged, as he did throughout the trial, that his client was not a nice woman. "Hate her as much as you want for being a cheat, a liar, and a thief. But," he added, "you can't vote her guilty of murder." He told the jurors that she was a thief, not a murderer. Johnston was definitely a woman obsessed with money, but she would *never* have killed the man who was financially supporting her and her children and permitting them to live with him in his Balboa Coves home.

Hill said that during the two-week trial "Matt" presented circumstantial evidence, which did *not* prove his client conspired with Eric Naposki to murder Bill McLaughlin. There was no confession, Hill stated, and no evidence that life with Bill was not a happy one.

Speaking about McLaughlin, Hill stated, "He was perfect for Nanette. He was very rich. Why was he so perfect? He was gone three days a week. What better person to cheat on? You've got no eyes watching you and you can cheat on him over and over and over again."

Hill called "Matt's" closing argument "two hours of horse manure" and contradicted Murphy's contention that Johnston gave Naposki her pedestrian access key and a front door key for him to copy.

Hill stated that on Wednesday Murphy had said the pedestrian gate key was stamped with the words "Do Not Duplicate" on it and that is why she had to lend him her key instead of giving him one to copy, as she had presumably done with the house key.

Hill went on to say that after hearing Murphy's statement about the key yesterday he decided to go to the tray of evidence and pick it out. And in the most dramatic moment of the trial, Hill stated, "There was *not* a stamp on the key." In other words, it did not say: "Do Not Duplicate," so it was *not* Nanette's key. Hill then walked right up to Murphy, dropped the key on his table, and challenged him to explain such a discrepancy.

Murphy could hardly wait. He jumped out of his chair and, uncharacteristically red in the face, told the jury that he *never* said or even implied that the key was stamped with the words "Do Not Duplicate." He said that Hill was simply "inventing a Perry Mason moment" and in "my one hundred and fourteen trials, I have never heard a defense do such a thing. Those words never came out of my mouth."

Murphy stated that when Nanette's key chain was examined on December 22, one key was missing—the key to the pedestrian access gate. But, he said emphatically, he never said or implied that the key found on the mat said: "Do Not Duplicate."

Murphy went on to say that the closing argument that Hill offered the jurors was "two hours of crap in an Irish accent."

Although the jurors tried hard not to show their emotions, several found it difficult to suppress a laugh.

After Murphy concluded his rebuttal, the case went to the jury for deliberations. It was late Thursday afternoon and the jurors were given their instructions. Since jurors had the day off on Fridays, deliberations would begin in earnest on Monday, stated the judge.

On Monday, when the jury reconvened, it didn't take long.

After approximately three hours of deliberation, the nine-woman, three-man jury sent word to the judge that they had reached a verdict. Obviously, they had been been convinced one way or the other by the testimony.

As a solemn judge and even more solemn defendant entered the courtroom, TV cameras were poised to capture everyone's reaction. The McLaughlin family sat hopefully in the second row, as they had throughout the trial. And it didn't take long before the word they hoped to hear was said. "Guilty," stated court clerk Laura Hoyle.

All eyes turned to Johnston, but she showed no reaction. Lishele, Johnston's adult daughter, however, cried uncontrollably upon hearing the verdict and had to be escorted from the courtroom. McLaughlin's daughters, holding hands, smiled and cried at the same time.

Once she gathered herself together, Kim went over to Johnston's third husband, McNeal, and gave him a hug. And McNeal, for his part, shook Ross Johnston's hand.

When Johnston was first arrested, her youngest child—the son she had had with McNeal—was a baby, only five months old. Now the boy was three. After the verdict, McNeal told Frank Mickadeit from the *OC Register* that their son didn't remember her. "He's well-adjusted, and I've already sought professional advice about what we have to face down the road" in terms of learning about her.

Interviewed after the verdict, a relieved-looking Kim McLaughlin said, "It was a long time coming," referring to the seventeen years since the murder. "But this is closure for us," she added with a smile.

Because of the verdict, Johnston faced a life sentence without the possibility of parole. The McLaughlins couldn't have been more pleased.

On May 18, 2012, Nanette Johnston, 46, was led into Judge Froeberg's courtroom to hear what her sentence would be for murder with special circumstances. She had already been in prison for three years and was desperately hoping that the court would be lenient on her. Living in a tiny cell was certainly a huge sea change from her heady days as the wealthy OC wife of several millionaires—and she prayed that one day, in the not-too-distant future, she would be reunited with her children and could put this whole, messy situation behind her.

In the hushed courtroom, spectators sat quietly, anxiously awaiting the decision. Would Nanette go to prison for life without the possibility of parole, or would she receive a more lenient sentence? It didn't take long before the word came down.

"Life in prison without the possibility of parole," stated Judge Froeberg emphatically. It was the harshest possible sentence she could have received, but again Johnston showed no emotion at all. Instead, she sat expressionless next to her lawyer in the jury box, perhaps too shocked—or callous—to react.

Although Johnston didn't show her feelings, the McLaughlin family did not hold back. After exchanging hugs and kisses, Kim and her sister stood up and delivered heartfelt impact statements.

Looking directly at Johnston, Kim began. She stated, "[Your] destructive trail of deceit is astounding. The fact that you, Nanette, destroyed so many lives, including my Dad's, is vile. . . . You had absolutely no right to take him from us for your own selfish reasons. He was incredibly good to you for four whole years." Kim continued, "What a despicable, disgusting disgrace you are to your family and the children you dared to bring into this world."

A tearful Jenny then spoke about her father. "I feel very grateful to have had such a wonderful father in my life for as long as I did. I wish he could have stayed with us longer and that God would have chosen his time to leave, rather than a person with a gun and a greedy heart."

Patrick McLaughlin, the deceased's brother, wrote an impact statement, which was read by a family friend. In it, he declared that Nanette was a true black widow.

Outside the courtroom, Murphy didn't hold back his feelings either. "She has to use contraband for her hair dye and she has to grind up magazines to be used for make-up. She looks haggard; jail has not been kind to her. She got what she deserved."

Continuing to express exactly how he felt, Murphy moved on to Naposki, who refused to appear in court, choosing instead to remain in a holding cell, listening to the proceedings and speaking by way of a microphone. "He is a coward for not being here today and facing the family of the victim," Murphy said. "They have a right to be heard by him. This is his final blaze of no class."

Hill filed a notice of appeal on Nanette's behalf, which lets the court and the other side know that the defendant is appealing the court's decision. The notice of appeal went to an appellate attorney. Hill was no longer involved in Nanette's case.

Although Naposki's sentencing was due to take place on the same day as Johnston's, Naposki's date was postponed until August 10, due to his attorney's request for a continuance.

Clearly, Froeberg was not pleased with the further delay. "I'm not particularly thrilled about this," he stated. "Ten months later and we still are not proceeding on this matter. After this," he declared in no uncertain terms, "there will be no more continuances."

As it turned out, Naposki had requested a new trial because, according to Murphy, he had come up with a "fifth story." Clearly miffed, Murphy stated, "I'm confident the new trial will go nowhere."

Even though they had already waited nearly two decades for justice, the McLaughlins would have to wait a little while longer before they heard what Naposki's sentence would be. However, they were hopeful that they might be able to begin the process of healing now. They knew that nothing could bring back their beloved father, but the justice system can—and did—hold those responsible for his murder accountable. And considering the circumstances, it was the best outcome they could have hoped for.

For Naposki, however, it was an entirely different story. He remained in prison, hell-bent on proving his innocence—and swearing that he would. After all, he said, "The truth counts. I know I will walk out of here one day, a free and exonerated man."

To that end, in early May 2012, Naposki's legal team got in touch with *48 Hours Mystery* and asked if they would come back to prison and interview him again. They said that Naposki wanted "to reveal the identity of the real killer."

Eager to hear who it was, *48 Hours* returned to the prison to interview Naposki for another hour-long segment. It was aired in late May.

During the interview, Naposki told interviewer Troy Roberts that he always knew who Bill McLaughlin's murderer was, but that he withheld the information from the police because he feared they wouldn't believe him since he didn't have any hard proof.

"Nanette paid for the killing. . . . she hired somebody," Naposki said. Going into greater detail, he stated that after Nanette told him that McLaughlin sexually assaulted her, he called a buddy and told him all about it. His friend said that he could easily understand "why I was so angry" and continued by stating, "I have people that take care of things like this, you know? I have people who don't like rapists."

Naposki went on to tell Roberts that he didn't take the person seriously because "a lot of people talk about a lot of stuff in this town." Instead, said Naposki, he wanted to find out all about the connections his friend had in Hollywood because he was hoping to break into the movies. In fact, continued Napski, "He got me an extra part in a movie." The two even began planning to start a film production company—with Nanette's help, of course, since she was so good at writing up business plans.

Explaining more, Naposki said that he never, ever took his friend's offer of finding a hit man seriously, and since nothing happened in September, October, or November, Naposki felt certain that nothing was *ever* going to happen in that regard.

However, Naposki said, in early December, he noticed that a 9mm Beretta was missing from his car. Since it was actually Nanette's gun, said Naposki, "I asked her if she took it. She denied she did."

About two weeks later, said Naposki, "Nanette called me and said that McLaughlin had been killed." When he asked her if she had had him killed, Naposki said that Nanette replied, "Absolutely."

Naposki stated that he then immediately visited the Hollywood producer to find out if it was true. "He told me, you know, he did what she wanted him to do." Furthermore, the acquaintance stated that the gun used to commit the murder was a gun that Nanette had given him—one, in fact, that she claimed she had taken from Naposki's car.

Now, Naposki told Roberts, "I was forever tied to the murder of Bill McLaughlin."

During the *48 Hours Mystery* episode, Roberts also interviewed DA Murphy about this revelation of Naposki's. Murphy reported that Eric had also told him about this supposed hit man, so "we thoroughly investigated" the man. According to Murphy, "The man's an unlikely suspect. What I can tell you is that . . . he was completely cooperative in every way. He has never been arrested before . . . he's legitimate as far as his business dealings go."

Roberts then returned to Naposki. "You're telling me that a businessman with no criminal history carried out this murder for $50,000?"

"I can only assume that's the amount of money that's missing from her cash withdrawals," said Naposki.

"It's kind of hard to digest, Eric. Fifty grand?"

"Troy, is it easier to digest that I did it for nothing? No houses, no future, no happily ever after?" Then, continuing in his own defense, Naposki pointed out that in December 1994, right around the time of the murder, he took out a loan for $10,000. "Does a guy need a loan for ten K," asked Naposki, "when he's about to make a million?"

At the end of the show, although Roberts originally intended to reveal the name of the supposed hit man, he decided against it, mostly because Murphy was so adamant in saying that the businessman had nothing to do with the murder. "Everything that comes out of Eric Naposki's mouth is a lie," said Murphy on camera. "Eric Naposki went into that kitchen that night and he murdered Bill McLaughlin and we have proven it. And everything he does since then is pointing fingers someplace else."

Chapter Thirty-One

Naposki Sentencing

On Wednesday, August 8, 2012, in a jailhouse interview at Theo Lacy in Santa Ana, Eric Naposki once again proclaimed his innocence. "I am not a murderer. . . . We're just one phone bill away from proving my innocence."

Naposki was once again declaring to anyone who would listen that he was an innocent man—two days before his sentencing. In the two-hour interview, Naposki claimed that Johnston, "a pathological liar," set him up, but he added that he is going to reveal the name of the person who is the "real" killer.

Naposki went on to state that his 8:52 p.m. call from a Denny's pay phone meant it would have been impossible for him to have had time to drive to the McLaughlin home and kill Mr. McLaughlin. "You can't be in two places at once," he said. "There is no way possible I could have killed Bill McLaughlin that night. I never set foot in that home at 67 Balboa Coves. And I sure as hell never went in there to kill Bill McLaughlin."

Naposki admitted that he made many mistakes along the way. The biggest, he said, was protecting Nanette and not putting her away fifteen years ago. Another was not testifying in his trial. "My lawyers told me I didn't need to, that they [the prosecution] didn't present enough evidence to convict me. You have no idea what I would have done to Matt

Murphy. But I listened to my attorney's advice. It was another mistake."

Talking about himself, he spoke in the third person: "Eric Naposki is not a murderer. Eric Naposki is a father. Eric Naposki is a pro athlete, who's worked hard all of his life. There are people in this world who can kill another person. I'm not one of them. Absolutely, positively, I'm not that guy."

Summing up, he stated, "I just thank God I didn't make the mistake of doing what they said I did."

The next day, Thursday, August 9, a little over a year after Eric Naposki was convicted of murder, Judge Froeberg ruled on a defense motion for a new trial that Naposki's lawyers had been working on for a year. In the motion, the lawyers contended that because of the many years between the murder and their client's trial (over fifteen), Naposki had been prejudiced. They said that Naposki's previous lawyer, Julian Bailey, had lost a phone bill that could have definitively proven Naposki's innocence.

Murphy begged to differ. He stated that Naposki—"a buffoon . . . the more he talks, the less people listen"—did, in fact, receive a fair trial. On top of that, said Murphy, Naposki lived a full life for fifteen years—during which time he should have been incarcerated. Murphy stated that even if the phone bill appeared, it would still not exonerate him. "His fundamental problem is he doesn't understand the concept of an alibi. An alibi means that he couldn't have been there to commit the murder, and we proved otherwise."

Once again, lawyer was pitted against lawyer and Judge Froeberg would make the final decision. After having read through the papers submitted by the defense and carefully considering both sides, Froeberg ruled in favor of the prosecution. He stated that the circumstantial evidence in the case was "overwhelming."

The motion for a new trial was denied.

The next day, Friday, August 10, was the day of Naposki's sentencing. The McLaughlins had waited a long time to hear the words they prayed would be spoken: life without the possibility of parole.

Naposki, now 45, entered Judge Froeberg's courtroom in handcuffs and wearing a pink starched shirt. For a man who had spent time behind bars, he looked surprisingly healthy. He was still seemingly in great shape, cleanly shaven, and smartly attired. Naposki sat down between his attorneys, Pohlson and MacDonald, and talked quietly with them as he awaited his turn to speak.

To a packed courtroom, before sentencing, Naposki spoke in his own defense. Handcuffed and with his notes in front of him, he proclaimed his innocence in a strong, clear voice. "I can't imagine that there's any evidence that I could have committed the crime. To be tried as somebody's boyfriend—I admit I might have made some bad decisions as far as handling the police and I might have made a very bad decision in who I chose to be my girlfriend, but I was never ever convinced by Nanette Johnston to commit a murder, and the audacity of someone to say that they proved it when you know it didn't exist.

"Am I seventeen years late in coming forward with the information on [unclear], the person that Nanette paid cash money to kill Bill McLaughlin with? Absolutely. Did I make a bad decision by not coming forward seventeen years ago? Yes."

But, Naposki insisted, he was not the murderer of Bill McLaughlin.

It was then Kim McLaughlin Bayless's opportunity to give her victim impact statement. Haltingly and through tears, Bayless looked directly at Naposki. Naposki stared straight back at her. At times, when Naposki disagreed with something Bayless said, he stated his own point of view.

"Our dad planned his life around family time," said Bayless. "Sunday brunches, family dinners, and family vacations—any excuse to enjoy each other and get that quality time together. And because of Eric's selfish reasons, he decided to take my dad away from us." After a tearful pause,

Bayless continued, "Thankfully, there is one thing that [he] cannot take from us no matter what. That is the intense and abundant amount of love my dad gave us all the years we got to spend with him."

After taking a moment to collect herself, Bayless, staring straight at Naposki, said, "Change your horrific ways and honor the man you murdered."

Bayless stated that Naposki lied when he said he had never set foot in the Balboa Coves home.

"That's a lie," retorted Eric from his seat.

"You are full of lies," Bayless said right back to him. "Somehow during your lifetime you have learned that you can get away with these lies and these lies can get you where you want. Well, look where it's gotten you now, and where you will go forevermore."

And with the word "forevermore" echoing in the courtroom, Bayless turned away from Naposki and took her seat.

When it was time to hand down the sentence, a grave Judge Froeberg gave his statement as Naposki closed his eyes, his lips pressed together tightly. "Life without the possibility of parole," said Froeberg. Naposki's lawyers, MacDonald and Pohlson, looked deeply pained. Although the sentence was predictable, they nevertheless seemed heartbroken by its finality.

It wasn't long after that officers began to escort Naposki—feet in shackles, hands cuffed to his waist—from the courtroom. But Naposki was not done yet. As he was being led out, Naposki looked at Murphy and said, "You f_____blew it."

Murphy retorted, "Bye-bye."

Hell-bent on having the last words, Naposki said, "I'll see you again," as the door closed behind him.

It seemed highly unlikely that Naposki would get his way.

Epilogue

As I researched and wrote this book, many people close to this case were so fascinating that I yearned to find out more about them—to get their thoughts on their own challenges, investigative techniques, and the process of seeking justice. As a result, I called or e-mailed several people and asked if I could interview them. As it turned out, many graciously agreed.

It was not feasible to include all the details from these interviews within the chapters of the book. Such information would have broken the narrative. But here you can get to know some of the key people in this case—in their own words.

Detective Dave Byington

Detective Dave Byington was on the McLaughlin case from the very beginning, seeing it through from before the first police interview with Eric Naposki to the arrest of Nanette Packard McNeal fifteen years later.

"When I look at people," said Byington, when asked about his approach to arrests and interviews, "I try to put myself in their shoes and wonder if their reaction is appropriate for the situation. When I went to arrest Nanette [in 2009], for example, I knocked on her door in the high-end neighborhood where she was living. Truth is, she was no longer the beauty she was years before. She was cute, that's about it. As soon as she opened the door, she blocked it with one leg and said, 'What can I do to help you?'

"I said, 'I have an arrest warrant for murder.'

" 'For who?' she asked.

"And right there," said Byington, "I'm wondering, how many people did she murder?

" 'For William McLaughlin.' "

It was then, according to Byington, that Nanette realized the gravity of the situation. "She stumbled and her knees buckled. But then, she quickly regrouped and came out with this: 'Why would I want him dead? He was worth more to me alive.' "

Byington continued, "And I'm thinking that is not the way I would respond if someone was arresting me for murder. She put it in perspective for me. It was all about money, and all this time later, that was the first thing out of her mouth."

In the years that followed his involvement in the case, then detective sergeant Byington was involved with many other cases, but the McLaughlin murder was never far from his mind. Aside from his firm belief that Naposki and Johnston were guilty of the crime and it was just a matter of time until they got their due, each year, the McLaughlin daughters would send the department a lovely holiday basket. "The note would simply say: "Happy Holidays." So on an annual basis, we got reminded. Their case was kept in the forefront."

Byington doesn't mince words when he sums up his feelings about Nanette: "She must have had a trapeze in her bedroom because she's hooking these guys right and left." Continuing, he stated, "Every one of her relationships, she gets the guy, hard-core. There was one boyfriend after another. She was a decent looker." He further characterized her as a "seductress."

Finally, consolidating his feelings about Nanette, Byington stated, "She gives a bad name to sluts and whores."

Byington retired from the NBPD in 2010.

Detective Joe Cartwright

Detective Joe Cartwright was a detective in the Robbery-Homicide/Crimes Against Persons section at the NBPD when he was assigned to work the McLaughlin cold case in 2007. "I was immediately drawn into the tragedy. This was a huge responsibility and a total honor," he said. "Looking at the photos and realizing that this man was just relaxing in his home when someone walked into his kitchen and murdered him, that is shocking enough—but then I listened to the nine-one-one tape and it brought tears to my eyes. Kevin was struggling, trying so hard to just get some help for his dad. It was heartbreaking."

Cartwright was involved with many aspects of the case, but perhaps the most memorable was arresting Naposki. "When Larry [Montgomery] and I flew to Connecticut, I remember how physically imposing and confident Eric was, which might have explained the steroids we found in his car. Larry and I had prepared quite a bit because we listened to past interviews and we knew he was a strong personality who liked to take over an interview.

"I remember Eric being completely defiant. This is a man who, according to him, has an alibi, who didn't do this, who has been set up—and now we were giving him a chance to explain himself.

"He brought up the supposed phone record, and I said we don't have it and we didn't ever have it. And I'm thinking if I was innocent, I would carry a copy of that phone record in my wallet. I would tattoo it on my back.

"I asked him to describe the phone record, but he wouldn't. He kept cutting us off and demanding a trial. 'Take me to California right now. I want a trial today. You guys ruined my life fourteen years ago—you're about to do it again—but this time, you're gonna pay.'

"If a guy didn't do the murder, that's not the approach you'd expect."

Speaking about his finding Mike Tuomisto in Sweden, Cartwright said, "When I called Tuomisto, he was surprised to hear from me. He said that nobody had contacted him regarding Eric Naposki—ever. When I asked him about his relationship with Naposki, he stated that basically, he didn't have one. He said that he was a bar manager at the Thunderbird back in 1994 and that security guards didn't report to him, so, he continued, 'I would have had no reason to page Eric Naposki.' Tuomisto stated that in late December of 1994 he was fired from the Thunderbird, but he stayed local. So," continued Cartwright, "I say to myself, here was Tuomisto, in the area for a couple of years after the murder, and if I was Eric, and Tuomisto was my alibi, you can be darn sure I would go to him and say, 'Hey, let's go to the police station right now, and you're gonna tell them about this call.' But Eric never went to Tuomisto."

After Nanette's trial, Cartwright stated, "I got to spend some time with the McLaughlin family and was reminded of what exceptional people they are. It is so gratifying to get to know them and be a part of something like this—and it's also pretty nice seeing Eric and Nanette together again, right where they belong."

Attorney Mick Hill

When Nanette requested a public defender in August 2009, the case was assigned to Mick Hill.

Born in Cork, Ireland, Hill and his family moved to the United States while he was in college. Once here, he attended Loyola Marymount Law School. Today, his Irish upbringing still influences his approach to justice.

Speaking about why he decided to become a public defender, Hill stated, "Growing up in Ireland gave me a strong sense of justice and empathy for those accused of crimes. I grew up during 'The Troubles' in Ireland, when many Irish people were being released from English prisons for crimes they didn't commit—after years of investigations that proved that the cases had been fabricated by corrupt police officers and the defendants had been denied fair trials due to a flawed justice system.

"One of the greatest things about the United States is that its Constitution guarantees every citizen a right to a fair trial and the right to be represented by counsel. I truly feel honored to be able to fight for something I believe in every day."

For Hill, the McLaughlin case was different from most of the previous cases he has handled in a number of ways.

"First, I was representing a woman charged with murder—which is uncommon it itself.

"Second, it was a fifteen-year-old homicide. The investigation in the case was very demanding since they were trying to resurrect evidence from a decade and a half previously. This created huge hurdles for us.

"Third, the media attention in this case was high from the very beginning, so that came with its own challenges. For example, having the TV show *48 Hours* air its story on Naposki's trial six days before my case was set to begin in November 2011 created a set of unforeseen hurdles and drew additional unwanted attention to my client, which I think had an impact on the potential jurors."

Speaking of his courtroom style, Hill said, "While trying a case, I tend to be on the informal side. I like to inject a lot of humor, often self-deprecating humor, and I tell a lot of stories so that I can draw analogies from external events and experiences to the particular facts of my case.

"Some of my fellow PDs complain that I get away with conduct for which they would be sanctioned because I have an accent and am given significant leeway by judges." Plus, he looks a bit like a pupil at Eton. Except for his "mature" wrinkles, his face is incorrigibly youthful.

Smiling broadly, Hill said, "I think that they are just jealous."

Attorney Angelo MacDonald

When Eric Naposki was arrested, the first call he made was to his childhood friend John Pappalardo, a New York attorney who worked with Angelo MacDonald. "John and I were both shocked," said MacDonald. "I'd known Eric as an acquaintance through John for many years. John grew up with him. There was no way Eric committed the crime he was accused of."

MacDonald related a story that John Pappalardo told him about Eric. "When John and Eric were in high school, John played basketball and Eric played football. One day, John was being harassed by a mob of thugs in the gym and it seemed that there could be some damage. Eric, who was lifting weights in the next room, heard the commotion. He walked right onto the basketball court and said, 'If any of you wanna fight someone, you gotta go through me first.' With that, said MacDonald, the trouble ended and John and Eric were sealed as friends for life."

Because MacDonald handled the trial cases in Pappalardo's firm, Papallardo asked him to get involved in the Naposki case. "It gave me a chance to stretch my wings. As an attorney, you don't get many opportunities to go to California to try a capital murder case."

Regarding his trial style, MacDonald said, "I like to take the approach that I'm in control of the courtroom. I am quite energetic. I like to keep witnesses on the edge of their seats. I can speak very loudly or quite softly, depending on what I think might work best. I ask a lot of questions— some slow, some machine-gun-like just to keep witnesses on their toes or to catch them in something I can capitalize on."

Speaking of what makes a good courtroom lawyer, MacDonald cited two things—the ability to think on one's feet and common sense. "Plus," he added, "if you're inquisitive and curious and a thoughtful and good listener, you should make an excellent attorney."

MacDonald sees the courtroom the way some people view Mount Everest. "It's a huge challenge. I go into court every day and learn something new. I'm always trying out new stuff at every trial, always thinking of better ways to get the jury to see things my way."

Talking about the case, MacDonald said that it was purely circumstantial. "There was no direct evidence. In some ways, these cases can be more persuasive for the prosecution. You build little piece after little piece after little piece, and then the jurors say, 'How *can't* it be that?'"

MacDonald believed that circumstantial cases were not "weak" cases, as the average person may think. "Murphy was very adept at focusing on those separate little pieces that added up to a jury saying, 'How could it *not* have been Naposki?' When you look at motive, innuendo, and inferences about his connection with Johnston and the unresolved questions about the gun, his suspicious behavior afterwards, the license plate on the piece of paper in Naposki's car—so many things—it's difficult to overcome especially when your defense is an alibi that is fifteen years old and almost impossible to recreate. The defense had to attack every single thing, and if not successful, the result generally goes in the direction of the prosecution."

Asked about some of the discrepancies in Naposki's statements over time, MacDonald offered this explanation: "He was getting the feeling, actually it was quite obvious, that the police were trying to blame him. And when you have a young kid in his early twenties who doesn't have experience dealing with police officers and detectives with a lot of experience, you do a lot of things that come back to bite you in the behind later. I think he started to toy with them in a defensive way: 'I'm gonna hold my ground, match wits with them, deal with them the way they deal with me.' I think that backfired. A lot of that goes to immaturity. The other part was his belief and attitude that he could be on the same mental level with them.

"It just doesn't happen," said MacDonald. "Police officers are experienced people. It's not easy to outsmart them."

Because MacDonald has been on both sides of the fence—prosecutor and defense attorney—he can speak from both points of view. "As a prosecutor, you have to be-lieve in the person's guilt. I always believed in their guilt when I prosecuted defendants. If I didn't, I would have the obligation *not* to prosecute or to question it and do further investigation.

"The troubling part of being a defense attorney is when you really have an innocent defendant, someone you believe did not do what the government or law enforcement is say-ing they did. because that's a very, very difficult position to be in personally. For me, that was this case."

For lawyers, every case is different; yet over a lifetime of trying cases, some stand out. For MacDonald, "This case stands out because I had the opportunity and privilege to try a case in another State-jurisdiction. And because I had an acquaintance with the defendant."

After the closing, the defense team was somewhat opti-mistic. "I thought we had a shot. But I am also very much of a realist. I'm aware of what the conviction rate is for most cases. It is always an uphill battle."

Kimberly McLaughlin

Growing up, Kimberly McLaughlin knew she was blessed. "We had a fabulous childhood and a very sweet family. My parents wanted to make sure everything we did included the whole family, so we would attend church together every Sunday often by bike and afterward enjoy long Sunday brunches around the table. We would all be together and enjoy quality time.

"My parents' friends and their families, our friends and their parents, as well as neighbors, would often come to our house. Some wanted to ask my father's advice in business matters. Others just liked the atmosphere. It was always lots of fun and really interesting.

"When we were kids, we had neighborhood concerts be-cause we all played the piano. People would pay a quarter to listen.

"As a family, we'd travel a lot because Dad thought it was important for us to see different places. He would take us on business trips, even to Europe. Mom was a seamstress then and still is now, and she would make us all matching outfits when we would travel. We were probably all under ten, and we'd be sightseeing in these sweet matching outfits. I think we stood out starkly as tourists.

"Dad encouraged us to go out and help others in the community. We would visit local nursing homes and entertain by playing the piano or doing gymnastics or dance routines. Dad was a very generous spirit. He was all about helping others and passing on our good fortune. He wanted to make other people's lives easier.

"When my mother and father were together, my mom was in charge of raising us; that was her job. Dad's job was to be the provider and businessman of the family. He ran the finances, but Mom would pay the monthly household bills. Often, my dad wouldn't share what was going on in his business with my mom because he felt it was too stressful, like when he didn't know where he'd get money to pay his employees. One time, he had to refinance the house. He didn't want Mom to know.

"In 1990, my parents, who had been married for twenty-four years, got divorced. It was devastating. Then, only about a year later, tragedy struck. Kevin was twenty-one when he was hit while skateboarding, in 1991. It was a terrible time for us all, but especially for my dad. His one and only son, and a person he was so close to, might never wake from a coma. Then, when Kevin miraculously woke up, my father feared that Kevin would never walk or talk. When Kevin finally could do a few things for himself, my father still was afraid that Kevin would never be able to take care of himself. It was extremely devastating to my dad."

Thinking about how Nanette came into her father's life, Kim believed that the main reason her father attracted Nanette was because he was at a very low point in his life. "His divorce. His only son, whom he had really counted on, had been hit by a drunk driver. But not only that.

"His former business partner Hal Fischel was suing him for a good part of his income and my dad knew it was wrong. My dad felt that Fischel breached the contract they had formed, so he had the company stop paying him. Fischel sued the company, Baxter, and my father. It went on for a very long time and my father had to travel to San Francisco during the week and fly back to OC for the weekends. He was getting really tired of it. He thought there was no real reason for the lawsuit in the first place, and was angry that he was spending so much time on it and on lawyers' bills.

"So," said Kim summing up, "my dad was feeling kind of low and that was one reason he attracted Nanette. Nanette made him feel good—or at least better—on a day-to-day basis."

Kim recalled that her father set up the same arrangement with Nanette as he did with her mother. "He would put money in an account for her to pay household bills. Nanette was interested in learning about businesses, and he was going to mentor her and do some businesses with her, for example, a hairbrush that takes out water. So one of the reasons he appreciated Nanette was because she did tasks my mom had done, which would leave him free so he could concentrate on managerial stuff."

In August of 1994, Kim left for Japan to teach in an international school for a two-year stint. She had been an elementary teacher and "I wanted a change. . . . My parents supported me—and my siblings—in practically everything we did, although my dad was a bit bummed that I would be moving so far away. However, he gave me his blessings."

But after only three and a half months in Japan, Kim received the heartbreaking call from her mother telling her that her father was dead.

In the years following the murder, Kim said that she lost hope that the case would ever be solved. "After two years, in 1995 and 1996, we kept discovering new things Nanette had done—cheating on my dad, stealing money, forging signatures, buying motorcycles after the funeral—and we were sure she'd be arrested any day, but then she wasn't and nothing happened, so we started to lose hope. And then, the detectives presented all they had to the DA, and *she* turned the case down. We were really low then. We thought for sure that my dad's murderer would never be found.

"We knew we had to move on with our lives. Having been involved with all this—learning about Nanette and things she had done to my father and the kind of mind she had—it was bringing our morale down, as a family. She was making us crazy. We started seeing how evil the world was and it was making us negative and lose hope in society.

"In time, I moved on with my life and so did Jenny and Kevin. My mom moved back to Hawaii, and although there was no resolution to my dad's murder, we were at least trying to move on. Kevin decided he wanted to be nearer to our mother, so he moved to a guesthouse behind hers in Hawaii. Every day, he would take long walks on the beach and take a swim and try to surf. Surfing was his passion in life. He was a very, very good surfer. Throughout his whole recovery, what drove him to go on was his goal to surf again. He was a short boarder preaccident but was never able to get back up on short board. My mom got him surfing lessons and every once in a while he could stand up on a long board. It was very frustrating. He had little muscle and nerve coordination. His muscles would take a long time to react to what his brain was telling him.

"We were worried about him surfing in the rough waves. But we couldn't chain him down. We had to let him have his freedom."

But then, about five years after Bill McLaughlin was murdered, a second, unfathomable tragedy occurred. "Kevin drowned. It was another devastating loss.

"Almost a decade passed after Kevin's death and still, there was no news as to the resolution of my dad's murder. But then, at the end of 2008, fourteen years after the murder, Matt Murphy and Larry Montgomery called Jenny and me and asked us to come to their office. We answered a bunch of questions.

And once again, nothing at all happened in the months

after the interview, and once again, the McLaughlins lost all hope of the case ever being solved. "But then six months later," said Kim, "Newport Beach detective Joe Cartwright called us. He said, 'Do you know where I am?' And I said I had no idea. Then he told me he was in Connecticut and he had just arrested Eric Naposki. I screamed. I was in shock. I was elated. It came out of the blue."

Kim stated that she didn't really know Murphy or Montgomery until she and her sister were being briefed on how the trial was going to go and what their part would be in it. "Then," Kim said, "there was a two-day pretrial and we saw how they worked. Once we saw them in action and saw how meticulous they were, our hopes soared.

"People told us Murphy was a great DA, but we had no idea what that meant. We hadn't ever been exposed to the justice system. I'm in education, and Jenny is in finance. But when we saw Matt in action, we knew what they meant. We were in awe of him. He is a modern-day hero. He is truly amazing. Our family and my dad's family in Chicago, we thank God every day that Matt Murphy entered our lives, because he is the reason those two will get what they deserve.

"We learned how Montgomery had gone over all the audiotapes and Thousands of pages of evidence, all with a fine-tooth comb, and found so much just by taking the time and being so meticulous. He, too, was our hero. And to know that he had been on the case for two years before we even knew he was on it was such an honor to us. To see that justice would prevail was so inspiring and gave us so much hope and faith in the system—because the system really hadn't worked for us."

Giving details, Kim stated, "In fact, the system had disappointed us twice. First, there was Kevin's accident. When Kevin was hit by a drunk driver, that man got one night in jail, his car was taken away for a short while, and he was required to perform one thousand hours of community service. However, the guy never performed *one* single hour of service. Back then, drunk-driving laws were very lenient. If he had killed Kevin, he would have gotten years in jail, but because he just barely didn't kill him, he got off.

"And then there was my father's murder. That Nanette and Eric could get away with this heinous crime and go about their lives was an extreme indignation.

"Their arrests were soooo satisfying. And then, there was Eric's conviction—finally justice was prevailing and the system worked as it should.

"During Eric's trial, we learned so much more about how Nanette had taken advantage of my dad, things we didn't know before because the case was confidential. The information made us sick to our stomachs. He did so much for her and her kids, and for her to be so evil behind his back was really hard to take in."

When asked about what she did immediately after the verdict was read at Eric's trial, in the summer of 2011, Kim said, "I saw Eric's fiancée sitting in trial every day and I knew who she was. She was similar to my age and she was also a teacher, like me. Plus, I knew that she had flown in from the East Coast to sit in trial every day, all alone. I put myself in her shoes and was feeling empathy, sympathy for her. I realized that she truly believed that he was innocent. They had never talked about this, so while she was sitting through all the trial and believing he was innocent she must've been in denial and hopeful that he would be released. Then he was convicted by twelve jurors, and I felt her pain in the loss of her hopes and dreams and I went to her and put my hand on her shoulder and said, 'I'm really, really sorry.'"

Then, another bit of wonderful news came Kim's way, in 2012. Nanette's trial took place and after only three hours of deliberation the verdict came back. Guilty. "The system really, really does work."

Speaking of the years since her father died, Kim said, "It has been lonely and hard without my dad around, not to have him there at my wedding, walking me down the aisle.

It was really hard not to have him around when Kevin died, to give us guidance and comfort.

"For five years after the murder, I kept waking up in the morning and thinking he'd be there, or I'd get in a car and turn around and think he'd be there. In continuing to handle his businesses, I'd think he'd walk into a meeting. It is still so hard to think he is really, really gone."

Speaking of how she has come through the tragedy, Kim said, "I feel my dad is on my shoulder every day in whatever I do. Kevin, too. I feel proud of the fact that I had so many incredible years with both of them. And we really had a special relationship and there is nothing I regret in our relationships. I treasure every time we spent together. And we did spend a lot of time together. Very few people get to do that with their families.

"Those memories of the love my dad gave me can never be taken away. That is what I take with me every day."

Investigator Larry Montgomery

Investigator Larry Montgomery became involved in the McLaughlin cold case in 2007. At that time, Montgomery was a part of TracKRS, whose mission was to review old unsolved cases with a fresh set of eyes. And that is exactly what Montgomery did—and his diligent work led directly to the case being reopened.

The McLaughlin case meant a lot to Montgomery. "I think the family were very nice people, and for fifteen years they thought nothing was happening. So it was nice after all that time to come back to them and say, 'We think we have solved it and will bring the people to court and hopefully get some justice.'

"They were very appreciative. That meant a lot, especially in cold cases when people think nothing is ever going to be done. That is especially gratifying."

Montgomery's reputation is legendary in police circles in

the LA area. When asked what makes an effective investigator, he said it's several things. "Interest is one. I am fascinated by this stuff and would do it even if I wasn't getting paid for it. Experience is really valuable also. I was lucky enough to spend twenty-three years doing investigative work with the police department and eight years at TracKRS, so I've had a lot more time to learn the trade. Plus, there's tenacity. I never give up.

"Being open-minded is really important, too," continued Montgomery. "I've had cases in which it really looked like the person was guilty because of the evidence that came in, but then something pops up that is not consistent with that. You always must keep an open mind if someone comes forward with new information and see if it is consistent or not with guilt or innocence."

When asked what it was like to testify at the trials, Montgomery said, "It was huge. I had over two hundred forty pages of single-spaced typewritten notes. I had to be prepared and not look like an idiot on the stand. I bent over backwards for the defense and I bent over backwards for the prosecution because all we wanted was the truth. If the defense had something that was true, and helped their client, that was fine with me. If it was a lie, you wanted to present and show that, too."

During the trials, Montgomery sat next to Murphy. "I take a lot of notes. Murphy doesn't have the time. I try to write down what witnesses say so that in the final argument we have the right stuff. We're looking for anything that helps or hurts either side. We are looking for the truth."

Speaking of how he and Murphy work together during a trial, Montgomery said, "During questioning, Murphy always pauses before saying 'no further questions' and looks to me to see if there is anything else he needs to ask. I'm not up there doing what he's doing, so I can kind of relax and think of things that he may not have a moment to think about. I get to be his second person to make sure we don't miss anything."

Attorney Matt Murphy

Commenting on the McLaughlin case after the Naposki trial, Murphy had a lot to say. "It was a media case. Two TV stations filmed opening arguments. They were interested in the various aspects of the case: a young pretty woman, an older rich guy, an ex–pro NFL player, the lifestyle in Newport Beach, and you can't forget Kevin."

Going into greater detail, Murphy continued. "Think about the victim," he said. "By all accounts, a really nice man. Factor in how much money he had and the lifestyle he lived. Then there's Kevin's story. He was really good-looking, played water polo, was an accomplished Newport surfer. And then he had this tragic accident while skateboarding. But then, he died in a surfing accident in Hawaii.

"There are the two other McLaughlin children who, although brought up with anything they might have wanted, were not spoiled, not pretentious, such nice people.

"And then you've got Nanette and the way she works men over the years—and how she manipulated Naposki.

"And finally, you've got Naposki himself. Arrogant, cocky, obviously a liar, grew up in New York, goes to the NFL.

"Taken all together," said Murphy, "you can't find a more interesting group of people for a murder case."

Speaking of the trial, Murphy admitted it was stressful. "It was among the most challenging cases I ever tried." According to Murphy, "Seventy percent of the cases we do, a trained monkey could do. There's incontrovertible DNA evidence, for example; there's the murder weapon, several eyewitnesses, or even a video of the event itself. There are no Clarence Darrow recitations. No great trial moments. The way these cases are put together, any rational jury will convict.

"However," continued Murphy, "this case was different. Every single piece of evidence had alternate explanations. You had to look at each individual item in light of every other one. My job was putting all the pieces together and showing the jurors in such a way that *they* could connect the dots."

Murphy explained, "There was denial all the way. Every time we talked to Naposki, he changed his story. Every time he opened his mouth, things changed." According to Murphy, "Naposki has adamant denial on top of a denial wrapped up in a lie followed by adamant denial." Then, after a pause, he added, "Classic Naposki."

Ultimately, for Murphy, the best part of the McLaughlin case was "that the two thought they'd gotten away with it. And, that we could bring some closure to the patient and truly lovely McLaughlin family."

Murphy credits his success on this case not only to the work of Montgomery and other law enforcement individuals but also to his two in-house colleagues Dena Basham and Susan Frazier. "They deal with my neuroses, but more importantly, they deal with every detail of the case. 'What about this? What about that?' they ask me. The PowerPoint is honed over and over again. They weigh in if there's too much here or not enough there. In truth," said Murphy, "this really is a team thing."

Basham's major role was helping develop discovery. Basham stated, "Everything that we receive from the police departments has to be discovered [given] to the defense. But before that happens, I need to number and index everything so we are able to find it easily.

"Then there's the cart that the prosecution rolls into court every day with many, many binders on it. Those are all the notebooks that I prepared for trial. I organize the case—all the police reports, subpoenas, search warrants—so that we are able to find everything we need easily during trial."

For the McLaughlin case, Frazier worked as Murphy's investigator. She had been a police officer for a total of twenty-two years with fourteen years in the DA's office. Frazier was fascinated with the McLaughlin case from the moment Murphy got her involved. "I remember when he first told me about the case, I was shocked. I thought it would be very tough. But as I learned more and more, it made more sense, until I thought it would be a winner."

Among other things Frazier did was get all the witnesses together when it was time to go to court. We prepare witnesses for their testimony, which sometimes includes providing them their previous statements for review.

"During the actual trial," Frazier continued, "it seemed to me that the case got even stronger, with the real estate person; Suzanne Cogar; Larry Montgomery; and Tom Voth."

For this case, Murphy worked things out in front of Basham, Frazier, and Montgomery, asking them what they thought about this and about that. "We met quite a lot to talk about strategy and witnesses, usually with the lead detectives from the police department as well," said Basham. "Matt usually asks for mine and Susan's thoughts and input during jury selection."

According to Murphy, "I need them to help me think. If they don't think we can make it, we don't file it."

What Murphy especially loves about his job is that he gets to help grieving families through the worst thing ever. "And it will sound corny," he stated, "but I can give them something. I can deliver retribution if I don't screw it up. It's important. I really enjoy pushing the envelope on difficult cases."

Asked what he would do if he wasn't a prosecutor, he said, "It's all I want to do. I would like to do this for another decade at least. My next step after prosecutor is either the bench or maybe I'll be one of those ex-pats living in Mexico, writing bad poetry, and eating churros. You never know."

Eric Naposki

Since his conviction, Eric continues to maintain his innocence in the shooting death of Bill McLaughlin.

"Nanette was evil," said Naposki in one of two interviews I had with him at Theo Lacy Facility, a maximum security jail in the City of Orange. "Everything that has come out of her mouth to me has been a lie: her relationship with Bill; that she was sexually abused by him; that she was a college grad; that she had a pilot's license.

"Bringing in Bill in that light [saying he had abused her] . . . She was trying to get me going toward Bill. I'm not that kind of person to have really bad feelings toward anything. I'm the furthest thing away from killer. I see a bug and open the door. I was the kid on the playground who saw a kid cry and I would cry. My mom would always tell that story."

Naposki is still not able to fathom how Nanette could have kept her two lives separate—one in which she was Bill McLaughlin's fiancée and another in which she had taken on Bill's persona as a wealthy inventor and was dating him. "As it turned out," Naposki continued, "I wasn't the only one who was taken in by her lies. Everyone at the gym was fooled into thinking she was a millionaire. And there is no way that Bill McLaughlin didn't know about me. Her kids were always with me. They surely spoke to him about me. She came to my house in New York and spent days there with my family. We went to Radio City Music Hall with the kids. Lishele said to me, 'You're my mom's favorite.' They must have told Mr. McLaughlin."

Before I was granted permission to interview Naposki in prison, I had to make specific arrangements, giving the exact dates and times I would be there. Then, once I arrived, I was told that they have a "no hostage policy." Explaining this, the officer told me that if I was taken hostage while in the prison, they would not necessarily come to get me.

Not a very auspicious beginning.

However, as it turned out, everyone at the jail was extremely cordial and helpful. They took me to a holding cell and then a few minutes later, Naposki was brought in. His hands were kept cuffed.

Naposki is a big man. At 6' 2", over 200 pounds, and bald, he presents an imposing figure. With tattoos—among others, a tribal tattoo from his back to around his neck and a dragon Barcelona tattoo on his leg—and enormous arms barely fitting in his orange jumpsuit, he doesn't look like someone to mess with. When I asked him how he kept in such seemingly great shape, he said, "I shoot baskets and lift weights. I gotta keep my 22-inch arms."

For several hours, Naposki answered any question I asked. He told me about prison life, saying he is currently in a two-man cell, in the bottom bunk. "Twenty-two hours a day I'm in the small cell. Then, I'm out for two hours. I take a shower, make calls, hang out in the dayroom, which is really just a bigger cell. I'm on the phone for hours with my fiancée. If it wasn't for Rosie," said Naposki softly, "I couldn't deal with this. She's a fantastic teacher, runs ten miles a day. She's waiting for me. I told her not to, but she loves me. She's the best thing that ever happened to me."

Continuing, he said, "In here, you can't talk. If people in here knew we were having this conversation, I would get my ass kicked at day room."

I wondered who, exactly, would be able to take him on, but I held my tongue.

After that, we began to talk about the trial. According to Naposki, Murphy made a big deal about his having McLaughlin's license plate number in his notebook. If he was given the chance to explain this, Naposki said, he would have told the jurors, "After I sensed something seemed off with Nanette, I called my friend Todd Calder and asked him to check up and see who Nanette's been hanging out with. He goes to her house. He sees the garage door open with a white Mercedes-Benz. Calder calls me and I jot down the license plate number. I didn't give it a thought until the trial, and then I hear all about this license plate number. I'm wondering why Matt made such a big deal about it. I was just checking up on Nanette because I had the suspicion she wasn't as clean as she pretended to be."

Recalling his surprise when he was arrested, Naposki gave some background. "When I left California, Julian Bailey was my attorney. As far as I knew then, we one-hundred percent had everything that was needed to show my innocence. Bailey had sent a letter outlining everything and expected to sit down and talk it out. But," continued Naposki, "they never called up to schedule a meeting. They never tried to get phone records.

"One thing was perfectly clear in Bailey's letter," continued Naposki. "We were looking forward to sitting down with them and exchanging information. But because they never followed up, naturally I figured they agreed with everything Bailey had written and I was a free man—totally off the hook for anything the cops might have thought about me. That's why I was so shocked when the SWAT team came to arrest me, fifteen years after the crime." Naposki said he was so stunned by the arrest, that when they took him to the police station, he couldn't stop hyperventilating and had to be rushed to the hospital.

Switching topics, we talked about some of the happiest and saddest moments of his life. Naposki said that among his proudest moments was the day he graduated from UConn, after having completed the final twelve credits he needed to graduate. "I quit before my senior year in order to support my family, and it took me a while to get back to school, but I did it. In fact," he said, "while I was living in Connecticut in the years before I was arrested, I graduated college, had a new fiancée, a new car, a truck, a bike. Everything was perfect—until Murphy decided I needed to be in jail."

Perhaps the saddest moment of his life, Naposki stated, was the day they told him his mother died. "I was locked down. She passed away in Florida and the funeral was in New York. I wasn't allowed to attend. My mom was my best friend in the whole world. I can't even talk about me and her."

Naposki is certain that one day he will be exonerated and will walk out of prison a free man. He cannot wait for that day, to be reunited with the woman he loves and his children. Naposki said that Rosie Macaluso visits him as often as she can, and that that's what keeps him going.

After spending a total of about five hours with Naposki, I got up to leave after my second interview. Naposki asked if I had a moment to take a look at some photos. Of course I did, I said. He then slipped under the glass that separated us about fifty or more photos of him and his family—his children and his current fiancée; his sister and nephew; his parents; and many others, including him sitting on a Harley with his son. They showed a happy father and fiancé; a man who seemingly had it all.

After telling him that I greatly appreciated his sharing the photos and talking with me, I got up to leave. "One day," he said trying to be upbeat, "I'll be out of here. And then, let's have a cup of coffee at Starbucks."

I said, "It's a date."

Detective Tom Voth

Speaking about the McLaughlin case, Detective Tom Voth mentioned that when he retired it was one of only a handful of cases that wasn't solved. "It bothered me. As the years passed, I wondered what was going on, all the time, hoping that something would break. That's what was needed: to find the gun or hear someone say he or she did it and this is how it happened. And then Matt Murphy came along.

"I heard that they were preparing to arrest the two of them and I was asked to help because I was the initial lead detective. I was happy to be called back and fill in the blanks for the investigators that were handing the case to the DA's office.

"Only Investigator Larry Montgomery and I testified at the prelim [the hearing to determine whether or not there was enough evidence to go to trial]. In California, we have CA Proposition One-One-Five, which allows any officer to testify to what any other officer did or what witnesses told another officer. This helps to speed up preliminary hearings. The defense asked lots of unanticipated questions. Sometimes you answer, 'No,' and it doesn't look good. But the judge presiding over the prelim saw through that and felt there was enough here to bring this case to trial, and that's what started the ball rolling."

Speaking about the original investigation of Naposki, Voth reflected, "He lied so much, and an innocent person doesn't lie like that in a homicide investigation. I can see lying about being with Nanette, because maybe you're protecting her interest in a civil trial for palimony. But once that's discovered, why continue to lie about things still related to it, and lying about who had his gun, lying about where it was?

"After Eric's conviction, Murphy, Mongtomery, I, and others interviewed Naposki, at Naposki's request, in prison. Eric had said he was going to tell us the absolute truth. But he was caught in lies. He named a person whom he said he introduced to Nanette and claimed that after that she made arrangements with that person to kill Bill.

"But," continued Voth, "here's the part, and this is pure Eric. He completely keeps himself out of any kind of criminal activity by trying to structure his answers so he is not involved at all. He said, 'I told her about this guy and the guy tried to get me to go with him, but I said I wouldn't have anything to do with it.' We knew that was a lie. He kept himself out of it."

Continuing, Voth related, "Eric said Nanette got his gun out of his car. Now, here's a guy who is a security person who hides it so cops can't find it, yet she is able to get the gun out of his car and keep [it] for a week without him ever knowing it. It's not believable.

"Then Eric says, 'I am one hundred percent sure my gun was used in this crime.' How do you make that statement if you have nothing to do with it? He messed up big-time."

Voth stated that he was well aware that Nanette was successful at getting men to do what she wanted, yet, he said, "how do you [bring] in a complete stranger from the outside [the person Eric said he introduced to Nanette], who may tell on you and put you in jail for life? How do you do that if you don't have something extremely damning on them to make them keep quiet?

"So it has to be Eric and Nanette and they are both there or Nanette is helping plan and execute the plan. That was our feeling in 1995 and absent Cogar's statements, and the talents of Murphy and Montgomery, we had a good case back then. We just didn't have enough to take it to court and feel confident that we would get a guilty verdict."

When asked what the best part of being a detective is, Voth said, "Following a case all the way through. Seeing the beginning of a case and following it from one end to the other, through the whole justice system, the ups and the downs.

"That's the way it was with the McLaughlin case, and that's a great feeling."

When I turned in the manuscript for this book to St. Martin's, Nanette Johnston's lawyer, Mick Hill, told me Johnston was unwilling to speak to any journalists at this time.